THE BRITISH ZION

THE BRITISH ZION

Congregationalism, Politics, and Empire,

1790–1850

Michael A. Rutz

BAYLOR UNIVERSITY PRESS

Cover Design by Andrew Brozyna, AJB Design, Inc.
Cover Image: Photographs and Prints Division, Schomburg Center for Research in Black Culture, The New York Public Library, Astor, Lenox and Tilden Foundations (digital ID 1249737).

Library of Congress Cataloging-in-Publication Data

Rutz, Michael A., 1970-
    The British Zion : congregationalism, politics, and empire, 1790-1850 / Michael A. Rutz.
        p. cm.
    Includes bibliographical references and index.
    ISBN 978-1-60258-205-7 (hardback : alk. paper)
    1. Great Britain--Church history--19th century. 2. Missions--Great Britain--History--19th century. 3. Evangelicalism--Great Britain--History--19th century. 4. Missions--South Africa--History--19th century. I. Title.
    BR759.R93 2011
    322'.10917124109034--dc22

                                        2010021149

Printed in the United States of America on acid-free paper with a minimum of 30% pcw recycled content.

For
Shelly, Ethan, and Sage

Contents

Acknowledgments   ix

List of Abbreviations   xi

Introduction   1

1   The Evangelical Revival and the Origins of the Missionary
     Movement   9

2   Itinerancy, Religious Liberty, and the Rise of Evangelical
     Politics   31

3   The Missionary Movement and the Politics of Abolition   53

4   Missionary Politics in Britain and the Cape Colony   75

5   Church, State, and Dissenting Politics in the Age of Reform   97

6   Church, Race, and Conflict in the Cape Missions   115

Epilogue   141

Notes   147

Bibliography   173

Index   187

Acknowledgments

Every book is a collaborative effort. My name might appear alone on the cover, but I cannot take sole credit for this work. I offer my most sincere thanks to all of the persons and institutions that contributed to its completion.

The staff at Baylor University Press have been patient, encouraging, and professional throughout this process. I am grateful to them for the opportunity to make this first book a reality. I also wish to thank the librarians and staff at the SOAS Library, Dr. Williams's Library, the Guildhall Library, the Edinburgh University Library Centre for Research Collections, the Cullen Library, Wits University, the Billy Graham Center Archives, and many more. Their cooperation and able assistance never failed to make my research a productive and pleasant experience.

My colleagues and friends at the University of Wisconsin–Oshkosh have been a consistent source of encouragement and support. The generous financial support of the university's Faculty Development Program made continued research and the completion of the manuscript possible. I am also grateful to the many friends and colleagues from my days at Washington University, and numerous conferences. Their collective wisdom, experience, and comments contributed much to this work. Special recognition must go to Richard Davis, whose steady guidance and learned advice have proven invaluable. I could not have asked for a better mentor and teacher. I have been fortunate to have also had the constant support of family, who did not always understand the process but never failed to stand behind me. Shelly,

Ethan, and Sage have shared all of the highs and lows at various stages. Without their encouragement, confidence, and patience I would not have made it this far. This book is dedicated to them.

List of Abbreviations

BL	British Library
BM	*The Baptist Magazine*
BMS	Baptist Missionary Society
CL/Wits	Cullen Library, Historical Papers, University of Witwatersrand
CM	*The Congregationalist Magazine*
CWM/LMS	Council for World Mission/London Missionary Society Archive
DUL	Durham University Library
DWL	Dr. Williams's Library
EM	*Evangelical Magazine*
GL	Guildhall Library
HMM	*The Home Missionary Magazine*
KP	Le Cordeur, Basil, and Christopher Saunders. *The Kitchingman Papers: Missionary Journals, 1817–1848, from the Brenthurst Collection*. Johannesburg: 1976.

LMS   London Missionary Society

MM   *The Methodist Magazine*

Parl. Debs.   Hansard's Parliamentary Debates

SACA   South African Commercial Advertiser

SOAS   School of Oriental and African Studies Archive

WMMS   Wesleyan Methodist Missionary Society

Introduction

*[T]he great vice of all missionary institutions, in the eyes of the
colonists, was that they enabled the Hottentot to learn that, as a human being,
he had rights; they taught him to claim these rights.*

—Richard Lovett
History of the London Missionary Society

This book examines the intersection among religion, politics, and empire in
early nineteenth-century Britain. The primary subject is the advent of the
political activity of evangelical Dissenters and its influence on the activities of the predominantly Congregationalist missionaries of the London
Missionary Society (LMS) between the years 1790 and 1850. During this
period, Protestant Dissenters and missionaries actively participated in political campaigns to open colonial territories to evangelization, to abolish slavery, and to secure civil rights for indigenous peoples. These positions often
set the missions against the interests of settlers, slave owners, and colonial
officials. My argument connects this political activism in the colonial sphere
with evangelical Dissenters' concern for the protection of religious liberty
and with the struggle to gain their own civil equality in Britain. Empire, and
especially the missionary movement, thus operated as a catalyst for, and a
means of advancing, dissenting ideologies about civil equality and religious
freedom at home and abroad.

Modern historians' consideration of evangelicalism's impact upon late eighteenth- and early nineteenth-century Britain dates from the monumental works of Elie Halévy in the early twentieth century. Halévy stressed the significance of evangelicalism and dissent for understanding the political development of British politics during the revolutionary era,[1] and his work helped to launch a rich historiography on the Dissenters' participation in the fundamental political contest of the era, that between "the traditionally privileged . . . old oligarchy based on the land and the aggressive and expanding middle classes of the country."[2] During the first half of the nineteenth century dissenting political objectives "increasingly aspired to reform society in line with the ideal of religious equality before the law."[3] First and foremost this meant repeal of the Test and Corporation Acts, accomplished in 1828. Following that, Congregationalists and Baptists especially turned their focus toward the disestablishment of the Church of England in the 1830s. While history and dissenting ecclesiology pushed them from advocating mere religious liberty toward demands for the separation of church and state, evangelical Dissenters engaged in a variety of other reform and even radical movements during the early decades of the nineteenth century, including antislavery and parliamentary reform. As such, evangelical Dissenters became increasingly important players in the political life of early nineteenth-century Britain, and this work argues that their influence reached far beyond the shores of Britain itself.

Examination of the links among evangelical religion, social class, gender, nationality, and ethnicity has also commanded the attention of scholars of nineteenth-century Britain.[4] They have sought to trace the association between religion and social movements, paying special attention to the place of religious belief in establishing mechanisms of social control and middle-class hegemony in nineteenth-century Britain. Scholars have looked to uncover the social, cultural, economic, and, to a lesser extent, political *uses* of religion.[5] These works have also begun to raise provocative questions about the role of foreign missions in the creation of a nineteenth-century British imperial culture and the influence of the missionary movement upon relationships between social classes.

Historians increasingly recognize that colonial societies and colonial politics were not simply products of the top-down transmission of Western influences to the colonies. Rather, they were clearly shaped "[b]etween metropole and colony."[6] That is to say, British society and culture were themselves products of the colonial encounter, and the character of that encounter within the colonies was also contingent upon conflicts and events within the metropole. Understanding the history of the British Empire requires us to see that the policies of the colonial governments were shaped not only on the ground, but also in response to social and political pressures in Britain. One recent example in this vein is Catherine Hall's study of the intersections between Birmingham and Jamaica in the mid-nineteenth century. She recounts the growing disillusionment of Baptist missionaries who saw their hopes for the conversion (religious and cultural) of the emancipated slaves dashed both by the increasing resistance of their flocks in the colony and by the shifting attitudes of their supporters in Britain. Hall argues that the ideals of missionary humanitarianism became increasingly less relevant as, by the 1860s, missionaries themselves began to split over the place of free blacks within colonial society and the ideas of the differentiation between white civilization and black savagery hardened at home. More importantly, the missionaries failed to achieve their goals because they were never truly committed to the idea of racial equality. On the domestic side, Susan Thorne examines the contribution of the missionary movement, and the LMS in particular, to the "making" of the British middle class through the interplay between the home and foreign missionary movements. Her argument concentrates on the use of religious organizations as a means of delineating class distinctions, and investigates the Congregationalist elite's use of the LMS as a tool for creating and asserting their middle-class identity. The study concludes that the liberal and egalitarian discourse of the nineteenth-century missionary movement in fact concealed ideologies of class subjection and racial supremacy within the middle class.[7]

There is no denying that British evangelicalism, and the missionary movement in particular, played a significant role in the development of what would eventually come to be widely known as Victorian values. Whether attempting to convert Welsh coal miners, the residents of London's slums, or the colonized peoples of Africa, most evangelicals certainly assumed that with salvation came civility and respectability. Liberal ideologies mingled concepts of social order, Christian morality, and economic advancement into a coherent model of civilization, which evangelists actively sought to cultivate among the "heathen" at home or abroad. For many Protestant Dissenters, however, these assumptions were also intimately connected to notions of equality and justice, which had the potential to serve as powerful arguments against the inequities produced by nascent industrial capitalism, religious discrimination, racial prejudice, or colonial expansion.

British Congregationalism was never so completely made up of, or controlled by, the upper-middle-class elite as Thorne's argument might suggest.

Accounts of the disaffection of the working classes with religion have been largely overstated, especially for the early nineteenth century. Considerable evidence exists to demonstrate that evangelical Dissent appealed most solidly to artisans and members of the so-called labor aristocracy. The evangelical spirit may not have always reached the poorest of the poor, but it is no longer tenable to characterize it as the exclusive property of the upper middle class. Without question, religion furnished an instrument for constructing collective identities, especially through the sense of community and purpose created within the chapel communities. The appeal of the chapel community, however, was clearly not confined to any particular social class. The most successful of the nineteenth-century evangelical movements were those that spoke to the social and political goals of a broad popular base during a period of significant socioeconomic and constitutional transformation.[8]

This study centers upon the involvement of evangelical Congregationalists in the budding missionary and humanitarian movements of the early nineteenth century. Congregationalists were by no means the only Britons concerned for the propagation of religious and humanitarian doctrines. Theological and philanthropic interests created the possibility for collaboration across religious and class lines in the interest of common goals, such as the protection of religious liberty or the abolition of slavery. Congregationalists allied themselves with, and sometimes contested with, various elements of metropolitan and colonial society in the politicized early nineteenth-century debates over the future and progress of Britain's constitution and its expanding empire. The diversity of religious and intellectual opinions engaged in the humanitarian movement present difficulties for any simple association of it with the hegemonic interests of a particular social class, such as the industrial middle class. Study of the relationship between evangelical politics and empire can highlight the complexities in the interaction of religion, race, and class in early nineteenth-century metropolitan and colonial societies.

Historians of empire tend to identify the surge of missionary enthusiasm as a central element of late eighteenth-century British imperial expansion. Missionaries frequently emerge from their accounts as the advance forces of colonial domination, transmitting the values of bourgeois society around the globe and paving the way for British hegemony.[9] Denominational historians, for the most part, give emphasis to religious developments and the Evangelical Revival in particular as the principal impulses for missionary activity.[10] Intent on making a clear distinction between the missions and colonial exploitation, their histories stress the positive influences of the humanitarian and educational efforts of the missionaries. Each of these categories of inter-pretation deals with admittedly significant aspects of a complicated set of relations between the missionary movement and imperialism, yet often fails to fully acknowledge or account for the merits of the opposing argument.

In recent years scholarship on the history of missions has increasingly moved beyond this dichotomy of agents of empire or Christian humani-tarians. Norman Etherington has contended that for too long historians of empire ignored missionary history, and historians of missions ignored imperialism. Both played important and related parts in the development of British colonialism, and historians must be careful to neither idealize nor demonize their role. Likewise, Andrew Porter has argued that while mis-sionaries often went into the field with noble intentions, they were clearly not immune to the ethnocentric and racist ideas of their times. Still, mis-sionaries and mission societies frequently found themselves opposed to colo-nial policies and imperial expansion. While missionary work in fields like education came to be closely associated with imperialism, the missionary movement cannot be neatly summed up as being proempire.[11] The history is far more contested and complicated. This study proceeds from the premise that it is possible to recognize the humanitarian and theological impulses of the missionary movement without sacrificing a critical examination of its impact upon the political, social, and cultural development of Britain and the Empire.

An ironic consequence of the recent trend toward examining the socio-cultural influences of religious movements has been the decline of serious consideration of their theology. All too frequently religious ideas fall by the wayside once the problems of social control and imperial hegemony are taken up. However, the rise of the missionary movements, home and foreign, reflected important developments in the character of British evangelicalism. Evangelical Dissenters' attitudes toward the evangelized were profoundly shaped by theological considerations that in turn fueled their concern for the rights and material welfare of those whom they sought to convert. Fol-lowing the pioneering work of Roger Anstey on the theological foundations of the abolitionist movement, I attempt to elaborate further upon some of the connections among evangelical theology, ideology, and political activity in a broader colonial context.[12]

The political and ethnically complicated situation of early nineteenth-century southern Africa offers a particularly rich history for exploring these issues. Some of the most exciting scholarship on the missionary movement in the past two decades emerged as a result of Jean and John Comaroff's extensive study of the interaction between the Congregationalist and Methodist missions and the Tswana.[13] At the heart of the Comaroffs' argument is the claim that the missionary project involved not only religious conversion, but also cultural transformation. British missionaries not only sought to save the souls of so-called African heathens, they sought to remake their minds and their daily lives as well. The refashioning of the mundane symbols of everyday life ultimately facilitated the incorporation of the Tswana into the modern, industrial colonial order.[14]

The Comaroffs also give considerable notice to what they call the politics of the missionary encounter and provide a fascinating account of the often-contentious relationships between missionaries and African chiefs. This focus on the politics of the personal encounters between missionaries and rulers sometimes elides the highly contentious public political discourse in southern Africa and Britain at the time. Consideration of the British political context of the LMS missionaries' participation in the vigorous political struggles of early nineteenth-century South Africa has understandably drawn the attention of many Africanists, and most works on early nineteenth-century southern Africa now include an obligatory chapter or two on the "British context" of missionary ideology and activity. Historians of nineteenth-century Britain, and British politics in particular, have largely failed to examine the issue in significant detail. This work seeks to interpret the actions of these missionaries from the perspective of the development of dissenting politics and to suggest that we must understand dissenting politics not merely as a domestic movement, but a movement that involved Britain's expanding empire during the early nineteenth century.

The stress placed by scholars such as the Comaroffs on the politics of the missionary encounter leads them to marginalize the position of the missions within the broader political context of British colonial policy. Furthermore, they suggest that the dissenting missionaries' involvement in colonial politics compromised their ideological commitment to the separation of church and state.[15] My argument proposes a different way of interpreting the relationship between missions and politics. Commitment to the separation of church and state did not necessarily mean that Dissenters, or dissenting missionaries, compromised themselves by becoming involved in politics. Throughout the early decades of the nineteenth century, as will be shown, evangelical Dissenters, the missionaries included, were among the most active and influential participants in British and colonial politics. As Porter's work has suggested, careful examination of evangelical and missionary politics offers one of the best methods for understanding an incongruity in British imperial history, namely, how dissenting missionaries often functioned in the seemingly contradictory roles of agents of the expansion of British religion, culture, and values and as vocal critics of British colonial policy.

Chapter 1, "The Evangelical Revival and the Origins of the Missionary Movement," provides an overview of the history of the Evangelical Revival, detailing its role in the origins of the missionary movement, and formation of the LMS. Chapter 2, "Itinerancy, Religious Liberty, and the Rise of Evangelical Politics," examines the emergence of evangelical dissenting politics within early nineteenth-century debates over religious liberty and missionary activity. The primary focus is the campaign against Lord Sidmouth's bill to regulate itinerant preaching in Britain and the campaign to open India to missionary work. Chapter 3, "The Missionary Movement and the Politics of Abolition," details how evangelical Dissenters' commitment to religious liberty spurred them to greater involvement in the antislavery movement and the particular role of Congregationalist missionaries in pushing the LMS to participate more aggressively in abolitionist politics during the late 1820s and early 1830s. In chapter 4, "Missionary Politics in Britain and the Cape Colony," the focus expands to issues of colonial politics beyond slavery. In particular, it examines the involvement of LMS missionaries in the campaigns for recognition of the civil and religious equality of free blacks in the early nineteenth-century Cape Colony. Chapter 5, "Church, State, and Dissenting Politics in the Age of Reform," returns to Britain to explore the difficulties faced by the LMS as a result of the increased political militancy and activity of its missionaries and supporters. Particular attention is given to the debates over government grants to missionary societies in support of educating the emancipated slaves. The final chapter, "Church, Race, and Conflict in the Cape Missions," examines the continued development of the missionaries' participation in colonial politics at the Cape. The chapter assesses the accomplishments of the missionaries, as well as examining the challenges posed by changing racial attitudes and the decline of evangelical influence in British politics in the mid-nineteenth century.

The missionary James Read Jr. presents us with one of the best symbols of the complex situation of the missions within the early nineteenth-century British Empire. His father was one of the most controversial LMS missionaries in southern Africa, and his mother was an African convert to Christianity. Read Jr. spent the majority of his early adulthood assisting his father's work among the Africans at the Kat River settlement in the eastern Cape Colony. In 1851, reflecting upon his career, and that of his often-maligned father, he neatly captured the dual nature of their missionary work. "As regards ourselves," he wrote, "we have tried to do our duty by the people of the Kat River settlement in promoting industry, education and godliness. . . . When they have been wronged, we have fearlessly, but in a constitutional way, sought redress for them."[16]

The constitutional redress of grievances and inequality formed the essence of dissenting political activity during the first half of the nineteenth century. The liberal humanitarianism of missionary figures like the Reads, and their engagement in colonial politics, was a direct extension of the dissenting interest and its politics beyond the shores of Britain. The following chapters attempt to trace out the influences at work in Britain and the colonies that helped to create these ambiguous figures on the landscape of Britain's emerging empire.

1

The Evangelical Revival and the Origins of the Missionary Movement

On the evening of 4 November 1794, eight men gathered at the Baker's Coffeehouse, a regular meeting place for London ministers, to discuss the creation of an organization to promote foreign missions. Two of these ministers, John Eyre and Matthew Wilks, inspired by the writings of an Anglican chaplain to Sierra Leone, Melvill Horne, had organized fortnightly meetings for prayer and discussion of the missionary cause.[1] Within a short time the group had resolved to "unite together . . . that we may bring forward the formation of an extensive and regularly organized society . . . of Evangelical Ministers and Lay brethren of all Denominations" for the purpose of establishing a foreign mission. These discussions led to the formation of the Missionary Society at an inaugural meeting on 22 September 1795. Organized for the "sole object" of spreading "the knowledge of Christ among the heathen and unenlightened Nations," the Missionary Society (or London Missionary Society [LMS] as it subsequently came to be known) was among the first and long one of the most important participants in Britain's missionary movement.[2]

True to the spirit of evangelical cooperation evident among its founders, the Society reflected their belief in Christian unity.[3] The directors adopted the promotion of Christianity without reference to specific sects or denominations as the "Fundamental Principle" of the Society. The Independent minister, David Bogue, famously declared the Society's inaugural meeting "the funeral of bigotry" and praised the numerous "Episcopalians, Methodists, Presbyterians, and Independents, all united in one society" for the promotion of the knowledge of the Christian gospel. The rising evangelical zeal among Christians of various denominations received a boost from the openly undenominational spirit of the Napoleonic era, which instigated cooperative efforts to carry out home and foreign missionary work. Nevertheless, from its inception, the LMS was closely associated with the Independents (or Congregationalists) who made up the majority of its founding members and its popular support. Encouraged by the accounts of Captain Cook's voyages in the Pacific, the Society sent its first missions to Tahiti, Tongatabu, and the Marquesas in 1796. A Dutch man, J. T. Van der Kemp, put himself forward for a mission to South Africa and set sail for the Cape with the assistance of the Society in 1798. By the first decade of the nineteenth century the LMS had further missions in Ceylon, Bengal, Canton, and Demerara.

During the final decades of the eighteenth century evangelical Protestants generally in Britain began to act with greater urgency upon their sense of the Christian duty to spread the knowledge of the gospel. This is not to say that the idea of Christian missions was wholly new in the 1780s and 1790s. The fervent piety of many late seventeenth-century churchmen had brought the Anglican Societies for the Promotion of Christian Knowledge (SPCK, 1699) and for the Propagation of the Gospel (SPG, 1701) into being nearly a century earlier. Moravian communities in Britain and Germany had initiated missionary efforts in North America, the Caribbean, and Africa in the early decades of the century. Among Dissenters, the influential evangelically minded Independent minister and educator in Northamptonshire, Philip Doddridge, had asked in 1742 "whether something might be done in most of our congregations, toward assisting in the propagation of Christianity abroad?"[4] Nevertheless, the 1780s and 1790s marked an important turning point in missionary history. For the first time British Christians organized themselves on a large scale for the primary objective of converting the "heathen" around the globe. Whereas chaplains of the SPCK and SPG had directed their attentions primarily toward Britain and the colonial populations of North America and the Caribbean, the object of the new missionary enterprise was to reach the "far more than half the inhabitants of the earth ignorant of God . . . to proclaim the tidings of salvation . . . and . . . turn them from darkness to light."[5]

The first substantive efforts to undertake foreign missions to the "heathen world" took place in the 1780s. Thomas Coke, a leading Wesleyan Methodist, published a plan for a missionary society in 1783 and personally helped to finance a Methodist mission to the West Indies. Melvill Horne's

Letters on Missions, of 1784, foretelling the pan-evangelical character of the Missionary Society, called upon concerned Protestants of all denominations to join forces to promote missionary ventures. That same year the Northamptonshire Association of Baptist Churches called for evangelical Christians to join in prayer for "the spread of the Gospel to the most distant parts of the habitable globe." The response to the Prayer Call of 1784 within Baptist, Independent, and even some Anglican churches across Northamptonshire and beyond made the monthly missionary prayer meeting a regular event in evangelical congregations for decades to come. The birth of the modern missionary movement is largely credited to Northamptonshire's William Carey, a part-time shoemaker, schoolteacher, and Baptist minister. Carey's pamphlet *An Enquiry into the Obligations of Christians to Use Means for the Conversion of the Heathen*, and a rousing sermon which challenged his colleagues in the Northamptonshire Association to "expect great things from God" and to "attempt great things for God," led to the formation of the Particular Baptist Society for the Propagation of the Gospel to the Heathen in 1792.[6] The first evangelical organization devoted solely to the purpose of evangelizing the non-Christian world, the Baptist society sent Carey himself among its first missionaries to Bengal in 1793.[7]

Carey's example spurred others within the evangelical community to seek opportunities to advance the nascent missionary cause. The Independent minister David Bogue (one of those present at the Baker's Coffeehouse) urged paedobaptist evangelical Dissenters to consider "though we endeavour *personally* to live to [God's] honor," whether "our obligations are fulfilled, while we have employed no methods *as a Christian body*, to lead our brethren in Pagan lands to glorify him also?"[8] The failure of evangelical politicians, led by the Anglican William Wilberforce, to obtain official support for missionary work in the 1793 renewal of the East India Company Charter also motivated the religious public to action. William Ellis, a director of the LMS, noted with regret that in 1793 a "corporation of Christian men had by their determined hostility excluded all sanction from the English nation for the entrance of a single treatise of Christianity to the heathen inhabitants of that vast empire." The "retention of power, and the interests of trade" had superseded the cause of the gospel.[9] Yet the cause continued to gain momentum with the formation of several new voluntary organizations dedicated to supporting missionary work. The formation of the LMS in 1795 was followed shortly afterward by the Anglican Church Missionary Society (CMS) in 1799 and the coordination of the various Methodist missions into a national society in 1813.

The rise of the missionary movement at the close of the eighteenth century coincided with the expansion of British colonial possessions around the globe and the onset of industrialization, as well as with important shifts in the character of Protestant evangelicalism in Britain. While scholars frequently associate the evangelical values that launched the missionary movement with those of the Victorian middle class, the simple equation of earlier evangelical with Victorian values often elides the complicated process by which those values came to prominence in British society. Over the course of the century following its revival, the evangelical religion in Britain changed in response to numerous theological, social, economic, and political pressures. In considering the factors that contributed most to the formation of the missionary movement, we must pay special attention to the development of British evangelicalism in the late eighteenth century and its relationship to the fundamental transformations taking place in British society during that time.

The Origins and Impact of British Evangelicalism

Some sense of the revolutionary impact of the Evangelical Revival on British Protestantism, and Protestant Dissent in particular, is apparent in the prefatory remarks to the first edition of the *Evangelical Magazine* in 1795. "In the beginning of this century," the editors declared, "there were few persons of evangelical principles in the kingdom; but now . . . there are more than three hundred thousand Calvinists, and many others, savingly converted to God, who trust in the merits of Christ alone for salvation."[10] The numerical evidence of the transformation was in itself remarkable. In the early eighteenth century Dr. John Evans, a London Presbyterian, estimated the strength of English nonconformity at about 1,840 congregations. By 1851, thanks largely to the impact of the Revival, the religious census conducted by the London barrister Horace Mann counted 17,019. In 1851 nonconformist chapels outnumbered Anglican churches by 5,420. More than one-half of these chapels were Methodist, a new denomination that had emerged out of the established church and owed its very existence to the Revival.[11]

The dynamic growth of evangelicalism represented a response throughout Britain (spontaneous revivals occurred in England, Wales, and Scotland), Germany, and North America to a sense of profound crisis that pervaded the Protestant churches of the eighteenth century. Protestant morale "was at a low ebb" in the decades prior to the 1730s and 1740s, the result of

a Catholic resurgence on the Continent, the threat of advancing rationalism in European intellectual circles, and a deep sense of moral and spiritual
decay within society and the church.[12] Although largely independent in origin, the revivals shared an emphasis upon the Reformation doctrine of jus-
tification by faith, the importance of personal conversion, and the hope of
rescuing the Christian world from a period of apathy and decline by recap-
turing "the religious fervor of an earlier age."[13] The movements also inspired
among leaders and followers alike an intense interest in evangelization, so
that from its very origins the Evangelical Revival contained the impulse that
would drive the missionary movements of the nineteenth and twentieth centuries. The remainder of this chapter considers several theological and social
developments that gave rise to the Revival, and ultimately to the birth of the
modern missionary movement.

The most significant religious movement in eighteenth-century Protestantism, the Revival awakened a spiritual fervor and an ardent desire to
propagate the Christian gospel in men and women throughout Europe and
North America. Religious developments of the sixteenth and seventeenth
centuries, such as Puritanism in Britain and Pietism in Germany, provided
the soil from which the Revival sprang. Yet theological and social developments during the half century before the 1730s contributed much to the
dynamic rise of the evangelical movement. Among these influences in Britain was the emergence of the religious societies, inspired by the German
immigrant turned Anglican clergymen Anthony Horneck, and which provided an important early impulse toward evangelicalism. From the 1670s
onward large numbers of clergymen, artisans, and skilled craftsmen gathered in small groups to encourage holy living and the promotion of Christian principles. Samuel Wesley, the father of John and Charles, was among
many clergymen who formed religious societies to develop the "piety and
humility" of the young men of their parishes. Their impact was evident on
Samuel's sons, whose Holy Club at Oxford, the highly organized activities
of which gave Methodism its name, clearly reflected its origins in the turn of
the century religious societies. The societies themselves continued to thrive
into the 1720s and 1730s in localities as diverse as Gloucestershire, York-
shire, and London. Leading figures in the Revival, such as Wesley himself
and George Whitefield, maintained close ties with several of the organizations, preaching before them on numerous occasions and maintaining a
regular correspondence with their members.[14]

The spirit of the religious societies contributed to the creation of larger
organizations for the promotion of Christian morality. The 1690s saw the

formation of societies for the reformation of manners, intended to counteract the proliferation of Sabbath breaking, blasphemy, drunkenness, gambling, and prostitution associated with the lax moral atmosphere of the restoration era. Moral reform societies incurred considerable public resentment as a result of their efforts to rigorously enforce the laws against vice and immorality. Such counterproductive efforts to regulate the manners of the English public soon gave way to an ambitious project to promote religion through education. The SPCK and the SPG played particularly prominent parts in this endeavor. Thomas Bray, one-time commissary for the church in the Maryland colony, spelled out the societies' intentions to

> promote and encourage the erection of charity schools . . . to disperse both at home and abroad Bibles and Tracts of religion . . . to advance the honour of God and the good of mankind by promoting Christian knowledge both at home and in the other parts of the world by the best methods that should offer.[15]

Enlisting the participation of clergy and the laity, the societies undertook the task of advancing Christian education in Britain and the colonial settlements of the American colonies. While charged primarily with the religious instruction of white settlers, enterprising agents of the SPG also made largely unsuccessful attempts to evangelize the Native American populations. Wesley himself made an ill-fated journey to Georgia in 1737 in the service of the Society, and the failure of his missionary work contributed directly to the personal crisis of faith that preceded his conversion in 1738. In their efforts the SPCK (in England and Wales) and the SPG (in foreign lands) anticipated the close connection between home and foreign evangelization that, I shall argue, was a defining characteristic of the evangelical missionary movement of the late eighteenth and early nineteenth centuries. Although not possessed of as fully developed a concept of a mission to the "heathen world" as their evangelical descendants, in their design and composition they foreshadowed the emergence of the modern missionary movement a century later.

Perhaps the most significant contribution of the SPCK to the Revival, however, was its promotion of the charity school movement. By the mid-1720s the Society claimed to administer more than 1,300 schools, instructing over 23,000 scholars in the Bible, the catechism, and other devotional works.[16] The rapid growth of the charity schools reflected a general consensus between clergy and influential laymen that, as well as spiritual benefits, the maintenance of social stability required the reformation of public morals and manners, grounded in religious faith. In the schools children of the lower orders, and many adults, received an introduction to religious instruction and the values of thrift, sobriety, and humility. But the Sunday school movement was not merely an exercise in the imposition of values from above. To common people, the advantages of "cheap literacy and self-improvement" made the Sunday schools the most popular religious institutions of the eighteenth and nineteenth centuries.[17] Attendance at Sunday school did not necessarily guarantee regular attendance at church, but significant numbers of persons did absorb their religious message as well as the benefits of learning to read or write. While institutions like the SPCK and its schools were not of the Revival itself, the emphasis given to personal piety, proper moral behavior, and charity clearly provided the fuel within upon which the Revival would later feed. In other words, they "laid the tinder to which the Methodists put the spark."[18]

John Wesley's career, and his journey from a personal crisis of faith to prominent leader of the evangelical movement, paralleled that of eighteenth-century English Protestantism from crisis of faith to Revival. Wesley traveled to Georgia under the auspices of the SPG with the express purpose of reaching beyond the colonial community to evangelize the Native American population. His mission ended in utter failure, yet during the journey he formed a relationship with Moravian missionaries in the colony that would have significant consequences. At the instigation of their patron Count Zinzendorf, the Moravians had established themselves in London under the direction of Peter Bohler. Upon his return from North America Wesley sought out Bohler, and thus strengthened his ties with the Moravian sect and its evangelizing activities. Wesley's famous conversion, on 24 May 1738, took place at the Moravian meeting house in Aldersgate. His new conviction of personal faith channeled Wesley's formidable severity of character and feelings of obligation to God into a career that would make him the greatest single figure of the Revival in Britain.

Wesley's Arminian theology, which emphasized the abundance of divine grace available to all, drove his tireless work as an evangelist across many times the length and breadth of England, proclaiming the Christian gospel to all who would hear him. His theology caused tensions in his relationship with the Calvinist George Whitefield, and determined the denominational affiliation of many of their auditors; but to many more the difference was probably not apparent. In any case, all the converts of both men became evangelicals of one sort or another, swelling the great Revival.[19] Their techniques were identical. Itinerant preaching became the means by which both men helped to transform the religious landscape of eighteenth-century Britain. The practice had appeared first in Wales, where the labors of Howell Harris and Daniel Rowland led to the establishment of a network of nearly four hundred congregations between the 1730s and 1850. The example of Harris and Rowland, and the increasing frequency with which Anglican clergy refused Whitefield the use of their pulpits, led him to take up field preaching. He introduced Wesley to the practice in 1739 by prevailing upon his colleague to take charge of his societies in Bristol during one of Whitefield's many journeys to North America.

More significant than their theological differences were the divergent approaches of the two evangelists toward the organization of their followers. Renowned as a field preacher, and famous for his constant travels throughout Britain, Wesley came to believe that his work as an evangelist could only "be sustained and spread by a tightly disciplined connexion linking [his] new societies together." He organized his followers into classes, which helped to sustain their new faith after he had moved on, and placed itinerant lay preachers at the head of regional "circuits" to ensure that his adherents had access to gospel preaching in his absence. All of these he brought under the control of a national "Conference," made up of the circuit preachers, through which "he maintained an authoritarian control over what he had created."[20] This system, initially implemented in the 1740s, allowed for the emergence of Wesleyan Methodism as a distinct sect by the time of Wesley's death in 1791. In time, some individuals and groups chafed at the authoritarian nature of Wesley's leadership and split from his "connexion." However, Wesley's model of circuit itinerancy and the organization of followers into "classes" influenced virtually every effort at home and foreign evangelization that would follow it.

Although Whitefield was, by all accounts, the more accomplished preacher, he lacked Wesley's genius for organization. He traveled even more often and more extensively than Wesley, making numerous trips across the Atlantic to participate in the North American revival. His constant travels hindered his ability to effectively organize his large following in Britain, and he does not appear to have shared Wesley's inclination toward exercising a strict control over his flock. Left without an institutional structure to secure them, Whitefield's followers ultimately gravitated toward evangelical communities among the Countess of Huntingdon's Connection, the Baptists, and the Independents. Thus, while Wesley's legacy lay in the formation of what became the largest evangelical sect in nineteenth-century

Britain, Whitefield's contribution was to ultimately strengthen the diffusion of evangelical principles within the ranks of Calvinist Dissent.[21]

Evangelicalism and Social Class

The revivals launched in the middle of the eighteenth century by Wesley and Whitefield in England, and by Rowland and Harris in Wales, succeeded in large part through their ability to provide reassuring answers to the doubts and fears that plagued many eighteenth-century Protestants. The experience of religious conversion offered "direct evidence of God's spiritual presence, countering the skepticism of deists and rationalists who spoke of a distant and impersonal God." The emphasis upon religious community, first embodied in the religious societies and then the Methodist classes that succeeded them, evoked a sense of the primitive church and of a return to a purer form of Christianity. They also helped to transcend social barriers. From an early stage the evangelical movement drew followers across a wide social spectrum. Evangelists also stressed the importance of moral reform, anticipating, in the words of Wesley, "a reformation not of opinions . . . but of men's tempers and lives; of vice of every kind."[22] The central message of the Revival, the free and immediate availability of God's grace and the assurance of saving faith, appealed strongly to many dismayed by the state of the moral and religious fiber of British society and increasingly shaken by the socioeconomic changes taking place throughout the eighteenth century. Any examination of the Revival or any attempt to understand how and why the religious ideas and practices peculiar to it gained such wide popular support must, while by no means ignoring them, look beyond the theological and religious influences to social, political, and economic factors. Developments in all of these areas contributed greatly to the dramatic expansion of Methodism and evangelical Dissent in the eighteenth and early nineteenth centuries. The intensified efforts of evangelical ministers, itinerant preachers, and lay persons increasingly attracted the attention of those whose interests and identities were challenged by the emergence of new social, political, and economic forces. Evangelicalism thrived "amidst the erosion of old structures and the weaknesses of the established denominations"; it grew especially on the margins of a society in the early stages of the transformation to the modern world.[23]

Historians have long identified the social and political upheavals of the revolutionary era, and the advent of industrial production, as key contributors to evangelicalism's success in Britain. One such historical account goes like this. The turmoil of warfare, scarcity, and aborted political revolution created a psychological mood, famously described by Edward Thompson in the phrase "the chiliasm of despair," which enabled evangelicalism to prosper.[24] Set into the context of the birth of industrial capitalism and the emergence of the English working class, this interpretive model classifies evangelicalism as an agent of bourgeois social control: conditioning the working class for the drudgery of factory labor, repressing sexual behavior, and inhibiting popular forms of recreation and protest. Yet the analytical assumptions that place the growth of evangelicalism into the context of class formation and middle-class social engineering raise as many questions as they propose to answer. How do we explain evangelical religion's dramatic success in mostly rural areas? How should we interpret its seemingly paradoxical appeal to both middle- and working-class populations?

Part of the answer lay, as noted above, in the movement's ability to address the growing doubts and concerns of Protestant Christians of various social backgrounds. Part lay in its ability to exploit weaknesses in the establishment and to locate itself in communities poorly ministered to by the Anglican Church. In one sense the Revival occurred largely on the margins of British society. It took deepest root among those people, and in those places, beyond the effective reach of the established church. Although born out of the church itself, the Revival ultimately flourished among the laborers and skilled craftsmen of rural freehold parishes, market towns, seaports, industrializing and mining regions, and other communities where the church's institutions were weakest.[25] From an early period, it also touched some of power and influence in society, as well as large numbers who would become so as a result of rapid economic and social change. During a period of war, rapid population growth, agricultural crisis, economic depression, and revolutionary potential, the assurance of faith and the stability offered by religious community seem to have held great appeal for a wide spectrum of the British public. The chapel, the Sunday school, and the auxiliary missionary society contributed substantially to building the sense of community and sociability in which numerous historians have located the early formation of middle-class identity in nineteenth-century Britain. Yet these same institutions were also adopted from below by "people searching for cohesion and security" amid the significant socioeconomic transformations of the age. Popular evangelicalism succeeded in Britain when and where it responded to the social, political, and economic pressures of a changing world with institutions and beliefs in which ordinary people could find meaning. To reduce it to a set of values and principles imposed from above, or to treat it as a mere tool of middle-class social control, is to refuse to recognize the variety of ways that working people shaped and reshaped their own religious beliefs and traditions.[26]

When considering the sociopolitical consequences of the Revival, we must not lose sight of the tendency for popular evangelicalism to threaten a "world order in which Christianization of the poor was regarded as the exclusive function of politically manipulated and spiritually pragmatic state churches."[27] The seemingly unchecked expansion of evangelical religion in late eighteenth- and early nineteenth-century Britain alarmed defenders of the establishment who feared its challenge not only to the religious, but also to the political and social order. That challenge appeared particularly distressing amid the social and structural transformations of the decades surrounding the turn of the nineteenth century. During this time, the proponents of evangelical religion became increasingly forceful advocates of religious liberty against coercion by agents of the state or the established church. The Church of England, inefficiently funded and institutionally weak, had little chance of countering the outburst of itinerant preaching, cottage meetings, and missionary fervor that marked the high point of the Revival. During the first decades of the nineteenth century, defenders of the church and state made repeated calls to strengthen the church, financially and structurally, against the rising tide of the evangelical sects.

The Impact of the Revival on "Old Dissent"

The impact of the Methodist revival, as noted above, included the spread of evangelical opinion within the denominations of Old Dissent. Independent and Baptist congregations in particular benefited from the steady stream of Whitefield's disciples who joined their ranks following his death in 1770.[28] The rise of Methodism was not, however, the only force behind the growth of evangelical Dissent at the end of the eighteenth century. Religious conflict played a role in the spread of evangelical influence within English Dissent as well. The rise of Unitarianism within the Presbyterian denomination factored prominently in the growth of Dissent in counties such as Lancashire. Independent congregations frequently split from churches where ministers had "wandered away into the mazes of Humanitarianism and Unitarianism."[29] Many of the Independent churches originating from these doctrinal disputes were later infused with a vitality that spurred the expansion of evangelicalism after 1780. Evangelical sentiments steadily broke down the adherence to rigid Calvinist doctrines and the customs of the settled pastorate that had proved obstacles to the growth of the movement within the older sects. By the turn of the century, as is demonstrated by Lovegrove, evangelicalism and itinerant preaching were rapidly transforming English Dissent.[30] In Lancashire, William Roby epitomized the new style of Independent minister and itinerant preacher advancing the evangelical message across the county. While minister to the Countess of Huntingdon's chapel at Wigan, Roby "paid regular visits to the surrounding towns and villages," and he kept up the practice after moving to Manchester's Cannon Street Independent Church in 1795. His early home missionary activity, which also included the formation of an Itinerant Society, took Roby as far afield as the Scottish border. On the weekends he preached twice daily in open fields, tents, or barns, traveling "on average about twenty miles a day."[31]

The adoption of the Methodistical practice of itinerancy reflected an important theological shift away from the high Calvinist doctrines that epitomized most of eighteenth-century English Dissent. Independents and Baptists, touched by evangelical sensibilities, came to recognize the advantages of organizing itinerant practices along the lines of the Wesleyan system. Dissenting ministers formed regional and county voluntary associations that allowed for better organization and the pooling of limited resources without sacrificing the autonomy of individual congregations. Roby participated in the implementation of the Lancashire Congregational County Union's scheme to evangelize the rural areas of the county. In 1801, the "Itinerant Society" formed by the Congregational ministers sent its first home missionary, George Greatbatch, into the vicinity of Southport. The society provided Greatbatch with a salary of £80 to support his family and to keep a horse. On horseback, Greatbatch made daily trips to the villages throughout the region, establishing small congregations, and frequently returning home "at midnight, drenched with rain and benumbed with cold."[32] The Lancashire society was just one of many such local associations that sprang up among the denominations of "Old Dissent." By the 1830s Independents and Baptists had formed as many as sixty-eight associations devoted to promoting itinerant preaching. Many of these, at least thirty-five, were interdenominational organizations such as the East-Kent Association formed in 1798.[33] There, Independents, Baptists, and members of the Countess of Huntingdon's Connection joined "to devise means of mutually aiding and assisting one another in the work of the Lord; and to consult about whatever may tend to promote the interest of true Religion in our respective situations and neighbourhoods."[34] The development of evangelical dissenting academies ww TH.

devoted to training evangelists contributed further to the increasing influence of itinerancy. Extensive use of the students of the Blackburn Academy in the Lancashire countryside, for example, assisted in the establishment of new congregations in Belthorn, Great Harwood, Ribchester, and several other nearby villages. The academies provided a steady stream of pastoral candidates who developed the skills on the preaching circuits and on many occasions eventually settled themselves as the ministers of the new congregations.[35]

The considerable variety of forms in which itinerant evangelization appeared reveals the advantages of the flexibility of itinerant preaching that enabled evangelicals to overcome the diverse challenges of limited resources and geography. Lay persons frequently supplemented the work of ministers on several levels: as preachers, as Sunday school instructors, or through financial support. Lay evangelists cut across all levels of society from the Scorton mill owner George Fishwick to textile workers like William Hayhurst of Blackburn. A member of the Chapel Street congregation, Hayhurst began preaching at a mill in the village of Knowle Green in 1827. Within three years he had raised a following of more than one hundred forty at two services every Sunday morning and evening. Hayhurst eventually moved himself and his family to Knowle Green, where he "followed his occupation as a warper, and also as pastor of the infant cause." In time the congregation constructed a chapel, where Hayhurst fulfilled his pastoral duties for more than three decades, all the while supporting "himself and his family" through his secular calling.[36] Lay evangelists never eclipsed the importance of the settled minister, as is evinced by Hayhurst's ultimately settling with his new congregation, and lay preaching generally took place under the watchful eyes of dissenting clergymen. However, the expansion of lay evangelism significantly recast the nature of the lay-ministerial relationship within the dissenting churches and demonstrated the increased willingness of the religious public to take part in the work of the evangelical cause. The growing participation of the laity in home evangelization also encouraged greater participation in the various voluntary organizations that became the driving forces of the missionary movement.

As suggested above, the increased interest of Dissenters in evangelization is conventionally understood as the result of a decline in the high Calvinist doctrines that had characterized dissenting opinion for more than a century.[37] Still, precedents for the participation of Calvinist Dissenters in the missionary movement may be traced as far back as the seventeenth century. John Eliot, the Presbyterian pastor of Roxbury, Massachusetts, worked among the Pequot Iroquois during the 1630s. Eliot ultimately "gathered about 3,600 Christian Indians" into his flock, and translated the Bible into the "Moheecan" language.[38] At home, Thomas Collier of Surrey, a preacher of Baptist and Calvinist views, itinerated widely during the 1630s and 1640s, and Particular Baptist ministers in 1689 appointed itinerant preachers "for the task of collecting and re-organizing . . . congregations which had been scattered during the years of persecution."[39]

Toward the latter half of the century, many Dissenters came to hold a more "open ended, progressive view of the divine purpose in human affairs" which worked to moderate their Calvinist beliefs. It seems clear that during the second half of the eighteenth century Independents and Baptists became increasingly comfortable with reconciling the apparent incongruity between the doctrine of the elect and the Christian responsibility to spread the gospel message. Whitefield, and the early Welsh evangelists, had found no trouble in actively pursuing evangelization while professing Calvinist theology. A "marriage of traditional theology with the more positive concerns of the Enlightenment" produced a more favorable view of missionary work within the ranks of Old Dissent.[40] Evangelical Dissenters did not, by and large, reject Calvinism, but adopted more open-minded and optimistic views of the workings of divine providence in the process of salvation. The theological shifts corresponded with broader changes taking place within Dissent, which emphasized the duty of Christians to spread the gospel and to make the effort to defeat the obstacles that hindered the advance of the Christian religion.

Leading evangelical ministers, such as Roby, made decidedly more favorable estimations of the number of the elect, rejected more pessimistic views, and openly encouraged evangelization. The inward focus and theological quarreling that marked early eighteenth-century Dissent gave way to a more outward view of the role of the church and a growing concern for the unchurched and unconverted at home and abroad. In 1786 the elder John Ryland reputedly censured William Carey's enthusiastic appeals on behalf of missionary work by asserting, "Young man, sit down: when God pleases to convert the Heathen, he will do it without your aid or mine." Ryland's alleged challenge represented something of a last stand for the old Calvinist sensibilities against the rising tide of evangelical enthusiasm.[41] Carey's moderate Calvinism was gaining the ascendancy by the time of the publication of his *Enquiry*, and the formation of the Baptist Missionary Society in 1792.

Calls to take action upon, in the words of David Bogue, the "obligations we are under to pity those who are sitting in sin and darkness and in the shadow of death" intensified in the final decade of the eighteenth century.[42]

They received further encouragement from evangelical expectations "bourne up by the continuing impetus of the Evangelical revival, . . . the study of biblical prophecies, . . . the events in France, and . . . the expansion of British influence throughout the world." Evangelical interpretations of historical developments incorporated a form of Enlightenment rationalism with the biblical concept of divine supremacy over the natural and moral orders. Human history unfolded not as an arbitrary process, but rather through the progression of natural laws and divine ordinances directed toward the fulfillment of God's purposes. Primary among those purposes, in the estimation of late eighteenth-century evangelicals, was the propagation of Christianity throughout the earth. The assumption that history "was the story of the divine preoccupation with the furtherance of the gospel of salvation" informed evangelicals' interpretations of contemporary events and their expectations for the furtherance of the missionary movement.[43]

The significance of such providentialist thinking showed itself repeatedly in evangelical publications, and in sermons before the annual meetings of the LMS, such as the Rev. John Griffin's "The Signs of the Times Favourable to the Cause of Missions." "Prophecies and promises," said Thomas Grove, "combine to encourage every exertion to send the gospel to all nations."[44] Evangelical ministers also stressed Britain's special and divinely appointed role in the process of evangelizing the faraway and unenlightened corners of the globe. The religious public observed the "shaking of the foundations of the old order in Europe caused by the French Revolution" with increasing interest and a sense of almost apocalyptic expectancy. The missionary enthusiast Melvill Horne stepped up his calls for evangelical cooperation in missionary work, reading the affairs on the Continent as a sign that the "latter ends of the world are fallen upon us."[45] The apparent decline of Catholicism in France and the defeat of the popish Antichrist excited evangelical enthusiasm for promoting the knowledge of "true Christianity" throughout the globe. Thomas Coke, the Methodist preacher, crossed the Channel in the fall of 1791 with two French-speaking preachers in hopes of establishing a mission in France.[46] "The downfall of popery, by the arms of Infidel France," asserted a mid-nineteenth-century history of the LMS, "had . . . considerable weight" in encouraging the formation of the Society.[47] "Consult the state of Europe," Jehoiada Brewer told the LMS meeting of 1798. "When were the signs of the times so portentous" for the cause of the gospel?[48]

More significantly, the expansion of British power and territorial possessions that resulted from the wars with France strengthened the momentum of the missionary cause. Britain's status as a military and commercial power increased the religious public's sense of the nation's obligations to the non-Christian world and channeled the attention of the evangelical public toward the foreign mission field. The acquisition of new territories populated by millions of new subjects of the British Empire "destitute of the knowledge of the Gospel, and sitting in darkness and the shadow of death . . . falling down before stocks and stones" captured the imagination of many within the evangelical community.[49] Increasing interest in foreign missions manifested itself in a supreme confidence in divine providence and the belief that the "remarkable extension of [British] commerce . . . arising from our lately acquired superiority of the seas" was part of God's plan to spread the knowledge of Christianity.[50]

Evangelicals believed strongly in the "regenerative role of lawful commerce within the providential order" and understood "colonization and commerce" as essential parts of the process of civilization and "the great means of ameliorating the condition of man."[51] The divine purpose behind the extension of British influence and trade seemed abundantly clear: to open avenues for the diffusion of Christianity throughout the world. Connections between commerce and Christianity showed themselves most clearly in evangelical campaigns against slavery, beginning with William Wilberforce's first calls for "legitimate" forms of commerce to replace the slave trade in the late 1780s. At the same time, the relationship between evangelicals and commercial interests was, without question, a contentious one, and Andrew Porter has demonstrated the skepticism with which many early supporters of the missionary movement viewed commercial enterprises.[52] The LMS required its candidates for missionary service to disavow any intention to withdraw from their "proper duties" in order to "pursue the worldly advantages" which the mission field "may present." The society's directors harshly criticized the East India Company for its persistent hostility toward religious instruction that might interfere with the interests of trade in India.[53] The general consensus of the evangelical public at the end of the eighteenth century was that commercial interests, in order to benefit Britain and the inhabitants of its colonial possessions, must be tempered by the influence of Christian principles. As John Griffin made clear in his address to the annual meeting of the LMS in 1807,

> The hope of accumulating property for personal enjoyment is a strong motive, but the satisfaction of communicating happiness to others is a motive which gives dignity to the soul . . . and . . . tends to moderate the selfishness of the other motive, and, at the same time affords a

powerful spring of action, tending to increase the temporal interest of the individual.[54]

A proper balance between commercial interests and Christian obligations stood to profit not only the conditions of colonies but Britain itself. In the advance of Christianity and civilization among the indigenous populations of the Empire, claimed Wilberforce, "we shall soon find the rectitude of our conduct rewarded, by the benefits of a regular and a growing commerce."[55]

A second conclusion upon which evangelicals, as a whole, could agree was that the providential expansion of British economic power increased the obligation of Christians to seize the opportunity to spread Christian knowledge. David Bogue put the question as clearly as could be:

> Do ye suppose, ye men of commerce, that the great end of God in this dispensation is, that the manufacture of England might find a more extensive and profitable market, and minister to our convenience, luxury, and affluence?

Bogue answered, definitively, no. "These are the false imaginations of worldly men," he declared; "God in his Providence has discovered these to us, and given us intercourse with them, that a door might therefore be opened for the entrance of the gospel."[56]

The Relationship between Home and Foreign Missions

The attention which the expansion of British commerce and influence drew to the nation's obligations toward the "heathen" subjects of its empire, also worked to raise evangelical concerns about the "heathen at home." It seems no mere coincidence that the creation of foreign missionary societies in the 1790s was accompanied by the formation of the earliest dissenting organizations to promote home missions, such as the Lancashire Congregational Union's Itinerant Society. There are good reasons to believe that evangelical Dissenters saw both foreign missions and evangelization at home as part of the same obligation to spread knowledge of the gospel. Early nineteenth-century evangelicals readily drew parallels between the lands of the "heathen world" abroad and the remote, so-called "dark corners" of the English countryside. Reflecting upon his early career as an itinerant evangelist, George Greatbatch recalled that he had "little thought there was a station for me at home, which so much resembled the ideas I had formed of an uncivilized heathen land."[57]

In 1798 the Lancashire Congregationalist Samuel Greatheed observed how the "institution of the Missionary Society" and the example of the "pious mechanics and a few Ministers" who put themselves forward as missionaries, had inspired many "Ministers and private Christians" to consider "whether it was not their duty to do likewise." Greatheed noted that while circumstances prevented most from entering the foreign mission field, "they felt with new force that they ought not to leave anything undone that they could do at home." As a result, village preaching and other forms of itinerancy "revived by degrees pretty generally" among Dissenters. Moreover, "the example of association offered by the Missionary Society . . . had considerable influence in disposing Ministers to associate in their respective vicinities for the purpose of spreading the Gospel around them."[58] Greatheed and William Roby not only devoted themselves to the formation of the Lancashire Congregational Union's Itinerant Society, they also served as county directors for the LMS. At the same time that Roby was convincing George Greatbatch to remain and to evangelize in Lancashire, he regularly nominated to the directors of the Society in London candidates for service in foreign missions. When the Rev. Joseph Jefferson stood before the annual meeting of the LMS in 1811 and declared himself "unfit to be a missionary . . . except in village excursions, among the heathen at home," he expressed a common belief that "missionary" work comprised evangelization at home as well as abroad.[59]

Individuals did, in some instances, differ over which project ought to take priority. Letters to the *Home Missionary Magazine* frequently asserted that "[h]ome . . . has the first claim on our attention," as did hymns, which declared,

> Shall we hold the bright lamp of Missions on high,
> And leave all around us in gloom?
> And regard not the claims of the millions who die
> In heathenish darkness at Home?[60]

Alternatively, William Carey responded to those who emphasized the "multitudes in our own nation . . . as ignorant as the South-Sea savages" by claiming that while "our own countrymen have the means of grace, and may attend on the word preached if they chuse it . . . but with them the case is widely different who have no Bible, no written language, . . . no ministers." "Pity, therefore, humanity, and much more Christianity," he declared, "call loudly for every possible exertion to introduce the gospel among them."[61] Some historians have taken this evidence to emphasize the competition between home and foreign missionary interests, to suggest a contradictory or opposing relationship between the two movements.

Even scholars who recognize a more complementary connection nevertheless stress the "Primacy of the Foreign Field."[62] They point to the consistently higher incomes of foreign mission societies compared to those for home evangelization, and the leaders of the home missionary movement's repeated complaints of the challenges of contending with the exotic and adventurous nature of foreign missions in the contest for financial support. The statistical evidence of the ascendancy of foreign missions is compelling, yet it remains unclear that this is the best way to assess the relative strength of the two movements. During the decade of the 1820s the annual income of the LMS averaged £34,570, while the total income of the Home Missionary Society during the same period was a mere £14,476.[63] On this evidence the primacy of the foreign field seems obvious, but such a conclusion fails to take account of important differences between the organization and operation of the two causes.

The missionary societies, by drawing together the voluntary contributions of individuals and congregations and effectively channeling the enthusiasm of the religious public, provided evangelicals with a solution to the unique challenges of attempting "big things . . . like the evangelization of the world."[64] In practical terms the voluntary society made it possible, in a way that individual congregations could not, to enlist missionaries, train them for the mission field, and provide them with the supplies and transportation necessary to send them to the far corners of the globe. These tasks, as the directors of the societies repeatedly reminded their supporters, required considerable financial resources. Without the mobilization of the religious public through the societies, the foreign missionary movement could not have existed.

The case of home missions, on the other hand, involved a different set of challenges and circumstances. As we have seen above, evangelicals facilitated the expansion of the Revival through a variety of localized initiatives, such as itinerant preaching and Sunday schools. Individuals, or congregations, could advance the progress of the home missionary movement in ways impossible in the foreign field. Roger Cunliffe, a prominent Blackburn banker, "concerned about the moral and spiritual welfare of the people" in his native Great Harwood, built a room for preaching and religious services "at his own expense."[65] William Hayhurst, the textile worker who gathered his own congregation in the village of Knowle Green, demonstrated the possibilities for enterprising laborers committed to the evangelical mission.

A consequence of these circumstances was that national societies directed toward home missionary work were slower to develop than their foreign counterparts. Far more common were county organizations like the North Bucks Association of Independent Churches and Ministers. It directed the resources and time of the ministers and members of the congregations in Aylesbury, Olney, and Winslow toward itinerant preaching and Sunday schools in "the more remote and destitute villages" of northern Bucks.[66]

A Congregationalist home missionary equivalent to the LMS emerged only gradually over the course of the first two decades of the nineteenth century. An association of ministers known as the Societas Evangelica commenced labors in the late 1790s, and John Eyre, secretary of the LMS, also founded a village itinerant society of his own. Nevertheless, no effective organization emerged on a nationwide scale until 1819.[67] Even then, its founders intended for the Home Missionary Society to "strengthen District and County Associations, and Sunday-school Unions" not to supplant them.[68] Home missions remained primarily a county and regionally focused movement that did not require the same kind of resources or sophisticated national organization as the foreign cause to succeed.

Leaders of the home missionary movement, who were often also prominent supporters of foreign societies, clearly recognized the popularity of foreign missions. Repeated references on the part of home missionary publications to the "dark quarters of Cumbria" and their inhabitants "no less . . . interesting" than those of foreign lands "because they are at Home" reflected efforts to attach some of the allure and exoticness of foreign missions to the home efforts.[69] Still, complaints about the challenges of raising funds for home missions ought not to be read simply as hostility toward the foreign cause. The popularity of foreign missions, in fact, offered one of the strongest arguments in favor of supporting evangelization at home. Every new convert made in Britain provided one more potential supporter of the endeavor to convert the "heathen" abroad. The home and foreign missionary efforts were, without question, separate enterprises, but historians can overstate the extent of the competition or contradictions between them. Differences in their structure, practice, and organization were real, and it is difficult to deny that foreign missions more readily caught the attention of the general public. Nevertheless, the religious public at the turn of the century, as a whole, viewed home and foreign missions as two parts of a greater movement to carry news of the gospel to all places "where Christ was never named."[70]

This chapter has traced the roots of the missionary movement back to the resurgence of Anglican piety at the end of the seventeenth century, leading to the appearance of the religious societies and Sunday schools that helped to set the stage for the Evangelical Revival within the church. Groups organized for the improvement of Christian knowledge, such as the SPCK and the SPG, presaged the missionary societies of the late eighteenth century that expanded upon the scope of their predecessors by turning to the voluntary support of the religious public and emphasizing a global mission. In England, the Methodist revival of John Wesley and George Whitefield ultimately transformed the religious landscape by expanding the influence of evangelical religion and the practice of itinerant preaching. In time evangelical ideals, and itinerancy, made their way into the denominations of Old Dissent, reviving them from the doldrums of the midcentury. The accompanying decline of Calvinist precepts and inwardness increasingly turned the attention of the dissenting religious public to the condition of the "heathen" at home and abroad.

The expansion of British strength and influence overseas increased the evangelical public's interest in the missionary endeavor as the hand of God seemed to be directing Britain toward a leading role in the promotion of the gospel and humanitarian causes. The rise of the missionary societies, dependent upon the support of a mass membership that drew from across denominations and social classes, facilitated the realization of a global mission to the "heathen." Significantly, missionary enthusiasm contributed to the redoubling of efforts for evangelization at home. County associations, and ultimately national societies, coordinated a multitude of local initiatives by ministers and lay persons to take the gospel to the "dark corners" of the countryside. The resultant surge in the numbers of itinerant preachers, the dramatic expansion of evangelical religion in both its Methodist and dissenting varieties, unsettled defenders of the established church. During the uncertain times of the revolutionary era, conservatives viewed popular religious movements with increasing suspicion. The enthusiasm of the religious public for the home and foreign missionary movements, and the unease that it instilled within the establishment, at length brought calls to stem the tide of sectarianism. The evangelical public's response to the answer to that call would mark a crucial turning point in the practice and culture of dissenting politics.

2

Itinerancy, Religious Liberty, and the Rise of Evangelical Politics

In May 1811 Henry Addington, Viscount Sidmouth brought before the House of Lords a bill to address "the abuses which had arisen in the interpretation and the execution" of the Toleration Acts, which had protected nonconformists' freedom of religious worship since 1689.[1] The origins of Sidmouth's bill lay in the growth of evangelical nonconformity examined in the previous chapter. The expansion of evangelicalism aroused considerable anxiety among the defenders of the establishment, who feared the consequences of the eroding influence of the Church in British society. Sidmouth stated the risks involved with exceptional clarity. If the establishment failed to respond to the threat posed by the growth of evangelical Dissent, "we shall be in danger of having a nominal established Church, and a sectarian people."[2] He, and his supporters, viewed his bill to regulate the licensing of nonconformist ministers under the Toleration Acts as an appropriate measure to protect the status and influence of the established Church. For Dissenters, on the other hand, the bill represented a virtual repeal of the principle of religious liberty and acted as a catalyst to the emergence of evangelical nonconformity as a significant and influential force in nineteenth-century British politics.

Sidmouth's fears of the rise of a "sectarian people" were not without foundation. The number of licenses granted to dissenting preachers under the Toleration Acts had risen from fewer than one hundred in the 1760s to more than one thousand in the first decade of the nineteenth century. Furthermore, many of those receiving licenses no longer fit the image of a traditional minister. This new kind of preacher, "less well educated than the older sort of Dissenting minister" and often an itinerant, was usually associated with the Methodists or evangelical congregations among the Independents and Baptists.[3] Magistrates' liberal application of the Toleration Acts, according to Sidmouth, allowed any person "calling himself a protestant dissenter, of whatever age, or condition, however ignorant, however exceptionable in conduct and character," to obtain a license. He objected to such "self appointed preachers . . . wholly destitute of ordinary attainments" in education and training. Although he declined to interfere with the tenets and doctrines of dissenting congregations, he believed "to endeavour that . . . they should not be preached and taught by the grossly ignorant and the profligate" did not infringe upon toleration.[4] Sidmouth's comments implied that his bill was primarily intended to check the licensing of the poor, uneducated, itinerant preachers primarily responsible for the growth of evangelicalism among the lower classes.

In these opinions Sidmouth was not alone. An 1807 tract the by Rev. Josiah Thomas of Somerset typified establishment reactions to the growth of evangelical nonconformity, and Methodism in particular. Thomas protested against religious toleration that had "nearly obliterated from the common mind" all distinctions between law and disorder "by allowing to every man the privilege of thinking and of acting as he pleases, with regard to religious concerns." In his estimation, the expansion of evangelical Dissent and "clamours for religious liberty" had "drowned all sense of religious order and moral decency" in British society. The "confusions . . . discontents, and the religious madness," which Thomas attributed to the advance of evangelicalism, had "increased to such an extent as to endanger . . . the constitution in state and church."[5] To men of Thomas' and Sidmouth's opinions the establishment of the church and state constituted the bedrock of law and order. Political or religious dissent from the establishment, which in the minds of many were frequently combined, posed a serious threat. The unchecked growth of evangelical nonconformity endangered the stability of the entire social order.[6]

The bias of churchmen and numerous magistrates against uneducated, lower class preachers who obtained licenses under the Toleration Acts was reflected in the attitudes of numerous correspondents who encouraged Sidmouth to bring forth his measure. The Bishop of Durham warned against "modern sectaries" assembling "in barns . . . or in other buildings of the most improper kind, to hear the wild effusions of a mechanic or a ploughboy . . . destitute of the first rudiments of learning, sacred or profane."[7] The

chairman of the Stafford quarter sessions lamented that "low and illiterate fanatics" claiming divine inspiration "should be allowed to disturb the
order of society, and delude the weak and unwary."[8] The Rector of Sedstone,
Hertfordshire, decried a Methodist preacher who taught his flock that while
"all the knowledge of the clergy was only bought . . . *his* knowledge was
inspired."[9] To defenders of the establishment, evangelical claims to divine
inspiration posed a serious threat to the position of the church, its clergy,
and the catechism. Evangelical preachers instilled contempt for the religious
and civil institutions of the nation and sowed the seeds of discontent and
sedition among the lower orders of society.

Opinions of this sort intensified in the unpredictable and tumultuous years of the revolutionary era. Excluded from civil offices, effectively
second-class subjects, politically active Dissenters were of necessity advocates of civil liberties and reform. So-called Rational Dissenters, such as
Richard Price and Joseph Priestley, were notorious for their support of the
revolution in France and helped to make all religious Dissenters potential
Jacobins in the eyes of conservative churchmen. Agitation for the repeal of
the Test and Corporation Acts, which coincided with the early years of the
French Revolution, compounded suspicions about the loyalty of Dissenters.
In 1790, even the relatively moderate *Gentlemen's Magazine* maintained that
"a Dissenter, whatever may be his integrity and piety . . . is an unfit person
to be entrusted with command, authority and influence. . . . Ill will to the
establishment must, in all governments, belong to the Dissenter, if he be
an honest man."[10] Some evangelicals made their own contributions to the
suspicions of the agents of the establishment. Early praise for the revolution
in France, driven largely by excitement over the apparent collapse of papal
"tyranny," kept the Congregational minister Rev. David Bogue and other
evangelicals under the careful watch of the authorities. Conservative forces
reacted with dread to signs of religious enthusiasm that evoked recollections
of the religious tempests of the seventeenth century. "The descendants of
the puritans are still found among us," the *Anti Jacobin* alleged in 1800,
making the connection between religious enthusiasm and the threat of revolution explicit.[11]

In contrast with the concerns expressed by Sidmouth and other defenders of the establishment, scholarly interpretations have regularly emphasized
the conservative influences of evangelical religion. Elie Halévy's famous
thesis suggests that "England was spared the revolution toward which the
contradictions in her polity and economy might otherwise have lead [*sic*]
her, through the stabilizing influence of evangelical religion, particularly

Methodism."[12] Eric Hobsbawm identifies Methodism as an "anti-radical" force in popular politics, although not sufficient to have prevented revolution on its own, and Edward Thompson stresses the role of Methodist conservatism in impeding the revolutionary development of the English working class.[13]

Bernard Semmel and Alan Gilbert instead emphasize that it was the liberal, rather than the conservative, nature of evangelicalism that was most significant. Semmel connects Wesleyan Arminianism to a liberal revolution centered upon individual responsibility and laissez-faire economics. Gilbert asserts that many ordinary Methodists rejected the Wesleyan leadership's conservatism and instead embraced (along with evangelical Dissenters) a "moderate radicalism" that although critical of the establishment did not encompass revolution. According to Gilbert, this moderate evangelical radicalism operated as a "political 'safety valve' for the pressures of early industrial politics."[14]

In *The Methodist Revolution* Semmel further argues that in response to calumnies of the establishment, Wesleyan Methodist leaders attempted to dampen radicalism "by rechanneling . . . potentially disruptive evangelizing enthusiasm into foreign missions."[15] The Methodist mission party consciously tried to use foreign missions as a safety valve for the religious and social tensions resulting from evangelization and religious enthusiasm, attempting to lessen the fears of Sidmouth and the government by moderating itinerancy and evangelization at home through the encouragement of foreign missions. Semmel's thesis implies that the Methodist leadership cynically manipulated the home and foreign missionary movements to their political advantage to quiet attacks from conservative supporters of the established church and state.

Susan Thorne also identifies tensions and divisions within Dissent between the home and foreign missionary movements. She suggests that the turmoil of the revolutionary years, and the fear of connections between all branches of Dissent and Jacobinism, strengthened the supremacy of foreign missionary work over home evangelization. The compounding of "metropolitan social tensions" throughout the era, she argues, led to the "privileging" of the foreign missions over the home missionary movement. Shocked by the increasing radicalism of the events in France, "propertied Dissenters" began disassociating themselves from home missions, "whose social structure (large public meetings addressed by plebeian enthusiasts) if not their political discourse closely resembled mass mobilizations on the continent." As a result, the home missionary endeavor was left to "impoverished and politically vulnerable plebeian and radical elements within evangelical Dissent, from whom their respectable counterparts were increasingly alienated." Thorne considers this development a further explanation for the Dissenters' "negligible" support of home missions as compared to the foreign societies and a significant factor in shaping the attitudes of the "governing classes" toward potential dangers or benefits of itinerancy and foreign missionary work. As evidence of the differing "level[s] of concern" with which the ruling classes viewed the two movements, she contends that while the British government, through Sidmouth's bill, took "measures . . . to restrict the movement of itinerant ministries" at home, it pressed the East India Company to open its territories to foreign missions.[16]

If such conclusions were true, we might expect to find a reasonable amount of support for Sidmouth's measure among the respectable and propertied leaders of the dissenting interest. Sidmouth himself made a concerted effort to win the support of the nonconformist leadership, heeding the Bishop of Gloucester's warning that "there must be no force in matters of religion."[17] He assured the Lords that he had met with prominent Dissenters and confidently wrote to his brother, "I should think the measure *in itself* will be well taken by them."[18] In these meetings he stressed his "desire to render a benefit to the dissenters in general" and to "promote the honor, dignity, and sanctity of Religion."[19] He endeavored to convince the leading Methodists, Thomas Coke and Adam Clarke, that it was to their benefit to support "just and reasonable regulations tending to render their fellow-preachers more respectable and select."[20] Sidmouth confidently believed he had won the support of the Dissenters and the Methodist leaders and presumed that "he had done nothing which he would not have done had he been a dissenter" himself.[21]

Did the leadership of the movement, or "propertied Dissenters," share Sidmouth's concerns over the licensing of "cobblers, tailors, pig-drovers, and chimney-sweepers"[22] as preachers, or Josiah Thomas' fears of the impact of "fanatical seceder[s]" upon the social and political order? A careful examination of the Dissenters' response to Sidmouth's bill suggests that this was not the case. The Dissenting Deputies voiced several objections to the bill, attempting to "induce [Sidmouth] to relinquish his designs of bringing it forward," arguing that the "degree of learning" possessed by preachers was not the business of legislature.[23] Only days after his meeting with Sidmouth Coke wrote of his concern that the bill would disturb "the itinerant plan of the Methodists," and Clarke expressed fear that new restrictions "might be caviled at" by magistrates unwilling to license itinerant preachers.[24]

Sidmouth confidently believed that he had won the support of the Dissenters and the Methodists, yet in the nonconformists' view the bill could only "subvert the very basis of toleration." Far from distancing the leaders of the dissenting interest, or the dissenting public, from the home missionary movement, the debate over Sidmouth's bill brought them strongly to the defense of even humble and uneducated preachers in the name of religious liberty.

The Campaign against Sidmouth's Bill

Upon introducing his bill for its first reading Sidmouth assured the Lords that he neither intended nor wished to undermine the Toleration Acts. By limiting the automatic authorization of applicants without regard to respectability or education Sidmouth intended to ensure some minimum standard of competency and respectability among the dissenting clergy. Dissenters and churchmen alike, he declared, desired to prevent abuses that allowed so many "unfit" persons to receive licenses to preach. The bill proposed that applicants should not be granted licenses without the support of "six reputable householders of the persuasion to which [they] belonged" as proof of their moral and intellectual fitness to serve as preachers. Those unable to present the necessary householders to testify to their character and education would no longer qualify for licenses. Sidmouth also designed the bill to stem the growth of itinerant preaching by requiring that only applicants from "a known and distinct place of worship" be eligible to receive a license.[25] Sidmouth claimed that his bill went no further than to "render more efficient" the operation of the Toleration Acts, which, he alleged, had been explained and understood differently by magistrates in various counties.[26] In fact, the bill proposed a new test to require a minimum level of competency and respectability among applicants for licenses that Sidmouth believed would help to secure the status of the establishment by controlling licensing more tightly. He assured Wesleyans and Dissenters alike of the benefits of supporting a measure "designed to protect the respectable by eliminating the disreputable" among their preachers.[27]

Sidmouth's introduction of his bill to the Lords immediately "occasioned general excitement among the Dissenters." A Methodist MP wrote to Sidmouth that he had scarcely ever known any measure that had excited so universal an alarm in so short a period."[28] Opponents had only twelve days in which to mobilize against the bill before its second reading. The unified and overwhelming response that they produced was testament to their organization and a sign of the extreme threat to religious liberty that they perceived in the bill.

The Dissenting Deputies, the traditional representatives of the dissenting interest, responded under the direction of their chairman William Smith, the Unitarian MP from Norwich. They resolved unanimously to present a petition against the bill to Parliament, forcefully asserting that "liberty of conscience, comprehending the freedom of Public Assemblies for religious worship and instruction . . . [was] the individual right of all." The Deputies affirmed their "bounden duty . . . to protest against the principle of such a measure, and to point out the unjust and vexatious operations of the aforesaid bill" and distributed one thousand copies of the petition to ministers throughout the nation.[29]

The Deputies' petition clearly expressed their condemnation of the bill, and their representatives gave Sidmouth no encouragement in their one meeting with the former Prime Minister. Yet at the time many Dissenters expressed concern over the Deputies' apparent "lack of defense or zeal" in promoting public condemnation of the bill. John Gurney, their deputy chairman, felt compelled to explain the "apparent inactivity of the Deputies" in opposition to the bill to the Unitarian minister Thomas Belsham in June 1811. Gurney stated that since the Toleration Acts were then generally being enforced in a manner favorable to Dissenters, the Deputies had been reluctant to engage in a debate over the acts for fear of losing the advantages enjoyed under the current system. The Deputies "on the whole thought it better to lie still for the present inviting a more favorable opportunity" for a "full scale confrontation on the interpretation of the Toleration Acts." They hoped for the return of the Whigs to power (which seemed a real possibility in 1811), confident that under a Whig administration any decisions on religious toleration would be made in their favor.[30]

Memories of the violent reaction to the campaign for repeal of the Test Acts in 1789 and mob violence against Dissenters throughout the 1790s remained fresh in the minds of the Deputies and bred a fear of resorting to popular agitation. They scrupulously avoided public confrontations and preferred to work behind the scenes, as is evident in their efforts to persuade Sidmouth to drop consideration of the measure in 1810. As a result, the Deputies were neither anxious nor well prepared to lead a public campaign against the bill. Their failure to organize a strong popular response to Sidmouth left a vacuum in the political leadership of the dissenting interest that the forces of the evangelical nonconformists rushed to fill.

The evangelical response to Sidmouth's bill took shape on 15 May with
a gathering of Dissenters, Methodists, and Anglican supporters of the principle of religious liberty called to consider organizing opposition to the measure. Although the group "included Unitarians, and even liberal Anglicans,"
its principal support and leadership came from the ranks of evangelical Dissent.[31] Independents, Baptists, and Calvinist Methodists formed the core
of what was to become the Protestant Society for the Protection of Religious Liberty, the first predominantly evangelical organization dedicated
to that cause. The leading figure was John Wilks, the son of a founding
father of the London Missionary Society (LMS) and the *Evangelical Magazine*, the Rev. Matthew Wilks. The report of the meeting, published in
the *Evangelical Magazine*, declared "the right to worship God according to
individual judgment . . . an inalienable right superior to all social regulations." It rejected the principle "assumed as the foundation" of Sidmouth's
bill, namely, that the state retained the right to set limits on toleration, and
denounced it as "a precedent for future attempts at even more dangerous or
fatal experiments against religious liberty." Finally, the meeting resolved to
send a petition against the bill to the House of Lords and established a committee in London to coordinate the collection of "similar Petitions" from
"all congregations of Protestant Dissenters, and other friends of Religious
Liberty throughout the Empire."[32]

Adhering to their official position that they were not Dissenters, the
Wesleyan Methodists arranged their own response to Sidmouth under the
direction of the "London based connexional solicitor," Thomas Allan.[33]
Allan convened a meeting of the Methodist General Committee on 14 May
that denounced Sidmouth's measure as "subversive of the most valuable
rights and privileges which we as a religious society enjoy." The Wesleyans
saw the greatest danger in Sidmouth's attempts to restrict itinerancy, which
would "render it very difficult, if not impracticable, to obtain certificates
for the great body of local preachers and exhorters . . . whose aid is essentially necessary in the very numerous chapels and meeting houses in which
our congregations assemble." The committee concluded that the Toleration
Laws were neither "so ineffectual," nor was their interpretation "so uncertain as to render any bill necessary to explain them, much less curtail the
benefits intended to be curtailed by them." In language even stronger than
that of the Protestant Society the Wesleyans denounced the bill as "needless
and oppressive" and expressed confidence that Parliament would not adopt
a measure "so obnoxious to such a large proportion of the nation as our societies and congregations constitute."[34]

Most importantly the Protestant Society and the Methodist Committee took action in the orchestration of petition campaigns designed to show the strength of popular opposition to the bill. Representatives of both organizations across the country engaged in collecting signatures on petitions from dissenting and Methodist congregations. In London the leaders of the opposition devoted themselves to coordination of the campaign. According to Gurney, the Methodist Committee "held a permanent sitting . . . for nearly a week—almost day and night.[35] The Methodist connexional leader, Thomas Coke, wrote to Rev. Richard Gower that he had spent considerable time in London entirely consumed with fighting the bill.[36] The Methodists produced two hundred fifty petitions, with nearly thirty thousand signatures. The Protestant Society's campaign, combined with a late effort on the part of the Dissenting Deputies, brought the total number of petitions against the bill to almost seven hundred. Lord Holland recalled, "[F]or some days no places were to be had on the stage coaches and diligences of the Kingdom; all were occupied with petitions to Parliament against the measure."[37]

Evangelicals looked to the Whigs and especially to Lord Holland, the nephew of Charles James Fox, to conduct their opposition to the bill in the House of Lords. The Foxite Whig creed firmly supported the right to the kind of full religious liberty that Sidmouth and his allies found so dangerous. In response to Sidmouth's motion for the first reading of the bill, Holland declared that he opposed the intent of the bill because he was "of the opinion that every person had the right to preach those religious opinions that he consciously believed." He vigorously defended the principle of religious liberty and asserted that "all those who thought it their duty to interpret the Scriptures, should have the right to adopt their own mode of doing so." The bill infringed upon their "natural rights," and he conspicuously belittled the aspersions cast by Sidmouth against humble, uneducated preachers.[38] Many other Whig lords fell in behind Holland's opposition. Lord Erskine called the bill "declaratory" and "directly repugnant to the spirit and letter of the Toleration Acts."[39] Earl Stanhope declared his hostility to the bill and his hatred for the name Toleration Act "because he loved liberty."[40] Holland particularly objected to the requirement of testimonials.

[Applicants] must find six housekeepers to vouch for their morality. And who were those that were to have the power to bring forward six housekeepers to speak to character, or who was to deny to the dissenters the right of having humble men for their teachers? Suppose five hundred

paupers chose to hear religion from . . . a man of their own choosing and
of their own class, was it to be said, that the desire was beyond what might
be permitted? and where was this teacher to find his six housekeepers?[41]

The Whig's defense of the principle of religious liberty echoed the arguments made by the dissenting leadership and the evangelical public in their
response to the bill.

On the day of the second reading, 21 May, the results of the nonconformist campaigns demonstrated the extent of popular opposition to the
measure. The government, which was willing to support Sidmouth as long
as he seemed to have the support of the dissenting public on his side, moved
quickly to encourage him to withdraw the bill. Liverpool, the government
leader in the Lords, observed that "the objective to be attained was not equal
to the inconvenience arising from public agitation against the bill."[42] He
and the rest of the government feared that alienating Dissenters might lead
them into a political alliance with the Roman Catholics against the privileges of the established church. Privately, Liverpool rebuked Sidmouth for
stirring up the Dissenters against government for the first time in nearly
two decades. "We have hitherto felt the advantage of this conduct [refrain-
ing from public contests with the government] in all our contests with the
Catholics," he wrote, "and I own I am apprehensive that if the measure in
question is to be persevered in, we may unite the Catholics and all other
Dissenters in the same cause."[43] An obstinate Sidmouth refused to yield,
claiming that the opposition was the result of "great misconception and mis-
apprehension" on the part of the general public.[44] Holland chided Sidmouth
for thinking the Dissenters so "ignorant" as not to see the dangerous effect
of the bill on their own interests. Earl Stanhope called the day of the second
reading the happiest of his career in the Lords because of the "immense heap
of petitions that was strewed upon the floor, and piled upon their table, and
all against this wretched bill."[45] The house voted to delay the second reading
of the bill for six months, thus consigning it to legislative oblivion.

The issue of religious toleration, and what it meant, was at the heart
of the debate over the bill. Sidmouth conceived of toleration in the most
restrictive sense. In his view, the state and the established church tolerated
the beliefs of nonconformists and granted them a freedom of worship within
limits. By 1811 the practice of Toleration Acts had allowed such a great
expansion of Dissent that it posed a threat to the stability of the establishment. The most dangerous aspect, in the midst of the plebeian radicalism of
the revolutionary era, was the alarming success of evangelicalism among the
lower orders of society. Sidmouth's bill specifically targeted the uneducated,

itinerant evangelical preachers who were drawing the lower classes away from the state church.

Sidmouth may have believed that his bill would affect only the lowly elements of evangelical nonconformity, so-called "Ranters," Primitive Methodists, and the like. However, the premise of the bill struck at the core principle of Dissent, what was coming in the early nineteenth century to be called religious liberty. The infringement upon religious liberty was certain to cause opposition from even the most "respectable" and "propertied" Dissenters, who believed that all people possessed the right to express the views they conscientiously held free from all penalties of the law. The Unitarian divine, Thomas Belsham, characterized religious liberty as "the great principle of Toleration" and affirmed that "in defense of it Dissenters of all denominations, Trinitarians, Arians, Unitarians, Calvinists, Arminians, Presbyterians, Independents, and Baptists, and the vast growing body of Methodists, would all unite as one man."[46]

The Politics of Toleration and Religious Liberty

The response to Sidmouth's bill proved him correct. The public opposition to Sidmouth demonstrated the determination of nonconformists, and now emphatically evangelicals, to defend their rights. The strength of their opposition was not lost upon the government, which quickly backed away from Sidmouth and began to consider removing legal restrictions upon Dissent. In April 1812 the Prime Minister, Spencer Perceval, informed the Dissenting Deputies and representatives of the Methodists of his intent "to bring forward, or support an application to Parliament for the purpose of offering relief" to the Dissenters.[47] Perceval, and following his assassination the new Prime Minister, Liverpool, carried through their professions of good will in the form of a new Toleration Act which interpreted the law to the nonconformists' satisfaction and repealed the Conventicle and Five-Mile Acts. By 1813, "the spirit of toleration so prevailed that even the Unitarians were extended a measure of relief," in the form of a Unitarian Toleration Act.[48] The smoothness with which these extensions of religious liberty passed through Parliament arose from the fact that the government had made a tactical decision to appease nonconformist opinion to keep them from making common cause with the Catholics. Liverpool conveyed this strategy to the Archbishop of Canterbury in 1812.

> I think it very desirable that whatever is granted those people [nonconformists] should be felt by them to be granted by government, and that

they should not be led to make common cause with those whose views would lead them to level all distinctions, and to make no discrimination between the necessary connections of Church and State, and the fullest toleration to the subjects of the country in matters purely religious.[49]

The government moved to pacify nonconformist sentiment in hopes of nipping in the bud any thought of a nonconformist alliance with the Catholics. Presented with the stormy and newly mobilized political voice of evangelical Dissent, Liverpool determined to keep the government on good terms with the Dissenters, and not least with their new evangelical majority. His fears of a dissenting and Catholic alliance were naturally heightened by the Whigs' reintroduction of the Catholic issue in 1812 and 1813.

The budding political organization of evangelical Dissent was forced on by these ostensibly Catholic Emancipation bills, which served to raise the political temperature of the debates over religious liberty. Holland saw great potential for creating Whig support among the evangelicals, whom, as was common at the time, he indiscriminately labeled "Methodists." Those with whom he had most contact, however, were not the Wesleyans but evangelical Dissenters (Independents, Calvinist Methodists, and Baptists). In particular, Holland had a close connection with the secretary of the Protestant Society, John Wilks, whom he often referred to as "my Methodist friend."[50]

In the days before the defeat of Sidmouth's bill Holland wrote to Lord Grenville,

> Certain I am that he [Sidmouth] will do great good if by this unprovoked attack on the Methodists he teaches them that it is their real interest to concur with other Dissenters in promoting and not with the Church in resisting all extension of religious liberty. His bill will be a warning to them and I hope they will not again take part with the cry of "no popery" when they see that "no Methodism" would be one fully agreeable to the high church party if an opportunity should occur of raising it with effect.[51]

He may have overestimated the evangelicals' willingness to give up the cry of "no popery," but Holland was entirely correct in his estimation of the value to the Whigs of the evangelical goodwill they won by their opposition to Sidmouth. In another letter to Grenville, he noted, "[T]he only body that can at all counterbalance the church is the Methodists and . . . they profess some obligation to me for my early opposition to Sidmouth's bill."[52] Cultivating the allegiance of his "Methodist" friends was central to Holland's strategy to obtain religious liberty for Catholics and Protestant Dissenters alike.

The Roman Catholic Relief Bill brought forward by Henry Grattan in April 1813 proposed to remove the requirement of taking the sacrament "according to the usage of the church of England," for "holding civil and military offices" or being "a member of any lay body corporate."[53] These clauses, in effect, negated the Test and Corporation Acts and would have removed the disabilities of the Dissenters without ever mentioning them in the bill. Grattan's intention was to kill two birds with one stone; if Catholic Emancipation succeeded in the form proposed, religious liberty for the Dissenters would be achieved as well. Lord Castlereagh, the government leader in the Commons, recognized the intent of the bill and observed that Grattan "had gone a little farther than he ought to . . . in wishing to reagitate now the question concerning the test laws generally." Taking Castlereagh's concerns into account, George Canning amended the bill in committee and returned it to the Commons on 20 May with the clauses concerning the sacramental test omitted.[54]

Having intended to remove the grievances of both Catholics and Dissenters, and having failed, the Whigs next had to decide whether to accept the bill in its amended form. Lord Grey feared that by accepting the omission of the clauses the Whigs would risk alienating the Dissenters, who might conclude that their interests had been sold out in favor of the Catholics. He argued that pressing forward with the amended bill was "such an admission of the necessity of maintaining the Test Laws" as to "materially . . . prejudice the future agitation of this question as it applies to Protestant Dissenters." In Grey's opinion the Whigs ought to "risk the fate of the Bill" rather than accept the exclusion of the clauses. If the "loss would be misfortune," Grey concluded it would be "compensated" by the "advantage, that it would probably unite the whole body of Dissenters in a cordial co-operation with the Catholics."[55]

Holland and Samuel Whitbread, on the other hand, insisted that the amended bill, "if well managed" could be "made palatable to the Dissenters" as a preliminary step on the road to full religious freedom. Holland had received indications of some evangelicals' willingness to support Catholic Emancipation. He wrote to Grenville, in January 1813, that "a person who has much weight with the Whitefieldite Methodists and . . . a very ardent friend of religious liberty including the Catholick cause," perhaps John Wilks or his father Matthew, was ready to "support it by writings and sermons . . . protests and counterpetitions." Furthermore, his "Methodist friend" suggested that "some leading people," among them the influential evangelical minister Rowland Hill, "would declare for the Catholicks."[56]

Holland was not willing to give up Grattan's bill, pointing out rather weakly that Catholics and Protestants would still be left "equally exposed" to the Test Acts. He, like Grey, did believe in the necessity of associating Catholics and Dissenters, and thus creating "a much larger body of men . . . interested in the repeal of the Test Act and consequently united in promoting it."[57] Holland's strategy, however, ignored Grey's main point. As the sacramental test was of little interest to *Irish* Catholics at any rate, the offending clauses would have mainly affected the Dissenters and had been introduced largely for their benefit.[58] Grey feared that the removal of the clauses was bound to be deeply resented by Dissenters, and in the end he proved the better judge of their opinion.

Already the rising political enthusiasm of the evangelicals had presented problems for the Whigs' strategy. Dissenters had from the first showed little enthusiasm for a repeal of the Test Acts achieved by stealth and intended to have the vindication for their first-class citizenship publicly proclaimed. Thus when Grattan's bill was first under consideration, Wilks communicated to Whitbread the Protestant Society's intention to move "in force after the second reading of the Catholic Bill, to have obtained their own objects in that Bill." Both Whitbread and Holland advised against this, arguing that if the Dissenters just kept quiet, with the bill's passage "their object was equally attained." Whitbread confessed to Holland that while Wilks had "paid attention" to his advice, he had indicated that it would be "difficult to control the [dissenting] Body" with regard to the issue.[59] Allies as well as opponents were forced to contend with an increasingly aggressive evangelical movement.

True to Grey's prediction, after the offending clauses had been removed from the Catholic bill, Holland received a letter from Wilks "full of disappointment at the change."[60] A nervous Grey continued to press upon Holland his fears that "in the event of the Bill passing in its present form the Dissenters will . . . probably complain that they have been deceived and their interests betrayed."[61] Holland replied that he intended to assuage this frustration by reasserting the Whigs' absolute commitment "to remove from Catholics and from Dissenters alike all these badges of servitude." He further pledged himself "to bring forward their questions in the way and at the time that they not I may think most advantageous."[62] Although Holland would loyally honor this pledge in the future, he could not remove the Dissenters' deep irritation at the time.

The Dissenters continued to chafe at what seemed to them the Whigs' fixed policy of putting the Catholic cause first. The Whigs' reintroduction of the Catholic question several times in the years following Grattan's bill reinforced this perception in the minds of leading Dissenters and was especially resented by evangelicals represented by the Protestant Society. In 1820 William Smith wrote to Holland, "Our Body is tired with the repeated delays to which I from time to time obtained their reluctant consent, principally with a view to our relationship to the Catholic Question." Smith added, with dismay, that too many Dissenters desired "to abjure all connection [with the Catholics] whatever."[63] Such sentiments did not weaken in the 1820s, with the Protestant Society the center of dissenting anti-Catholic feeling. Only clever maneuvering, and not a little obfuscation, by the dissenting leadership hid the divisions within the body over the Catholic issue and kept Dissenters united in their efforts to repeal the Test Acts, which finally succeeded in 1828.[64]

The defense of religious freedom in 1811 began the rise of significant political activity among evangelical Dissenters, but they soon turned their attention and energy in the direction of other issues. Among the first was the encouragement of Christian missions to India. In the early nineteenth century, while the number of missionaries in India continued to grow, their legal status remained uncertain. Persons entering British territory were required to obtain a license from the East India Company administration, which maintained a "cautious, almost hostile attitude towards missionaries."[65] The opposition of the Company to missionary activity led a sympathizer in the Admiralty Office to recommend to the Society to find ways to "introduce their missionaries into foreign settlements without any appeal to the executive government."[66]

Concern for the status of missionaries in India, and the heightened political activity of evangelicals, led the missionary societies to consider the possibility of achieving their goals through political channels. As early as 1793, Wilberforce had attempted, and failed, to secure the insertion of an amendment encouraging missions into the Company's Charter. The need to renew the Charter in 1813 provided a fresh opportunity to secure official recognition of the missions, and the directors of the LMS began to raise the issue in 1812. In April the directors sent a memorial to the government concerning the Company's policies toward missionaries. They expressed their regret at the lack of substantial missionary efforts in India. They saw this arising not from "any want of liberality on the part of the Government, but from some of the measures contained in the [East India Company] charters," namely, those that required missionaries to obtain licenses from the Company. This regulation, "intended to secure commercial privileges" to the Company, had "most unhappily operated to prevent the entrance of the divine light of revelation" into India. The directors encouraged the government to remove "every impediment . . . which would counteract the interests of Christianity there."[67] During the same period, George Burder, the secretary of the LMS, was in regular correspondence with Wilberforce on the developments in Parliament. On the eve of an important early vote on the question in 1812, Wilberforce urged Burder that "every possible effort must be used to procure the attendance of our friends. For on our not merely carrying the resolution but carrying it with a high hand may depend in no small degree, our influence with the government afterward when we shall begin to act upon the system agreed on."[68]

Thus in 1813 evangelicals began a new effort to bring the Charter into accord with the missionary cause. While Wilberforce again led the effort in the Commons, evangelical nonconformists organized much of the popular movement in support of amending the 1813 charter. The *Evangelical Magazine*, a Congregational publication closely associated with the LMS, declared that recent circumstances had made it necessary to "restrain, by law, that hostile spirit against Missions, which has been repeatedly displayed in our eastern possessions."[69] Evangelical nonconformists mobilized again for a campaign to influence Parliament.

On 30 March 1813, a deputation from the Protestant Society expressed their fervent commitment to the missionary cause to Liverpool and the Earl of Buckinghamshire, president of the Board of Control, through which the government exercised a broad supervision over the Company's handling of Indian affairs. The deputation received assurances from the ministers that it was their "intention, . . . their inclination, and their duty" to propose an amendment to empower the government to "grant permission to pious men of every sect to visit and reside in India," and to provide "all prudent facilities . . . [toward] . . . the Christianization of India."[70] Having secured a promise from the government to amend the Charter, evangelicals looked next to ensure that it would pass through Parliament.

With the example of the Sidmouth bill agitation still a recent memory evangelical Dissenters were confident in the ability of popular pressure to sway Parliament. The evangelical press explicitly described the campaign in terms of the expansion of religious liberty. The editors of the *Evangelical Magazine* urged "all friends of religious freedom and Christianity" to "express their sentiments with an unanimity and fervor worthy of the importance of the occasion, and which the Parliament and the Administration will not fail to respect." The *Methodist Magazine* printed a copy of a petition directed to the House of Lords to "serve as a model to others," with directions for forwarding petitions to the House of Commons as well.[71]

Political figures on all sides knew the significance of the bill to the evangelical public. Members of the Commons knew whence support for the amendment came and whom it threatened. Charles Marsh, who had served with the Company in India, declared with some hostility, "[T]he Church of England is to send out no missionaries at all . . . the supporters of the clause have reserved all their zeal for the sectarians . . . the whole task of conversion is abandoned to them."[72] Keenly aware of the feelings of evangelical public opinion, however, the government proceeded cautiously with its support for the amendment. Thomas Sutton objected to the measure's direct acknowledgment of "the object for which missionaries were to go to India." Fearful of the response of Indians to open parliamentary endorsement of the endeavor to convert them to Christianity, he suggested softening the language of the amendment to endorse sending persons to India "for various lawful purposes." Castlereagh, who expressed his own preference to leave religion out of the debate over the Charter, responded that the government "deemed the wording of the clause necessary to satisfy other feelings than his own," a somewhat delicate acknowledgment of the need to be sensitive to evangelical interests.[73]

In total, some 908 petitions signed by nearly half a million people were presented to Parliament in favor of the amendment. Such evidence of popular support played an important role in securing the passage of the amendment in the Commons by a majority of fifty-three and later in the House of Lords. The *Evangelical Magazine* congratulated its readers "and others who [had] joined in Petitions to Parliament for liberty to send missionaries to India" on their victory.[74] Evangelicals had recognized their potential to affect the outcome of the consideration of the question of Indian missions. Significantly, as we have seen, politicians of both parties were very aware of evangelical opinions and desirous of maintaining their goodwill. Once again mobilizing popular opinion and the religious public, evangelical Dissenters played a major role in attaining the amendment of the East India Charter against the reservations of the Company itself as well as those of several government ministers and members of Parliament.

The Politicizing of Evangelical Dissent

In the past few years, religion has regained a place of prominence in historical studies of early nineteenth-century politics, and scholars have recognized
the roots of the radical ideologies and politics in contesting the alliance of
church and state in late eighteenth- and nineteenth-century debates over
religion. Challenges to the *ancien regime*, as Jonathan Clark termed it, were
primarily challenges to the established Church.[75] So-called Rational Dissenters launched the assaults upon the Test and Corporation Acts in the
1780s and 1790s, and the ideas of Richard Price, Joseph Priestley, and
Andrew Kippis, among others, fostered the development of "political Dissent." In the late eighteenth century evangelical Dissenters frequently sought
to distinguish themselves from such political dissenters, often associated
with heterodoxy. In 1795 Rev. Thomas Hawies, a chaplain to the Countess
of Huntingdon, observed to the inaugural meeting of the LMS that evangelicals could expect little help in the missionary cause

> from such, as, separated from the established Church have renounced
> not only her forms, but the God we worship. Even of those who profess
> the tenets of barren orthodoxy, how many have turned their zeal from
> the power of religion to this world's politics? or gravely meet, merely to
> discuss the important means of promoting *the dissenting interest*?[76]

Leaders of the missionary and other evangelical movements encouraged
their followers to pursue religious rather than political causes. The most
serious ideological threat to the Anglican constitution, and the bulk of the
leadership in dissenting politics, came from Rational Dissenters like the
Unitarians.

In the early decades of the nineteenth century, however, though the
generals might have seemed familiar the army was rapidly changing. During the 1810s important elements of the political ideology of Rational Dissent were fast coming to be held by evangelicals whose theology had very
little relation to the views of Rational Dissenters. The tensions dividing the
church and Dissenters were increasingly caused by the loud and insistent
demands of an undoubtedly orthodox evangelical dissenting public and the
establishment's distress over the threat of the swelling ranks of evangelical
nonconformity to the church's position in British society. The sociopolitical
tensions of the revolutionary era intensified the establishment's apprehension of the plebeian, and thus potentially radical, revivals sweeping through
regions such as northern Staffordshire and Cheshire.[77] Sidmouth, and his
supporters, sought political and statutory solutions to the threat posed by

evangelical expansion. Such political action demanded a political response, and quickly. Faced with a serious challenge to their religious freedom evangelical Dissenters turned to those long in the vanguard of the cause of religious liberty—to Lord Holland, Lord Stanhope, Samuel Whitbread, and William Smith—men whose theological opinions were very far from their own, but whose politics were made to order for their purposes. Unitarians such as Smith, the chairman of the Dissenting Deputies, maintained a leading role in the cause; nevertheless, it was increasingly the evangelical rank and file that gave the dissenting movement its growing political power and influence. The Whigs, for their part, were eager to please evangelical Dissenters, in hoping to win their support for Catholic Emancipation. For the opposite reason, the government was equally interested in not antagonizing and indeed doing everything it could to mollify them. Following their successful opposition to Sidmouth's bill, their appetites whetted for further efforts, evangelicals pressed forward their demands for greater religious liberty and the promotion of Christian evangelization in India.

With the petition campaigns of 1811 and 1813 evangelical Dissenters claimed their place at the forefront of one of the most significant developments in nineteenth-century British politics. In a recent study of the role of pressure groups in communicating public opinion and exercising pressure upon Parliament on the eve of the Reform Bill of 1832, Peter Jupp notes the significance of the substantial growth in petitioning in an era "characterized by a general expectation that Parliament's function was to redress grievances." His conclusions suggest that the evangelical political activity spurred by the events of 1811 and 1813 was undiminished in the years that followed by identifying Catholic Emancipation, repeal of the Test and Corporation Acts, and abolition, all issues of considerable importance to evangelical Dissenters, as the "three great causes" of petition campaigns in the decade prior to the Reform Bill.[78]

Neither was the influence of evangelical Dissent upon the political life of the nation lost upon contemporary observers. In 1834 Wellington remarked to Lord Aberdeen,

> To tell you the truth, I am inclined to believe that that which for the last fifty years has been allowed to have such weight in public councils, I mean public opinion, was in fact the opinion of the opposition . . . or, in other words, of the Dissenters from the Church of England.[79]

During the first decades of the nineteenth century, given the modest demographic gains made by Unitarianism, such public opinion could have been

effectively demonstrated only by harnessing the support of the growing
numbers of evangelical Dissenters. Significantly, the successes of the 1811
and 1813 campaigns set them down the path of increasing political militancy. Their emerging political self-confidence was evident in their overwhelming support for the final campaigns against the Test and Corporation
Acts in 1827–1828 and in the culmination of the process in the 1830s as
Dissenting organizations and ministers unapologetically called for the disestablishment of the Church of England and an end to all disabilities.

In any state with an established church religious changes have political
consequences, and this was certainly true of early nineteenth-century Britain. This chapter has located the rise of evangelical political activity in the
debates over religious liberty and the threat posed to the Church of England
by the rapid increase in the number of evangelical nonconformist congregations. Lord Sidmouth designed his 1811 bill to restrict the licensing of nonconformist preachers to forestall the dangers of sectarian expansion in the
midst of the turbulent sociopolitical conditions of the revolutionary era. The
infringement of Sidmouth's bill upon the principle of religious liberty and
the common evangelical practice of itinerant preaching evoked the immediate and forceful opposition of evangelical Dissenters and Methodists. The
newly created Protestant Society for the Protection of Religious Liberty and
the Methodist Committee, in the first concerted efforts of evangelical nonconformists to act in defense of their vital interests, coordinated the popular
movement against the bill that threatened them.

Contrary to the suggestion that "propertied Dissenters" separated themselves from the home missionary movement during the early nineteenth century, I argue that Sidmouth's bill rallied the dissenting leadership, and its
evangelical base in particular, to the defense of itinerant preaching and a
broad principle of religious liberty, even for unlettered preachers of lowly
origins. Furthermore, the vigorous opposition of evangelicals to Sidmouth's
measure solidified their emergence as a political force capable of influencing
parliamentary decisions. The Whigs, champions of religious freedom, zeal-
ously worked to assist evangelical Dissenters in hopes of winning their support for the extension of religious liberty to Roman Catholics. For its part,
the government responded by expanding, not restricting, religious toleration
lest the Dissenters should ally themselves with the Catholics.

The impact of these events, however, was not confined to British soil.
Buoyed by their success in the Sidmouth bill agitation, evangelical organiza-
tions, such as the Protestant Society and the missionary societies, pressed
Parliament for official sanctioning of missionary endeavors in India. Far

from representing the "more receptive response" of the government to a missionary program that "facilitated its power in the colonies," government endorsement of the promission amendment to the Company Charter reflected a calculated response to the demands of the evangelical public. When Castlereagh declared to the Commons that government sponsorship of the amendment was a concession to opinions other than his own, no one would have doubted to whom he deferred.

The politicizing of evangelical Dissent between the years 1811 and 1813 furthered a process that had begun with the first campaigns against the slave trade in the late eighteenth century. The anti-slave-trade agitation was as much a moral and theological crusade as it was political, yet in these campaigns evangelicals developed the practices of petitioning and organizing pressure groups upon which the opposition to Sidmouth's bill was conducted. In the early nineteenth century these methods of political action came into their own through the formation of groups such as the Protestant Society. Significantly, as Lord Sidmouth and the defenders of the established church sought to stem the tide of evangelical sectarianism in Britain, white settler populations in the West Indies and South Africa made similar efforts to limit the extent and influence of evangelical missions in the colonies. These contests between the proponents and the rivals of religious freedom were also fought out in the context of shifting racial attitudes and colonial policies during the first half of the nineteenth century. The political concerns of evangelical Dissent would continue to center on questions of civil and religious liberties in both their metropolitan and colonial settings. It is to the further development of this process in the history of Britain's expanding empire that we shall turn in the next chapters.

3

The Missionary Movement
and the Politics of Abolition

"And, after all, it is merely about a poor missionary!" the antislavery MP Henry Brougham declared to the House of Commons, mocking the arguments of his opponents who would "shut [their] ears against all complaints" regarding the trial and condemnation of the missionary John Smith. Smith, an agent of the London Missionary Society (LMS) in the colony of Demerara, had died a "miserable death" in the colony's jail following his arrest and conviction for instigating a rebellion among the colony's slaves in 1823. The persecution of Smith, "a humble minister of the Gospel," by the Demerara planters created a stir within the antislavery movement upon which Brougham sought to capitalize when he rose before the House on the first of June 1824.

"It is the first time," he chided his opponents, "that I have to learn that the weakness of the sufferer . . . left single and alone to contend against power exercised with violence" should cause the House "to refuse to investigate the treatment of the individual." Brougham went on, not merely framing Smith's ordeal as a matter of the weak against the powerful, but in good Whig fashion as a matter of civil and religious equality. Did Smith's "connection with that class of religious people . . . separated from the national Church, alter or lessen his claims to the protection of the law?" Brougham was certain that it should not, and he celebrated Smith's dissenting connections.

> Mr. Smith . . . was . . . a faithful and pious minister of the Independents, that body so much to be respected . . . for the unshaken fortitude with

which in all times, they have maintained their attachment to civil and religious liberty, and . . . the great doctrine of toleration.[1]

That Brougham should begin his defense of Smith with a rousing defense of religious liberty reflects both the significance of the issue in Whig and dissenting politics that gathered strength as the decade wore on and the meaningful role it played in shaping the antislavery debate and its relation to the missionary movement.

Missionaries and their supporters opposed slavery in formidable numbers. Yet for fear of the reprisals of the West Indian planters and their allies in Britain, the missionary societies and their agents only hesitatingly participated in open agitation against slavery during the early nineteenth century. This chapter examines the advances of antislavery sentiments within the missionary movement in relation to the problems of religious liberty, the growth of the evangelical political lobby, and the influence of events both in the colonies and in the metropole. The religious public's advocacy of antislavery emerged amid the social, political, and theological transformations explored in previous chapters. Here I hope to illustrate how evangelical nonconformists' growing concerns for religious and civil rights, particularly in the context of missionary work, significantly promoted their participation in the agitation against slavery during the early decades of the nineteenth century.

Chapters 1 and 2 examined the rise of evangelical religion and its impact upon British politics in the late eighteenth and early nineteenth centuries. The tensions of the revolutionary era, the dislocations of the early stages of industrialism, the growth of the middle classes all worked to advance the expansion of evangelical dissent and to raise the fears of the defenders of the Anglican constitution. Evangelical nonconformists mobilized themselves for political action in response to challenges to their civil and religious liberties. The concurrent expansion of British power and commerce overseas also elevated the religious public's awareness of colonial questions, such as foreign missions and slavery.

Opposition to the slave economy, and the slave trade in particular, first attracted the interest of evangelicals during the final decades of the eighteenth century. Organization of the initial campaigns against the slave trade relied heavily upon the participation of Quakers and evangelical Anglicans. While evangelical Dissenters lent considerable popular support to the movement, their active participation in antislavery activity matured only in the early decades of the nineteenth century. Within the antislavery movement manufacturers, merchants, and artisans took up leading roles on the local and the national levels. The men behind the formation of the London Abolition Committee, which coordinated the 1788 and 1792 petition campaigns against the slave trade, were not merely "saints" but "practical men who understood about the market and consumer choice," men who sought to "create a constituency for anti-slavery through books, pamphlets and artifacts." On several important levels, the nascent antislavery movement was deeply connected to more extensive socioeconomic developments in the 1780s and 1790s.[2]

The socioeconomic context of the abolition movements has dominated much of the later twentieth-century historiography of British antislavery. More than a century after the emancipation of the slaves in the British Empire, Eric Williams' *Capitalism and Slavery* challenged the pervasive humanitarian and progressive accounts of the antislavery movement initiated by Thomas Clarkson's *Rise, Progress, and Accomplishment of the Abolition of the African Slave-Trade*.[3] Williams stressed the influence of economic factors in the process of abolition and launched a new historiography of the antislavery movement that connected it to the economic decline of the West Indian colonies. Histories of abolition in the following decades largely assumed, as a matter of fact, "that the value and viability of British slavery deteriorated before the emergence of British antislavery." Subsequent works questioned the basis of Williams' thesis and the implication that antislavery arose in Britain only after its slave colonies ceased to be profitable. Considerable evidence now suggests that the antislavery movement "occurred against a background of slave expansion, and at the peak of slavery's value to British imperial political economy." The influence of *Capitalism and Slavery* and its successors, however, meant that for much of the past fifty years historiographical debates over British abolition were conducted in largely economic terms.[4]

In any case, popular Protestantism provided both the initiative and the striking public support for the antislavery movement in Britain. This is reflected in the facts that religion supplied the "primary idiom of antislavery" and that religious networks produced the mountains of petitions that so impressed political contemporaries.[5] At the dawn of the new century the evangelical public already understood slavery in terms of its opposition to the divine providential order, as a system of human cruelty that got between God and his creation. Slavery, in short, impeded the ability of individuals (be they slave, slave master, or slave trader), as well as the nation, to maintain a proper relationship with God. Or as the great leader of the movement, William Wilberforce, put it, slavery was "the greatest of our national crimes." The abolition of slavery became not merely a matter of national interest, but a national obligation.[6]

Like the missionary movement, this attitude was another manifestation of the theological influences of the Evangelical Revival. Wesleyan Arminianism, as well as the progress of moderate Calvinism within Old Dissent, gave increasing importance to doing good, to the performance of benevolent action on behalf of mankind. This state of mind not only provided the primary stimulus to evangelization at home and abroad, but also spurred believers to strike out against manifestations of evil in the world. By the close of the eighteenth century evangelical Christians, in burgeoning numbers, came to view slavery as the outstanding evil that their religious principles called upon them to stamp out. This conviction was made even stronger by the social construction that evangelicalism gave to the working out of the divine plan for salvation. Providence held out the promise of redeeming not just the individual believer, but society as a whole. Even more significantly for the antislavery movement, evangelicals frequently alluded to this process in terms of freedom from bondage, thus making an explicit link between spiritual and physical slavery. Just as the gospel redeemed the individual soul from bondage to sin, so would it ultimately redeem the nation from the stain of its national crime and the slaves from their physical captivity.[7]

The belief that Christians were called to participate in bringing about the thousand-year reign of harmony that would precede Christ's return to Earth, or postmillennialism, played its own important role in the formation of the missionary and antislavery movements. Converting the "heathen" world and abolishing slavery fit well into a providentialist understanding of history that furthered evangelical convictions that they, and the British nation, had been made "partners in the salvation of the world."[8] "Great Britain is the nation which God, in his providence, appears to have selected to take a lead in evangelizing the world," Rev. B. W. Mathias told the supporters of the LMS in 1813. "[M]ay we not hope, that, as of old the Lord sounded out from Jerusalem, so, in the later days it shall proceed from Great Britain?"[9] Evangelical theology's stress upon the process of sanctification, or the "quest for individual transformation in the present," took on important social implications as well. The expansion of missions, abolitionism, and numerous other humanitarian movements in the early nineteenth century arose from the application of such ideas about redemption and sanctification to the world at large.[10]

Missions, Antislavery, and Colonial Politics

The condition, both spiritual and temporal, of the West Indian slaves thus attracted the attention of the supporters of the missionary movement from its beginnings. The Moravians, pioneers in so many of the eighteenth century's missionary endeavors, established themselves in Jamaica as early as the 1750s. Thomas Coke, who single-handedly initiated the Wesleyans' early missionary efforts, settled the first Methodist missions there in the 1780s. By the time of Coke's death in 1814, also the year of the formation of the Wesleyan Methodist Missionary Society, the Wesleyans operated mission stations on fifteen West Indian islands. Agents of the Baptist Missionary Society began work in Jamaica during the 1790s, and the presence of Wesleyans and Baptists in the largest and most important of the West Indian colonies led the LMS to concentrate its efforts in other parts of the world.[11] The society did not establish a permanent presence in the Caribbean until 1808, when at the request of a Dutch plantation owner it sent its first missionary to the colony of Demerara.[12]

During these early years, in spite of the growing strength of the movement encouraged by the successful abolition of the slave trade in 1807, the missionary societies shied away from embracing the antislavery cause. This was a purely pragmatic policy and no indication of sympathy for the position of the slave owners. To allay the already keen suspicions of the planters and colonial officials the societies adopted a standard rule of yielding "all due respect and subjection to . . . civil authorities" and refraining "from all interference in . . . political concerns" especially as related to the civil condition of the slaves. The Baptist society counseled its missionaries to show a "respectful demeanour" toward the colonial government, and Wesleyans likewise pledged to conduct as their "sole business" the promotion of the "moral and religious improvement" of the slave population.[13] Upon commencement of their own West Indian missions, the directors of the LMS also stressed to the Society's missionaries their duty to "point out" to the slaves "the way of salvation" and the "consolation of religion," rather than to "interfere with their servile condition." Such assurances, the societies hoped, would placate the planters and keep them from raising obstacles to the evangelization of the slaves.[14]

The directors felt the necessity for these policies because of the West Indian plantocracy's deep distrust of the missions and their connections to the antislavery movement in Britain. In several ways the planters' anxieties paralleled the fears of the defenders of the establishment at home about the challenges of Dissent to the Anglican constitution examined in chapter 2. Conservative forces saw in the expansion of evangelical Christianity a threat to the social order, despite evangelical claims that their home missionary work could only ease social tensions. The egalitarian spirit of Dissent defied a social ethic still ordered on "rank and patronage," much to the dismay of those who benefited from and believed in the old system.[15] This egalitarian spirit posed no less of a threat within the social and economic order of the expanding British Empire. In the slave colonies of the West Indies the tensions escalated as missionaries arrived bearing not merely the Christian message, but the notions of liberty and brotherhood inherent in nonconformist Protestantism. Try as they might to assure the planters of their determination not to meddle in the civil condition of the slaves, and however much they might repeat Paul's admonition to slaves to obey their masters, most missionaries could not ultimately escape the recognition of the "incompatibility . . . between the very system of slavery . . . with that which the Bible teaches."[16]

The response of the religious public to Sidmouth's bill illustrated the acceptance of advanced conceptions of religious and civil liberty by evangelical nonconformists who had recent experience of the religious disabilities under the Anglican constitution, and who now threw in their lot with traditional Dissenters and Whigs already committed to the cause. The abolitionist movement of the early nineteenth century gathered around this same nexus, augmented by more secular radical elements for whom chattel slavery in the colonies was also emblematic of the "political slavery of British subjects at home."[17]

During the first decades of the nineteenth century, this version of the protestant ethic was taken up by growing numbers evangelicals to whom the incongruity between slavery and Christianity was equally clear. Such views, common to all branches of nonconformity, were naturally anathema to the West Indian planters, whose economy and society depended upon the preservation of the slave system. The colonists' hostility to the missions increased with every advance of the antislavery movement in Britain, which the planters met with a growing array of obstacles to the evangelization of the slaves. Ambiguities in the law aided these efforts. While the degree of protection provided to the missionaries under the Toleration Acts (which defined the legal position of dissenting ministers in Britain) remained unclear, British nonconformists watched with anger and concern at what they rightly saw as the existence of the same issue in the colonies.

In the case of Jamaica, considerable confusion existed over the status of religious toleration in the law. The Colonial Assembly had passed legislation in 1728 incorporating into the laws of the colony all English laws enacted prior to October of that year. This meant, in theory, that the Toleration Act of 1689 was the law in Jamaica, and missionaries routinely appeared before the colonial magistrates to swear the oaths of allegiance to the Crown and receive their licenses to preach. This practice accorded with the procedures of the 1779 Toleration Act as well, although it seems to have had no formal legal basis in the colony. The procedures for the licensing of missionaries thus left considerable room for confusion and for the manipulation of procedures to check the growth of missionary influence.[18]

The fear with which the planters viewed the spread of missionary work as a threat to the social order of colonial society led them to attempt to limit the spread of evangelization in Jamaica nearly a decade prior to Sidmouth's bill in Britain. As early as 1802 the Colonial Assembly sought to prohibit preaching by persons "not duly qualified by law" and the evangelization of slaves by "ill-disposed, illiterate, or ignorant enthusiasts." Similar measures, enacted by the Corporation of Kingston in 1807, endeavored to prevent the "Profanation of Religious Rights and False worshipping of God" by "ignorant persons and false enthusiasts." The ordinance noted the "alarming" growth in the attendance of slaves and free blacks at religious meetings where "unseemly noises, gesticulations, and behaviours . . . [took] place." There, "the minds of the slaves [had] been so operated upon and affected by the fanaticism [of the preachers] as to become totally deranged."[19]

The similarities between these declarations and the concerns of the clergymen and magistrates writing to Lord Sidmouth at almost the same time are evident. Fears of the destabilizing effects of religious enthusiasm and its potential to disrupt the social order were as readily apparent in the colonies—probably more so—as at home in Britain. The magistrates of Kingston responded by establishing restrictions upon the times and places available for religious worship. They set fines to punish white and "coloured" preachers "not duly authorized" by the law, and property owners who made their "house, outhouse, yard, etc." available for unlicensed religious meetings.[20]

The colonists' fears of religious enthusiasm were multiplied by the "democratic manners" and the "rhetoric of equality," promoted by many of the nonconformist missionaries. Most planters did not condemn religious instruction per se and were quite prepared to admit that Christianity taught in the proper manner might work effectively as a means of improving the manners and morals of the slave population. It was, rather, the "sectarian" missionaries and their egalitarian ideas that the colonists explicitly condemned. Colonial newspapers, such as the *Essequebo and Demerary Royal Gazette*, denounced "the precarious preachers of a pretended enlightening doctrine, who announced equal rights, and universal liberty." The Jamaica Consolidated Slave Act of 1807 specifically encouraged the religious instruction of the slaves under the auspices of the Anglican Church yet at the same time prohibited the missionary work of Methodists and "other sectarians."[21]

These efforts to place restrictions upon missionary work among the slaves came to the attention of Dissenters in Britain during the same period that the rights of Dissenting ministers reached a crisis point at home.[22] Only a few months after the defeat of Sidmouth's bill in 1811, the Dissenting Deputies had turned their attention to protesting against "the violent measures adopted by the Assembly of Jamaica on the highly important subject of religious instruction." In a memorial to the Privy Council the Deputies labeled the actions of the Assembly "illegal and unjust," as well as "in opposition to the general principles of a just and liberal Toleration." They called upon the government to defend "the rights secured to every Protestant inhabitant of His Majesty's Dominions" and to disallow the Assembly's limitations upon the religious instruction of the slaves.[23] At issue were not only the rights of the missionaries but the rights of the slaves themselves to attend religious services. For the next two decades, leading up to the Emancipation Act of 1833, this question was the most prevalent source of conflict between the planters and the proponents of the missionary cause.

During the early years of the nineteenth century the colonists enacted legislation to hinder missionary work not only in Jamaica but also Bermuda, Angilla, St. Vincent, Tobago, and Demerara, the location of the LMS's earliest West Indian mission. The Society appointed its first agent to the former Dutch colony in 1807 at the request of a pious proprietor from Utrecht, named H. H. Post. John Wray arrived at Post's plantation, Le Resouvinir, in 1808 and diligently set to work building his congregation among the slaves. From the outset, Wray, an enthusiastic young man committed to his mission as an evangelist, encountered "much latent, if little open" opposition from the majority of the planters and other residents of the colony. New to the customs and society of the slave colony, and infused with the egalitarian sentiments of his dissenting heritage, he quickly aroused the suspicions and hostility of the colonists.[24]

In London, the Society and its directors did all they could to damp down any suggestions of political agitation or connections with the antislavery movement. In the field, missionaries, such as Wray, found it difficult to play the role assigned to them. Wray's success as an evangelist, he quickly learned, depended much upon his ability to win the confidence of the slaves to whom he ministered. This frequently meant defending them against the abuses of plantation life. Beginning largely as a pragmatic response to the challenges of missionary work, the process increasingly inclined Wray to take up the interests of the slaves against their masters. This is not to suggest that Wray or other missionaries went out of their way to stir up trouble. Rather, the circumstances of their task brought home to the missionaries a confirmation of the belief in the incompatibility of slavery and the Christian faith. In time, the attitudes of missionaries in the field more closely resonated with the sentiments driving the antislavery movement in Britain than with the policies of the mission societies, which encouraged keeping on good terms with the planters. Wray, like others, attempted to establish himself as an "arbiter," taking up the justifiable (as he viewed them) grievances of the slaves while trying not to completely alienate the slave owners.[25] As the examples of both Wray and John Smith, his successor at Le Resouvinir, illustrate, this was easier said than done.

In addition to the hostility of planters, Wray found little enthusiasm for his mission among his fellow clergyman, the minister of the Dutch Reformed congregation and the Anglican chaplain of the colonial garrison. The Dutch minister's persistent opposition to baptizing the slaves especially frustrated Wray, who referred to the man repeatedly as "an instrument of the Devil."[26] Governor Murray welcomed Wray with considerable trepidation. Although he saw some value in religious instruction for the slaves, Murray objected deeply to teaching them to read. He, like the planters, feared the consequences for the peace and stability of the colony if the slaves were educated and thus exposed to dangerous ideas associated with the missions. Wray faced further opposition from the plantation proprietors and managers who served on the colonial Court of Policy. From his first days in Demerara Wray's correspondence was filled with references to the Court's desire to force him out of the colony.[27]

In the face of the general hostility to his mission, Wray looked to London for assistance. Thwarted by the planters' demands for Sunday labor, which prevented the slaves from attending worship, Wray gathered evidence from among his small number of supporters in the colony and forwarded it to the directors of the LMS. They, in turn, passed the information on to Wilberforce, who secured a conference with Lord Bentinck, newly appointed to replace Murray as governor of Demerara and still in London at the time. This initial appeal was of little avail. Upon his arrival in the colony Bentinck proved unwilling to side with Wray against the wishes of the planters. In 1811, he went so far as to ban religious meetings at night, as the Jamaica Assembly and magistrates in other colonies had tried to do in the past. Although Bentinck's declaration ostensibly aimed only "to prevent . . . mutiny or rebellion," from the missionary point of view it led "to the total suppression of the assemblies of the slaves for religious instruction."[28]

Wray responded by determining upon a more direct course of action, and set sail for Britain to plead his case in person. In doing so, Wray opened a direct line of communication between a missionary in the field and influential political figures in Britain. Using the directors' connections with influential leaders of the antislavery movement Wray managed to confer with evangelical politicians, such as Wilberforce and James Stephen. The Society also made a direct plea to Liverpool, the Prime Minister. They appealed to "British values" and requested to government to assist in restoring the "religious toleration" previously enjoyed by the missions in the colony.[29] Never anxious to clash with the evangelical lobby, which had so recently marshaled effective public opposition to Sidmouth's bill and was now clamoring for the encouragement of missions to India, Liverpool showed sympathy for the Society's requests. Shortly thereafter, Peel, then undersecretary for the colonies, communicated to the directors the Prime Minister's determination to overturn the ban on religious meetings at night and to strengthen the government's support for the religious instruction of the slaves.[30]

John Smith and the Demerara Rebellion

In 1813 Wray accepted the offer of a new position in the neighboring colony of Berbice, where he hoped to find a more welcoming attitude to his mission and fewer of the hardships that he had faced in Demerara. After some difficulty finding a willing and acceptable candidate, the directors ultimately appointed John Smith to replace Wray at Le Resouvinir. A twenty-six-year-old former biscuit baker's apprentice from Northamptonshire, Smith had received training at the Society's seminary in Gosport and arrived at his new post in Demerara with his wife Jane in February 1817. The governor and colonists alike received Smith with the same skepticism that they had shown to Wray. Wray's appeals to London and the Colonial Office on behalf of the slaves had only heightened the planters' mistrust of the missions, and the governor granted Smith's license to preach only after a second request.[31]

Although Smith came to Demerara anxious to win the good will and cooperation of the planters, the tensions that had arisen between the colonists and the mission under Wray were only to intensify with his successor. Smith's journals depict the steady deterioration of the young missionary's relationship with the planters, and how he came to see the stark reality of the slave system's total incompatibility with the work of his mission. In his journal, Smith began recording and commenting upon the punishments handed out to the slaves by the plantation managers. During his second year in the colony, he wrote,

> [O]pposite my window is a poor Negro dancing to the lash of the whip . . . I counted 12 lashes. The old man thus punished is attending the manager's cows. Perhaps . . . the old Negro did not drive the cows up the other road. The way here is frequently not to tell a Negro of his error, but to punish him first and then tell him what to do.[32]

A sturdy and optimistic view of political economy further complemented Smith's moral and theological objections to slavery. In a letter of 1822 to the directors he compared the plight of the slaves to the status of laborers in Britain.

> The labourer in Britain is impelled to active and persevering industry by a motive to which the slave is a stranger. The one is stimulated by the expectation of an adequate remuneration, by a jealousy for his reputation, by the fear of losing his employment, by his numerous wants and, in most cases, by the necessities of a dependent family; and besides, if the work be beyond his strength he is at liberty to leave it.

No such inducements or liberties were afforded the West Indian slave, however. The slave, Smith noted,

> knows it would be vain to look for reward; and as for reputation, he is quite unconscious of any such thing. If he neglects his work he is punished; but that is attended with no dishonour . . . it is too common an occurrence to be accounted disgraceful.[33]

Like Wray, Smith clashed with the planters and plantation managers over actions that prevented the slaves from attending religious services and over punishments given to slaves who were active in the chapel. To Smith's dismay, planters frequently punished slaves who avoided Sunday labor to go to the mission. "Last Friday [the] master had nearly the whole of his men severely flogged because they would not work on the preceding Sunday," he wrote in his journal, "each receiving about fifty lashes on his naked skin. No wonder so many of the slaves speak ill of religion and say it brings them into trouble."[34] Nonetheless, as the years passed Smith had some success in continuing Wray's work at Le Resouvinir. By 1823 the "usual number" of slaves in attendance on Sundays was "200 to 300," provoking among the planters efforts to institute a pass system restricting the movement of the slaves off the plantations.[35] As tensions between Smith and the colonists rose, so did Smith's antipathy to slavery, and to those who perpetuated the system in Demerara. The missionary became more willing to use his influence among the slaves to frustrate the will of the slave owners. He engaged in repeated confrontations with Michael McTurk of Plantation Felicity, the captain of the local militia, a medical officer, and the man behind several of the measures to prevent the slaves from attending religious services on Sunday. "I have influence over the negro minds," Smith had once warned McTurk, "and I will use that influence to bring the negroes of the neighborhood to the chapel, and preach to them in defiance of all the authority you possess."[36] By 1823 Smith's opinions had moved well beyond those of even the sympathetic politicians in London who began to call again for reforms to "ameliorate" the condition of the slaves in the colonies. In his journal the missionary concluded, "[T]he rigors of Negro slavery can never be mitigated. The system must be abolished."[37]

As Smith waged his battles against the planters in Demerara, parliamentary opponents of slavery prepared to launch a new campaign to ameliorate the condition of the slaves as a first step toward eventual emancipation. By 1823 Thomas Fowell Buxton had assumed the leadership of the antislavery cause from the aging Wilberforce and opened a new debate on the regulation of the slave system on the floor of the Commons.[38] "The state of slavery is repugnant to the principles of the British Constitution and of the Christian Religion," Buxton assured the House on 15 May 1823. It "ought to be gradually abolished throughout the British colonies with as much expedition as may be found with a due regard to the well being of the parties concerned." The transformation of the slave population into "a happy, contented, enlightened free peasantry," he proposed, was the surest guarantee against turmoil and "dreadful convulsion" in the slave colonies. "If we wish to preserve the West Indies," warned Buxton, Britain must begin "by restoring to the injured race, those rights which we have too long withheld." He proposed a series of reforms to "improve the condition of the Negroes."

Buxton did not fail to remind the government of the popular strength of his cause. "The public voice is with us," he warned, "and I for one, will never fail to call upon the public, loudly to express their opinion, till justice has so far prevailed as to pronounce that every child is entitled to liberty."[39]

Well aware of the potential pressure public opinion might bring to bear on the issue, George Canning, now government leader in the Commons, took a conciliatory line toward Buxton's proposals. While stopping short of conceding the total incompatibility of slavery and Christianity, he acknowledged that the "Christian religion [was not] favorable to Slavery." More significantly, Canning admitted "that the spirit of both the British Constitution and of the Christian Religion [were] in favor of a gradual extermination of this unquestioned evil."[40] To that end, he submitted the government's own proposals for the reform of slavery in the West Indies. These reforms included the prohibition of the use of the cart whip and the flogging of female slaves, protection of the right of slaves to attend religious services on the Sabbath, securing legal protection for the property of the slaves, and the abolition of the "writ of *venditioni exponas*," by which the slaves of a single family were "sold separately" from the estate to which they belonged.[41] To the leaders of the antislavery movement the passage of these proposals for the "amelioration" of the slave system marked a significant step on the path toward the ultimate abolition of slavery.

News of the amelioration policy traveled swiftly across the Atlantic, and by midsummer rumors about the parliamentary debates over the condition of the slaves spread throughout the plantations. In May 1823 Governor Murray of Demerara forcefully reiterated the planters' rights to regulate the slaves' attendance at Sunday worship as granted in the Colonial Office's instructions to Governor Bentinck in 1811. Although these recognized the right of the missions to provide religious instruction for the slaves, they also granted the planters substantial powers to govern how this instruction took place. The instructions had tried to conciliate the interests of both the planters and the missions and were thus doomed to failure. Intended to give something to both sides, they ultimately pleased neither. In his journal Smith commented that the directives appeared to him coordinated to obstruct missionary work under the guise of complying with "the commands of His Majesty's Government."[42]

Governor Murray's actions sparked conflict on plantations across the colony as slave converts chafed under the repeated harassment of the planters and estate managers intent upon frustrating their desires to attend religious services. Into this environment of increased tension and mistrust came word of the actions of Buxton, Wilberforce, and the antislavery crusaders in Britain. Murray received the dispatches detailing the reforms passed by Parliament from Bathurst, the Colonial Secretary, in early July. For more than a month the governor and the Court of Policy, who by and large objected to such Parliamentary meddling in their affairs, took no action upon the dispatches while deciding how to proceed.

In the middle of August, the Court of Policy at last resolved to accept the reforms, but because of the widespread opposition of most of the colonists they did not make them known to the general public. Meanwhile, rumors had spread among the slave population that "new laws" had arrived from England promising freedom that Murray and the slave masters were withholding from them. During the early nineteenth century West Indian slaves showed a noteworthy awareness of colonial politics and the existence of the antislavery debates in Britain. In his *Journal of a West India Proprietor* Matthew Lewis recounted the story of a slave, known as the "King of the Eboes," who was hung for subversive activities, such as teaching his fellow slaves a song that included the verse "Oh me good friend, Mr. Wilberforce, make we free!" According to Lewis, the slaves claimed the "good King George and good Mr. Wilberforce" had given him "a paper" to set them free "but that the white people of Jamaica will not suffer me to show [it]."[43] Whites in the colonies spoke openly about the abolition question in front of their house servants who quickly circulated all that they overheard throughout the slave community.[44] As speculation about the "new laws" spread, slaves who attended Smith's chapel repeatedly asked him about the dispatches from the government. Smith, aware that reforms were under consideration in Parliament, attempted to dampen the rumors by telling them that while the "government at home wished to make some regulations for the benefit of the slaves," there were no new laws to make them free. This answer, as Smith himself observed, "scarcely satisfied" the slaves. In his journal the missionary criticized the colonial government for "very imprudently" withholding information about the reforms from the slaves, whose minds were "greatly agitated."[45]

This agitation, spurred by the firm conviction that the planters were denying them the freedom granted by the King and Parliament, boiled over into the slave rebellion of 18 August 1823. Rising up against their masters, the slaves released years of pent-up frustration and anger. They refused to go to the fields to work, and they surrounded the plantation houses. They ridiculed the planters and managers, putting many of them into the stocks commonly used to punish the slaves. The leading conspirators had given orders not to harm any whites, and the revolt was carried out with considerable restraint and little physical violence. What the slaves asked for was that the governor and the whites grant them the freedom that they believed had been given to them by the "new laws." Their demands reflected the extent to which many had become familiar with the antislavery movement across the Atlantic, as slaves not only called for their freedom and their rights but also appealed for them in the name of the King, of Wilberforce, and of other "powerful men in England."[46]

The rebellion, in spite of the lack of excessive violence on the part of the slaves, confirmed all of the fears of the white population about the dangerous influences of the missions and of parliamentary meddling in the social order of the colony. Having always been suspect in the eyes of the colonists, the missions became immediate targets of their hostility in the aftermath of the revolt. This hostility was intensified by the fact that the leaders of the revolt included several slaves connected to the mission chapels. Governor Murray declared martial law and relied upon the militia to quell the revolt by force. Within days, the colonial officials also turned their attention to Smith, identified him as a possible collaborator, and ordered his arrest. On the evening of 20 August, as Smith sat in his home at Le Resouvinir writing a letter to the secretary of the LMS relating the events of the revolt, representatives of the colonial militia arrived at his door and placed him under arrest. Smith never returned to the house; he was imprisoned at Georgetown, convicted by a court martial of aiding the slave revolt, and died in the colony's jail on 6 February 1824.[47]

The conversion of Smith into a martyr for the antislavery cause, as evidenced by Brougham's dramatic speech to the Commons, took place almost immediately. The newly formed Anti-Slavery Society and leaders of the abolitionist movement seized the opportunity to intensify their demands for the ultimate emancipation of the slaves. The response of the LMS to the Smith case combined bolder action by the directors in defense of their missionaries with a persistent reluctance to call their actions against the slave system political. The Society published a report on the Smith trial, which claimed to include "Documentary Evidence omitted in the Parliamentary Copy" of the proceedings, intended to publicly vindicate the missionary's role in the disturbances in Demerara. The directors also engaged themselves more directly with the abolitionist leadership in Parliament and the government to remove restrictions upon the West Indian missions and the slaves' freedom to attend religious services.[48]

The LMS, the Hankey Controversy, and the Politics of Abolition

The events of 1823–1824 intensified the pressures on nonconformist missions in other West Indian colonies, as slave owners more readily identified them as allies of the abolitionists and threats to colonial interests. Baptist missionaries in Jamaica faced "the chill wind of the planters' heightened antagonism," escalated by their denominational magazine's call for the "British nation to awake from its slumber" and to demand the gradual abolition of slavery in the colonies.[49] Jamaican magistrates refused to license newly arrived missionaries, and in 1826 the Jamaican Assembly completed a new consolidated slave law designed to severely limit the operation of the Baptist and Methodist missions on the island. The Colonial Secretary, William Huskisson, severely criticized the measure, noting, "Even were the law unobjectionable on every other ground it would be impossible to surmount the difficulty presented by the Clauses restraining Religious liberty."[50] Huskisson's rejection of the act in 1827 led the Assembly to appoint a committee to examine the conduct of "Sectarians and Dissenters" in the colony, in an apparent attempt to collect evidence of the missionary threat. The committee duly condemned the missionaries for promoting the ideologies of equality and natural rights as well as inciting insurrection, and the Assembly also openly condemned the principle of religious liberty as "utterly at variance with the institutions of Jamaica."[51] The continued efforts by the legislature to enact a revised slave law in 1829 solidified the religious public's impression that the planters intended to encroach upon the religious freedom of the missionaries and slave converts. The colonists' hostility to the missions contributed directly to the resentments that stirred the slave revolt of 1831, known as the Baptist War, and helped to turn British public opinion in favor of the demand for immediate emancipation.

The evangelicals' response to the planters' declaration of "open war on Evangelical Christianity" stoked the flames of the antislavery movement and made abolition, not political reform, the primary issue in the popular politics of the early 1830s.[52] The Methodist Committee and numerous nonconformist ministers urged members of their congregations to vote only for candidates willing to pledge themselves against slavery. Within this context, the question of religious liberty continued to offer an avenue for leaders of the missionary movement to publicly express their hostility to slavery. The Baptist Committee engaged the Dissenting Deputies to protest to the government against the colonists' attacks upon the civil and religious rights of their missionaries. The directors of the LMS continued to profess the Society's intention to avoid the "general question of Negro Emancipation" or the "civil condition" of the slaves. Yet they forcefully lobbied the government to retract any policies that gave the appearance of concessions to the planters on the question of religious freedom. In a memorial to the government responding to an Orders-in-Council of November 1831, the directors declared their right to object to "legislative enactments" intended to "shut out . . . Missionaries" from access to the slave population and the performance of their duties.[53]

The orders in question set limits upon the age at which slaves might attend religious services, the distances they might travel to do so, and the hours allowed for religious worship on the Sabbath. These regulations upon the "attendance of slaves at public worship" were in the Society's view "too narrow" and "seriously impeded" the missionaries' abilities to promote the "religious improvement" of the slaves. The directors also protested a second provision that infringed upon the "personal privileges" of the missionaries themselves, by placing the authority of their licenses "at the pleasure of Governors of the Colonies." As the governors were "exposed to the solicitations of the colonists" and generally sympathetic to the interests of the slave owners, the directors objected strongly that their missionaries might be "ruled without remedy or appeal by the arbitration of the Governors." At stake here was the same threat posed by Sidmouth's bill of 1811, the placing of a discretionary authority over the issuing of licenses to preach. The memorial condemned the new policy as opposed to the "acknowledged rights" of British subjects and "directly calculated" to obstruct missionary activity.[54]

By couching their arguments against slavery within the rhetoric of religious freedom, declarations of this sort may have strategically masked but did not supplant the Society's increasingly determined opposition to slavery. This is illustrated in an 1832 letter from William Ellis of the LMS to Buxton. Following the almost ritualized denial of the Society's intentions to engage in the politics of antislavery, Ellis went on to condemn the slave system in the strongest terms as an obstacle to the work of the missions. He resolutely professed the Society's support for the objectives of the Anti-Slavery Society (of which Buxton was a founding member), and its position that the "truth and precepts of the Gospel" afforded the best guarantee against any hazards associated with the passage from slavery to freedom.[55]

The events of Smith's trial, his death, the creation of the Anti-Slavery Society, the persecution of the Baptist missionaries and their congregations in Jamaica, the energizing of the parliamentary campaign for abolition, and the resultant renewal of popular interest in the subject all worked to drive the LMS and its leadership toward a stronger public stand against slavery.

Indeed, instigation from the Society's supporters and its auxiliary organizations at times pressured the directors toward positions with which they were exceedingly uncomfortable. One of the most prominent instances of this sort involved the Society's treasurer, William Alers Hankey, a leading Congregationalist and a London banker. A partner in the firm of Thompson, Hankey, Plummer, and Company, Hankey had served as treasurer of the LMS since 1816. He was also an elected member of the Dissenting Deputies, and thus a man of some stature in dissenting circles in London. As a partner in the bank, Hankey possessed a joint interest in a Jamaican plantation of which the bank had been mortgagee. During his tenure as treasurer of the LMS, Hankey had "laboured to free [him]self" as much as possible from any voluntary connection to the property.[56] Reluctant to invite controversy, and satisfied with Hankey's stature as a man of character, the directors had seen fit not to make an issue out of his circumstances. In the heated atmosphere of the abolitionist agitation of the early 1830s, however, his connection to the plantation became a matter of considerable contention and ultimately forced his resignation from office.

Hankey had met with the Baptist missionary William Knibb and the committee of the BMS concerning the provision of religious instruction for the slaves on the Acadia estate. By this means knowledge of his connection to the plantation circulated throughout the Evangelical Party in London. The information ultimately reached the committee of the Anti-Slavery Society, who called upon Hankey to either "instantly" emancipate the slaves on the plantation or resign his position with the LMS, "an office totally incompatible with possessing such property."[57] The Anti-Slavery Society further conveyed the information to auxiliary societies of the LMS throughout the country in hopes that they might pressure the directors to take action against their treasurer. Numerous auxiliary societies wrote to the London for clarification, or confirmation, of Hankey's status as an officer of the Society and "a proprietor of slaves in the West Indies." In November 1831 the Newcastle Auxiliary passed a resolution, forwarded to the directors, declaring all slave owners "unfit for any official situation in a Christian Institution" and demanding Hankey's resignation.[58] Illustrative of just how far antislavery sentiments had gripped the evangelical public, the Ebeneezer Juvenile Auxiliary Missionary Society wrote to the directors to condemn Hankey's connection with the Society. They threatened that "if the present treasurer continue[d] in office . . . we would rather devolve the proceeds of our labours to the funds of some other institution, than give the slightest degree of sanction to the crime of man-stealing."[59]

The directors, still anxious to avoid the appearance of playing politics, sought to defend their treasurer against the accusations of the auxiliary societies. As his connection to the plantation had "existed long before
his official relation to the Society" and was "altogether unavoidable," they
refused to subject him to the "indiscriminate censure" that his opponents
demanded.[60] Hankey also mounted a vigorous defense on his own behalf.
He branded the Newcastle Auxiliary, and others, as "inquisitors" meddling
in the "private affairs and relations of individuals." He condemned the
"degrading invasion of [his] independence, arising out of the spirit of the
times." Drawing upon the rhetoric of dissenting campaigns against the Test
and Corporation Acts, Hankey reproached his opponents' demands for "a
Test of qualification for office." The treasurer warned of the "precedent
for the introduction of such other Tests" as might repel "the cooperation
of . . . persons whose influence and authority may be efficacious in promoting Missionary labour amongst the negro population."[61] As such, Hankey
reiterated a position of standard policy in the missionary societies for several decades, namely, the advancement of the religious instruction of the
slaves by way of cultivating relationships with sympathetic proprietors. He,
and many others with influence in the Society, believed this to be among
the most fruitful means of preparing the slaves for their eventual emancipation. By the early 1830s, however, the position had become increasingly
untenable to the growing numbers of missionaries and members of the religious public calling for immediate emancipation. Hankey had, himself,
come to recognize this in January 1832. "Unwilling to become a subject of
discord . . . that I must become, if I continue in the office," he tendered his
resignation to the directors.[62]

In testimony before the parliamentary committee "on the extinction of
slavery," Hankey clearly presented his views on the question, which turned
on three key points. First, while opposed to slavery as a "national crime,"
and "at all times ready cooperate in any proper system to effect emancipation," he did not believe in immediate emancipation as a practical remedy.
In his opinion the slaves were not "at present in a state of preparation to
make a useful and proper use of the benefit" of freedom. Second, he believed
Christianity to be the best means to spur the "moral feelings and habits,
that will ameliorate the character and condition . . . of the negro population" and prepare them for emancipation at some later date. To that end, he
reiterated his objections to the "violent" and "injudicious . . . spirit of advocacy" of the Anti-Slavery Society and other groups that, to his mind, alienated planters sympathetic to the missions and slowed the spread of religious

instruction. "I am a friend to the object of the Anti-Slavery Society," he told the committee, "but not the means by which it carries on its object."[63]

Hankey's cautious and pragmatic approach to the question of abolition reflected not merely three decades' worth of mission policy but the mainstream view of most of the evangelical public in the years before the mid-1820s. The Smith case and the events in Jamaica not merely had instigated a resurgence of antislavery activism but had intensified the rhetoric of the movement. A greater sense of the incompatibility of slavery and Christianity fueled calls for the immediate abolition rather than the mere reform of the slave system. By the 1830s even relatively moderate organizations, such as the General Body of Dissenting Ministers, had taken up the call for immediate emancipation. As victory in the struggle for emancipation neared in 1833, the General Body unanimously resolved to petition Parliament in response to the government's call for a "safe and satisfactory" plan to abolish slavery. In no uncertain terms the petition affirmed that "for the measure to be safe [it] must provide for the immediate emancipation of the slaves," and "for it to be satisfactory [it] must ensure the complete extinction of the claim of property in the person and labour of the slave."[64] In 1800, a man in Hankey's position, or any slave proprietor committed to the cause of the missions and eager to arrange for the provision of religious instruction on his plantation, might have been hailed for his humanitarian spirit. By the 1830s, in most evangelical circles, he had become a "foul stain" upon the integrity and credibility of the LMS.[65]

The story of Hankey's resignation reflects the broader revolution of British values and principles brought about by the antislavery movement and completed by the passage of the Emancipation Act of 1833. The accomplishment of emancipation ultimately involved compromise, as the West Indian lobby retained sufficient influence to secure for the slave proprietors compensation and the institution of the apprentice system. Nevertheless, within the span of a half-century Britain had evolved from a leading nation in the trade and use of slaves to the leading opponent of slavery throughout the world. An "element of British political economy . . . considered to be of well-nigh vital significance in 1787" had lost nearly all of its power to shape British values or policy.[66] More dramatically, the shift from the campaign for a gradual end to slavery to the call for immediate and total emancipation occurred only in the decade prior to 1833. The missionary movement and evangelical Dissenters' commitment to religious liberty contributed significantly to this process of social and ideological transformation.

In its earliest stages the antislavery movement consisted of a broad coalition of evangelical Anglicans, Quakers, various Dissenters, and political radicals at the head of "a grass-roots network of abolitionists."[67] Under the leadership of men such as Wilberforce, Thomas Clarkson, and James Stephen it successfully abolished the British slave trade in the name of justice, humanity, and the national interest. Evangelical theology provided considerable stimulus to the religious public's desire to combat the evils of slavery, and as the numbers of evangelical Dissenters rose in the early nineteenth century so did their importance to the abolitionist movement. Throughout the 1810s and 1820s the antislavery cause came to rely ever more heavily upon the support of the growing rank and file of evangelical nonconformists.

The moral and theological objections to slavery ensured the broad sympathy of evangelical Dissenters for the cause; but it was within the struggle for religious liberty that the antislavery cause took on its political edge. As early as 1788 the Baptist minister Robert Robinson wrote of the "natural connection" between the abolition of the slave trade and the advance of "civil and religious liberty."[68] In the early decades of the nineteenth century the efforts of slave owners and colonial magistrates to restrict missionaries' rights to evangelize the slaves and to prevent the slaves from attending religious worship as well as their persecution of missionaries and slave converts evoked a response strikingly similar to that brought about by Sidmouth's bill of 1811. The defense of religious liberty also provided a legitimate avenue for antislavery protest by missionary societies wary of appearing too political.

The conviction that slavery opposed the fundamental ideal of Christianity and religious freedom emerged first among missionaries and the field and the religious public at home. These, in turn, pressured the leaders of the missionary societies and denominational organizations to assume stronger positions against the institution of slavery. This they did, especially in response to the persecutions instigated by the slave uprisings in Demerara (1823) and Jamaica (1831). Evangelical Dissenters' and their missionaries' interest in the protection of religious freedom in the colonies deserves recognition as a significant stimulus to the escalation of demands for abolition in the years preceding 1833. As in the debates over religious liberty in Britain, political observers did not fail to recognize the significance of evangelical nonconformists in shaping the public's opinion on antislavery. The public's interest in the "slavery question, . . . which [was] the work of the Methodists, and show[ed] the enormous influence they [had] in the country," astonished

Henry Greville in 1830. In 1833 Zachary Macauly remarked to Brougham on the significance of the "intense interest" of evangelical Dissenters in the issue: "[T]hey have not only caught fire themselves but have succeeded in igniting the whole country."[69]

In his work on the culture of antislavery David Turley locates emancipation within the "large-scale process of reorganization of both the constitutional framework . . . and [the] social and commercial policy" of early nineteenth-century Britain, which included the repeal of the Test and Corporation Acts, Catholic Emancipation, the Reform Bill, the New Poor Law, and repeal of the Corn Laws. Rather than the mythologized or idealized campaign of a select group of evangelical "saints," antislavery is better understood as an integral part of the shifting social, economic, and political structure of British society.[70] More significantly, the abolitionist movement illustrates how these changes were not confined to Britain, but were instead essential elements of the politics of Britain's continued emergence as an imperial power.

The central role of the missions in this process lay in facilitating the transmission of evangelical concerns for enlightened and humanitarian principles into the colonial sphere. The Methodist Richard Watson commented in 1830 "that all our Missionary enterprises . . . do . . . tend to increase our sympathies with the external circumstances of the oppressed and miserable of all lands." Watson concluded that "it is impossible for men to care for the salvation of the negro, without caring for his emancipation from bondage."[71] Evangelical Dissenters' interest in the civil and religious freedoms of the "oppressed and miserable" in Britain's empire ultimately expanded far beyond the West Indies. The relationship established between missionary societies, like the LMS, and the antislavery movement was to prove equally consequential for the development of the missions and colonial government in Africa.

4

Missionary Politics in Britain and the Cape Colony

In 1825 James Kitchingman, the London Missionary Society (LMS) missionary at Bethelsdorp in the Cape Colony, received a communication from colonial officials regarding the collection of annual property taxes, called the *opgaaf*. In order to avoid "difficulties experienced at the last *opgaaf*," the dispatch instructed Kitchingman to "attend [the] next . . . with a list of [the mission's] people . . . and to pay for them on the spot." Furthermore, the missionary "was called upon to pay out of his own pocket, the tax for absentees and defaulters." Kitchingman declared the orders "both unreasonable and . . . impossible for me to do," and vigorously protested against the imposition of secular responsibilities that would interfere with his duties as a missionary. "The whole of my time," he noted in his journal, "will be occupied in this and other things quite foreign to a missionary's work—it seems hard for a missionary to be almost wholly employed in things so contrary to the object for which he was sent out."[1]

Kitchingman's protests to the colonial authorities fell upon deaf ears, and the missionary turned to John Philip, Resident Director of the LMS in Cape Town, for assistance. Philip also forcefully objected to the efforts of colonial officials to impose upon the missionaries secular duties intended "to annoy and weary them out." He argued that "devolving such concerns into the hands of a missionary" threatened to make him "a kind of political agent, . . . a tool of government, and an instrument of oppression." The colonial government had "no more claim" on a missionary's time than it had "upon his property." Inasmuch as Africans laboring on white farms were exempt from the tax,

Philip saw the policy as a concerted effort to "force the mission Khoi into the service of the farmers." His protests to the Colonial Office in Cape Town led to a quick reversal of the instructions to Kitchingman. The "idea of compelling Mr. Kitchingman to collect the *opgaaf*, and of making him responsible for the tax," he wrote, "was abandoned." The "formidable attempt, which threatened the ruin of [the] missions" was averted.[2]

Kitchingman's story reflects something of the complex and contentious relationship between the missionaries of the LMS and the colonial administration of the Cape. Contrary to conventional assumptions about missionaries working "hand in hand with the colonial powers for the subjugation of black people and the territorial extension of the imperialist power,"[3] the history of the LMS in early nineteenth-century southern Africa suggests the pervasiveness of real differences between the interests and objectives of the missions, colonial authorities, and the settler community.[4] John Philip's accusations that colonial officers devised policies intended to "annoy" the missionaries, to "ruin" the missions, and to coerce Africans "into the service" of white settlers reveal the intensity of the antagonism born of a fierce debate over the economic and political future of the Cape Colony. This chapter examines the emergence of mission politics within this debate, its connections to the growth of evangelical politics in Britain. Special attention is given to the central role of John Philip, whose long career and energetic struggles on behalf of the African population made him a pariah among white society, a trusted ally to many Africans, and a heroic figure to supporters of the missionary movement in Britain.

The LMS and the Cape Colony

Founded in 1652 by the Dutch East India Company, the Cape Colony grew over the next century and a half from a remote outpost to a prosperous colony of white settlement based upon the production of wine, grains, cattle, and sheep. This production depended upon the labor of the indigenous African population of the Cape as well as slaves from the east coast of Africa.[5] The arrival of Protestant missionaries from Britain in southern Africa coincided, more or less, with the initial British seizure of the Cape Colony in the mid-1790s. At that time the European population consisted primarily of Dutch and German settlers who held substantial authority over the population of slaves and free Africans (principally the indigenous Khoi and San, known to the Europeans as "Hottentots" and "Bushmen," respectively) who worked as agricultural and domestic servants.[6] When the first missionaries of the LMS arrived at the Cape, the pressures of Dutch colonialism had broken much of the fabric of Khoi society and significantly diminished their economic autonomy through the appropriation of land and livestock by European colonists.

The presence of Christian missionaries almost immediately aroused the hostility of colonists, who complained that the Africans, and their cattle, drawn to the mission stations encroached upon their lands. Colonists also increasingly voiced charges that the missions deprived their farms of much-needed laborers. As one *landdrost*, or local colonial officer, protested, "it must be very hard" for "peaceable and quiet" farmers to see themselves and their farms "molested in a very unreasonable manner by a parcel of Hottentots, who, to nourish their laziness, pretend to be at school" (i.e., the mission).[7] Hostilities between colonists and colonial officials (often landowners themselves), on the one hand, and the missionaries of the LMS (over time the most vocal defenders of the Africans), on the other, persisted throughout the first half of the nineteenth century. Rather than a cozy relationship between the Bible and the flag, conflict between colonists and missionaries, especially over the questions of land and labor, increasingly marked the stormy landscape of Cape politics.

Missionaries of the LMS first appeared upon this landscape in 1799, led by the Dutch physician Johannes van der Kemp. A late convert to evangelical Christianity, van der Kemp eagerly took up the missionary cause before leaving Europe, translating LMS pamphlets into his native Dutch and assisting in the formation of a Netherlands Missionary Society. Not long after beginning his association with the LMS, van der Kemp applied to the directors for permission to establish a mission in southern Africa. The emergency brought on by the Khoi rebellion of 1799–1803 thwarted his initial plan to found a mission among the Xhosa beyond the eastern frontier. Still, van der Kemp eventually succeeded in establishing a permanent mission at Bethelsdorp and oversaw the expansion of several new mission stations within (and beyond) the Cape Colony before his death in 1811.[8] Colonial authorities hoped that the missionary presence might help to stabilize the situation among the rebellious Khoi and facilitate their reincorporation as a reliable source of labor for white farms and the colonial military service.

An ardent egalitarian, however, van der Kemp left his stamp upon the early LMS missions as a zealous opponent of such efforts to subjugate the Africans to the interests of colonists and government officials alike. Van der Kemp also violated the racial and social conventions of Cape society in his relations with Africans. He controversially purchased the freedom of and married a young slave girl from Madagascar and actively promoted the use of indigenous evangelists, or so-called "native agents," in the work of the mission. The work of Khoi "intermediaries" like Jan Hendrik and Cupido Kakkerlak, who established their own missions, contributed significantly to the rapid growth of Christianity among the colonial Khoi. During the first decades of the nineteenth century, van der Kemp and his small band of missionaries also frustrated colonial officials and white farmers with their persistent objections to the injustice of the colonists' treatment of the Khoi, inundating the colonial governors with complaints. He protested loudly against slavery, against statutes prohibiting the ownership of land by the Khoi, against the exploitative nature of the Cape labor system, and against the legal inequality of nonwhites in the colony. James Read, who was to succeed van der Kemp as superintending missionary at Bethelsdorp, encouraged Africans to bring accusations of mistreatment before the system of circuit courts established by the British governor, Sir John Craddock, in 1812. Colonists, on the other hand, protested against the Africans' efforts to obtain redress for the abuses of their masters. They especially condemned the missions for abetting the "malicious, collusive, and false accusations" of African laborers.[9]

As in the plantation system of the West Indies, the egalitarianism of the Society's early missions posed a direct challenge to the racial and hierarchical structure of colonial society. The Dutch Reformed Church (DRC) that served the white population generally excluded Africans, and ministers of the DRC had pushed administrators of the Dutch East India Company to shut down a Moravian mission in the western Cape in the 1740s. Missionary education also created uneasiness among colonists and government officials at the Cape as it did in the Caribbean colonies. Van der Kemp repeatedly complained of the governor's hostility toward the schooling of the Khoi at Bethelsdorp.

> The governor wished us to desist for the present from instruction of the Hottentots in reading and writing . . . but I could not . . . consent to a proposal so contrary to the apparent interest of Christ's kingdom, and so unworthy of the rights of a free nation, merely to stop the clamour.[10]

To the many Khoi already reduced by more than a century of colonial exploitation to the status of an agricultural proletariat, the mission stations offered a sanctuary from the worst indignities of the colonial society. Although life on the stations was often overcrowded and hard, the missions nevertheless presented opportunities for education and commercial activity not available in the service of the colonists or the government. A posthumous tribute to the work of van der Kemp lauded the opportunities available at Bethelsdorp and suggested something of the entrepreneurial spirit of its inhabitants.

> [T]he number of persons belonging to the settlement . . . amounted to one thousand, including men, women, and children. Industry continually increased. Matts [*sic*] and baskets were made in considerable quantities, and sold in the country around. The manufacture of salt was encouraged, which was bartered in the neighbourhood for wheat and other useful articles. Soap-boiling, sawing, and wood cutting for wagons also became a source of support.[11]

The mission stations, as we shall see, also facilitated the formation of a new identity for peoples decimated by the incursion of European society and economy upon their indigenous culture. Perpetuating the egalitarian nature of the missions, in time Bethelsdorp and other stations "became [foci] for the reintegration of Khoi society and the reassertion of indigenous political leadership." The process of evangelizing Africans, by placing them "upon equal footing with the [white] Christians," undermined Boer pretensions to sole possession of the divine word which had made Christianity a source of "social power" within early nineteenth-century Cape society. The mission Christianity of the LMS denied the differentiation between Christian whites and heathen blacks that had sustained and justified the domination of the African population.[12]

While the expansion of the LMS missions threatened to undo the foundations of the social order at the Cape, the Society nevertheless suffered from a series of internal conflicts over leadership and the defense of African rights during the years following van der Kemp's death. The disputes threatened the future of the LMS mission and initiated a prolonged debate over the proper role of the missionary in relation to the colonial government and the systems of African labor in the colony. While the egalitarianism described above is an accurate general characterization of the missions during the early nineteenth century, not all missionaries shared it with equal fervor. George Thom, sent in 1812 by the LMS to supervise the missions at the Cape, objected to what he perceived to be the antigovernment and pro-African agenda of James Read and the other associates of van der Kemp. In 1817 Thom called a "Synod" of missionaries in Cape Town to examine the status of the mission stations in and around the colony. Thom's correspondence with the Society's directors emphasized his opposition to Read's playing at politics, his concerns over Read having married a young Khoi woman from the mission, and his determination to rid the missions of what he deemed to be radical influences. The Synod condemned Read, and the Society suspended him on charges of fornication for having committed adultery with the daughter of Andries Pretorius, a deacon in the Bethelsdorp congregation. In the midst of this internal discontent the governor, Lord Charles Somerset, a high Tory suspicious of the motives of dissenting missionaries, also refused to permit the LMS to establish new stations beyond the borders of the colony. Thom and a second missionary, John Taylor, ultimately resigned to take up congregations within the DRC, which more closely reflected their own antiegalitarian sentiments. A third missionary, John Brownlee, accepted an appointment as a so-called government missionary among the Xhosa east of the colonial frontier. The discord among the missionaries in the years following van der Kemp's death left the Society's South African enterprise understaffed, in dire need of restructuring, and in danger of collapse.[13]

John Philip and Colonial Politics

In the hope of stabilizing the troubled mission and repairing its fractured relationship with the colonial government, the directors decided to send a delegation to the Cape, led by John Campbell and John Philip. Campbell and Philip arrived in Cape Town in 1819 to conduct an extensive tour of the mission stations in order to assess their effectiveness. Campbell would ultimately return to Britain to report to the directors, while Philip was to remain behind to implement reforms intended to return the Society's work in southern Africa to a sound foundation. In the following decades Philip's interests and actions were to have profound repercussions on the political and religious life of the colony.[14]

Born in Kirkcaldy on the eastern coast of Scotland in 1775, Philip was the son of a successful and intellectually curious handloom weaver. He grew up in the midst of the significant social, economic, and religious changes that characterized late eighteenth-century Scottish society and was exposed to many of the philosophical and literary works of the age. These experiences profoundly influenced Philip's work with the South African missions and his views of British colonial policy. As a young man Philip first encountered the evangelical influences making their way into the religious life of Britain, and which were especially popular among the skilled artisan communities of his birth. Of particular importance in Philip's religious development were Robert and James Haldane, leaders of the evangelical movement that opposed the patronage and dominance of the Auld Kirk, who inspired the formation of numerous Independent congregations across Scotland. The Scottish establishment viewed the Haldanes' movement with much the same suspicion with which its English counterpart regarded the expansion of evangelical dissent in the late eighteenth and early nineteenth centuries. The General Assembly acted as early as 1799 to restrict the access of dissenting and evangelical preachers to Scottish pulpits, which intensified the movement toward independent congregations as well as the commitment to religious liberty among the followers of the Haldanes and other Scottish evangelicals. Philip's participation in this world of Scottish Congregationalism greatly enhanced the development of his own sensibilities, especially his concern for religious liberty and his belief in the principle of independence.[15]

Through the influence of the Haldanite movement, and at the urging of the Congregationalist minister Thomas Durant, Philip, in his midtwenties, left his position as manager of a textile mill in Dundee in order to enter the Christian ministry. Following his training at the Hoxton Academy in England, Philip ultimately settled with the Independent congregation at Aberdeen in 1804. He enjoyed marked success in his ministry, attained considerable status within British congregational circles, and was even awarded honorary degrees from Columbia and Princeton for his service to religious and philanthropic organizations. Philip also vigorously supported foreign missions through the LMS and its Scottish auxiliaries, which had close ties to the Haldanite Congregationalist movement. This connection led to the directors prevailing upon him to accept a place with the commission to South Africa and to his appointment as "Resident Director" in Cape Town to oversee the reorganization of the missions in the colony. Although instructed to improve the Society's standing in the eyes of the colonial administration, Philip soon came to see British colonial policy itself as the greatest obstacle to the conversion and improvement of the African population. In the words of the centennial history of the LMS, Philip had gone out "under the conviction that the poor treatment of the Africans by the Dutch had been ameliorated by the transition to British rule . . . but he was soon undeceived of the notion when he got to the Cape."[16]

Upon establishing himself in Cape Town Philip set about the task of improving relations between the missions and the colonial government, but was quickly drawn into the intricate political debates of Cape society. His arrival in Cape Town nearly coincided with that of some four thousand British settlers on the eastern frontier of the colony in 1820. Government hoped that the settlers, part of the "most ambitious" state-sponsored emigration scheme of the time, would both alleviate the pressures of unemployment in the depressed British economy and provide a defense against the intrusion of the Xhosa along the Cape Colony's frontier. As early as 1809 Col. Richard Collins had suggested that the British might stabilize the eastern frontier by settling significant numbers of white colonists on small-scale farms along the border. A parliamentary grant of £50,000 in 1819 facilitated the launching of the scheme and the placement of settlers on one-hundred-acre farms in the eastern Cape. The poor quality of the soil, the poor weather, and the relative lack of agricultural experience among settlers who came primarily from the artisanal classes, however, doomed the plan almost from the start. By the mid-1820s a vast majority of the original immigrants had given up on farming and had established themselves as craftsmen and tradesmen in eastern Cape townships such as Grahamstown and Port Elizabeth.[17]

A Distressed Settlers Fund was also established to assist struggling immigrant families, and Philip was appointed its director, placing him at the center of one of the most intense political conflicts in the colony. The disgruntled settlers formed an unofficial party of opposition to the colonial governor, Somerset, who disdained the pretensions of the upstart lower gentry and artisans of settler party. Philip's relationship with Somerset deteriorated because of his association with the Settlers Fund and his cordial relations with two fellow Scots, John Fairbairn and Thomas Pringle, publishers of the *South African Commercial Advertiser* (*SACA*), a voice for settler complaints against the Somerset regime. Through their common Scottish and nonconformist roots Philip, Fairbairn, and Pringle shared a deep commitment to the principles of egalitarianism, free trade, and freedom of the press, all anathema to the conservative Somerset. The governor waged a persistent battle against the *Commercial Advertiser* and its publishers, whom he referred to as "arrant Dissenter[s] who scribbled."[18] In due course Somerset came to see Philip as the mastermind behind the paper's campaign against government corruption and censorship. Engaged in the defense of his office against attacks from Britain as well as the within the colony, the governor singled out the missionary leader with particular scorn:

> Dr. Philip is the Head Huntsman and . . . Mr. Fairburn [*sic*] Mr. Pringle and Paddy Wright are the whippers in. . . . The Dr. gave out . . . that he went out of his way to avoid the constant solicitations made to him to sign a memorial for a free press [that] those matters were not within his calling! Villain—Hypocrite! When he himself is the premium mobile.[19]

There is little evidence to suggest that Philip involved himself in, let alone directed, a plot to oust the governor. Nevertheless, as Dissenters, liberals, and proponents of a free press, he and his associates were natural targets for the ire of the Tory Somerset. Philip's involvement with the settlers, and the debate over freedom of the press, not surprisingly contributed to the derailment of his efforts to restore the mission's relationship with the colonial authorities.[20]

In the midst of the controversies with Somerset, Philip further set himself at odds with the colonial government by taking up the cause of the Khoi population in the colony. During his first years in Cape Town, Philip, influenced by the reports of Thom and others hostile to van der Kemp and Read, was skeptical of the missionary accusations against the colonists. His views changed dramatically, however, following a visit to Bethelsdorp, where Read presented substantial evidence to support his charges that colonial officials repeatedly coerced Khoi laborers into the service of the government and the white farms. From 1821, then, Philip began his campaign to demonstrate that the Africans deserved legal and economic equality and that they were, in his words, "fit to be free." This entailed, at first, directing efforts toward the improvement of the mission stations at Theopolis and Bethelsdorp. Philip repeatedly implored the missionaries to whitewash houses, clothe the children, and keep the people working and productive to counter allegations that the missions fostered laziness and bad habits among the Khoi.

In the autumn of 1821, Philip stressed to the Khoi at Bethelsdorp "the advantage which an improvement in their houses, and their industry and mode of living, would afford their friends, in pleading their cause." Reflecting the assumptions about the superiority of European civilization which characterized his age, Philip emphasized that "the world, and the church of Christ, looked for civilization and industry as proofs of [Africans'] capacity for improvement, and of the utility of our labours." "The man of the world," he claimed, "had no other criterion by which they could judge the beneficial results of the missions."[21] Governor Somerset's "criterion of a people's civilization," he noted dryly, "was whether the people used knives and forks."[22] Philip did not completely rise above the cultural prejudices of his age or the paternal tendencies of the Christian mission. Yet as shall be seen, he believed strongly in the humanity and the equality of the Africans. Addressing the American Board of Commissioners of Foreign Missions in 1833, Philip exhibited views on the "Natural capacity of the African Race" that directly challenged the racial hierarchy of the colonial society.

> So far as my observation extends, it appears to me that the natural capac-
> ity of the African is nothing inferior to that of the European . . . the
> people at our missionary stations are in many instances superior in intel-
> ligence to those who look down on them, as belonging to an inferior
> caste. The natives beyond the colony live in a world of their own, and
> they know little of our world, but we know less of theirs then they do
> of ours. . . . I have never seen anything in civilized society like the fac-
> ulty those people have in discerning the spirit and character of men. . . .
> Contemplated through the medium of their own superstitions, or that of
> their general condition, we might hastily pronounce them to be inferior
> to the white race; but on these points they lose nothing by a comparison
> with our European ancestors.[23]

The "backwardness" of the "African heathen," a favorite theme of mission ideology, derived not from an inherent inequality with Europeans
but from the conditions in which they lived. A necessary first step in the
improvement of the "heathens" required the improvement of their physical
environment.

As an advocate for the cause of the free African population in the colony
Philip also relied upon the Society's connections within evangelical circles
in London. He successfully lobbied William Wilberforce to have the condition of the Khoi placed under the consideration of the government Committee of *Enquiry* appointed to investigate the problems in the colony in
1822.[24] On the basis of information from Philip concerning the treatment of
the Khoi, Wilberforce assured the secretary of the LMS that he had

> seen enough to render me deeply interested in the questions at issue
> between your society and the government of the Cape. . . . I have again
> enforced on the Secretary of State, Lord Bathurst, the necessity and
> importance of rendering the Hottentots one of the primary objects of the
> Commissioner's attention.[25]

Philip judged that impressing the commissioners with the condition of the
missions would greatly aid his efforts to improve the position of the African
population. "I may be expected daily with some great men from England,"
he advised Kitchingman at Bethelsdorp, and "everything relating to the
Hottentots depends on the way in which we find things."[26]

The Committee of *Enquiry* and the question of the improvement of the
Khoi gave rise to fervent debate in the colonial press between colonists and
the supporters of the mission. A correspondent to the *SACA* questioned the
"facts brought forward to enable us to ascertain the reality of [the] alleged

improvements" at the mission stations. Repeating attitudes common among the colonists, he described the missions as "little else than so many receptacles of idleness, filth, canting fanaticism and squalid poverty." The letter suggested that "the Hottentots [were] improved only in psalm-singing, and that it [was] all cry and a little wool at Bethelsdorp."[27] Champions of the missions, in turn, vigorously defended them against the criticisms of the colonists. H. E. Rutherford rebutted the charges of "laziness" and "canting fanaticism" at Bethelsdorp in his own letter to the *SACA*. Rutherford favorably compared the productivity of the Khoi at the missions to that of Africans in the service of the colonists, praising the men "cutting and sawing timber, driving wagons, building [and] thatching" at the mission. He lauded the "six masons, two carpenters, two or three tailors and shoe makers, and others . . . handy at different branches of trade" among the Africans at the station. "I think it might be safely affirmed," Rutherford wrote, "that there is more work done, and beyond all question, more money earned by the 400 or 500 Hottentots living at Bethelsdorp, than by the 800 amongst the Boors."[28]

The message of the missionaries and their allies was clear. Khoi at the missions left free to make economic choices for themselves were more productive and more useful to the colony than those compelled to labor on white farms without any incentive for economic or spiritual improvement. Increasingly, Philip determined that the colonial system, not the colonists themselves, bore the largest share of the responsibility for the oppressed state of the Khoi. He escalated his criticism not against "settler capitalism, *per se*," but against a system which he believed encouraged "settler capitalism of an exploitative, coercive variety . . . predicated on subjection and dispossession."[29]

The *Researches in South Africa* and the Rights of the Khoi

As early as 1822 Philip concluded that the struggle to free the Khoi population would have to be fought in London as well as the Cape Colony. His determination to place the condition of the free Africans under the consideration of the Commission of *Enquiry* reflected this belief. So did a letter to the directors of the LMS in 1823, which noted that "everything possible has been done by me to bring the government to reason in order to avert this struggle. Nothing can now be of avail to save Africa but British statutes."[30] Dissatisfied with the slow progress made on the question of African rights by the government commissioners, Philip determined to make a direct appeal to the British government and public in London. In 1825 he obtained the Society's leave to return to Britain in order to make the case for African civil equality in person. Before leaving he made a final tour of the mission stations to collect the evidence he resolved to "lay before Lord Bathurst [the Colonial Secretary]," and should that fail to "lay the whole before the British public."[31]

True to this intention, while in Britain Philip published the *Researches in South Africa*, a tour de force of political propaganda and a bold statement of his views on British colonial policy in the Cape. The missionary leader was well aware of his Society's hesitancy about overt political activity, and he quickly realized that enlisting the support of the burgeoning abolitionist movement was crucial to his success. He deliberately sought to connect the antislavery cause with his efforts to grant Africans the right to freely bring their labor, or its fruits, to the market. Through his presence in London and his relentless lobbying of the antislavery leadership, he ensured that the plight of the Khoi was not lost amid the growing intensity of the parliamentary campaign against slavery. He convinced Wilberforce, Buxton, and James Stephen that the benefits of abolition in the colony would mean little if emancipated slaves were subjected to the oppression faced by the colonial Khoi. "If they aim at the abolition of slavery," he wrote to Buxton, "is it to put freed slaves in the position of 'free' Hottentots?"[32] Convinced, Buxton and Zachary Macauly encouraged Philip to publish the *Researches* in order to make his case directly to that portion of the religious public most likely to be sympathetic to the Africans' cause.[33] The remainder of this chapter will carefully examine the argument of the *Researches*, the influences that shaped Philip's opinions, and his efforts to secure a parliamentary guarantee of civil rights for the Africans of the colony. Considering Philip's work in the context of contemporary political and religious currents in Britain clearly illustrates the important role of the politics of evangelical dissent in shaping the concerns of missionaries in the colonial arena.

In 1807 Philip identified the abolition of the slave trade as a primary factor in greatly increasing the value of free African laborers within the colony. This circumstance intensified white resentment of the missions, which the colonists believed were responsible for allowing the Africans to maintain their independence, thus depriving the farms of an essential workforce. Ordinances enacted by British officials in 1809 and 1812, the so-called Hottentot Codes, established severe restrictions upon the movement and labor of the Khoi and other free Africans. The ordinances enacted a pass system, which made Africans caught without proper documentation from an employer subject to prosecution and assignment to the services of farmers or the government at the sole discretion of local officials. The system further established the practice of farmers keeping African children from ages eight to eighteen as apprentices, effectively trapping Khoi families in the service of individual colonists. Such arbitrary control by farmers and government officials over the labor and movement of the Khoi deeply offended the nonconformist Philip's commitment to the principles of independence and freedom of choice. He condemned the ordinances for legitimizing practices that he claimed were considered abuses under the government of the Dutch and for denying the Africans the fundamental civil rights of British subjects. This, Philip argued, constituted the greatest flaw in British policy in South Africa.

> Although the weakness of the Dutch government might compel it to wink at the manner in which the Hottentots were oppressed by the colonists, that government was not so deeply implicated in the oppression as the English government has been . . . the oppressions at which the Dutch government connived have, under the English government, obtained the sanction of law.[34]

Philip, as a dedicated missionary, believed in Christianity as the "true center and source of civilization," and his book clearly identified the gospel as the essential means of improving and civilizing the African population.[35] "Civilization, social order, and the charities which sweeten life," he wrote, "are among the . . . advantages which spring from the diffusion of genuine religion." Christianity was indispensable to the fulfillment of Britain's mission; "there [was] not a single example on the records of history of any philosopher or legislator having civilized a nation or a tribe without the aid of religion."[36] The successful completion of this process, however, required appropriate conditions in which the Christian religion might thrive and do its improving work. This conviction provided the incentive for Philip's forceful critique of the colonial administration at the Cape. British rule, "under which the Hottentots, at one time, had reason to expect a greater degree of liberty," in his estimation had "only added to the number and weight of their chains."[37] Government policy in the colony failed to secure the conditions best suited to encourage and advance the conversion and civilization of the indigenous population. For the sake of the missions as well as the Khoi, it had to be changed.

The analysis of the colonial administration and of the plight of the African laborers contained in the *Researches* drew heavily upon the influences of Philip's youth. These included the Scottish Enlightenment as well as nonconformist concerns about independence and civil liberty. The enlightened political economy of Adam Smith loomed large within Philip's work. Quoting Smith, he argued that laborers "when they are secure of enjoying the fruits of their industry . . . naturally exert [themselves] to better their condition."[38] "The Hottentots at the institutions," he stressed, "notwithstanding their oppressed condition, have stimulants to exertion which the Hottentots with the Boers do not possess."[39] Philip dismissed colonists' claims of the Africans' inherent laziness and lack of industry, citing Campbell's and numerous others' accounts of the mission stations that emphasized the diligence and productivity of the Khoi. "They are said to be idle," Campbell had written, "yet I have found among them eighteen trades . . . [and] . . . they have more cultivated land than I have seen in any one place in Africa." The missions provided models of a foundation on which a new and productive Cape society might be constructed, "the seedbed of a new society."[40] Imbued with the same egalitarian nonconformist zeal that helped drive the antislavery movement, Philip asserted that the Khoi were "as capable of being excited to industry as any other class of people, when they [had] the prospect of procuring, by the fruits of their labor, the objects of desire." The "more nearly these objects are placed within their reach," he contended, "the more we elevate their characters."[41]

The colonial government's policies, Philip argued, bore the primary fundamental responsibility for retarding the pace of this improvement. Of the white farmers, he wrote,

> [T]he power thrown into their hands by the weakness of government [and] their situation in the midst of a population over whom they can tyrannize without control, is as unfavorable to the civilization of the farmers themselves, as it is to the happiness and improvement of those under them.[42]

This marked an important strategic shift in the policy of the missions in the colony. During the previous decade van der Kemp and James Read had brought to the colonial courts individual cases of Africans wronged by colonists, and the enmity of the missions focused principally upon the colonists themselves. In the *Researches*, Philip completely changed the focus of debate, using examples of white farmers' mistreatment of Africans as a means to illustrate the shortcomings of government policy. "Bad laws generate bad morals," he asserted; "there is no greater obstruction to the improvement of a people, than bad laws in the hands of men who only think of employing them to enrich themselves at the expense of those whom they oppress."[43]

Philip's assertion of the necessity of civilizing the white colonists suggests the depth of the influence of enlightened thinking upon his perceptions of colonialism in southern Africa and its close connection to the abolitionist movement. Early nineteenth-century missionary texts stressed that the "backward" or "uncivilized" character of indigenous societies resulted from their environment and circumstances, reflecting enlightened belief in humanity's connection to the natural world and the advancement of all human societies "according to uniform laws of cultural development" toward civilization.[44] "The filth and indolence of the Hottentots have become proverbial," Philip wrote, "but these, like the other vices of which they have been accused, arise out of their situation."[45] In other words, circumstances mattered. Given the centrality of the belief in a universal humanity in early nineteenth-century missionary ideology, this applied to the white colonists as much as to Africans. Abolitionists repeatedly argued slavery was as harmful to the slave master as to the slave. Philip viewed the influence of Cape colonial policy upon the white population of southern Africa in the same way.[46]

In the preface to the work, he declared, "My object in the composition of these pages has not been to expose men, but measures." A reform of the colony's laws, his argument claimed, would accelerate the improvement of the African population not only to their benefit, but to the benefit of the colony as a whole.[47] Philip envisioned the transformation of powerless, landless, rural Africans into a productive and prosperous class of farmers and artisans. He argued that the benefits of such a transformation would extend far beyond the colony itself by creating a "new and extensive market . . . for British goods [and] increased consumption of British manufactures."[48] He believed that South Africa's future prosperity depended upon reforming its economic structures and securing for Africans the means for their economic and spiritual improvement.[49]

Recent scholarship on the impact of the missionary movement in southern Africa has connected the evangelical nonconformists' colonial agenda in southern Africa to the eighteenth-century "fall of the British yeomanry" and the "defacing of England-as-garden" brought about by the onset of industrialization in the northern counties and Scotland, from whence most of the early missionaries came. These missionaries, so the argument goes, saw Africa as fertile ground for the creation of an "independent [African] peasantry" and the re-creation of an idealized version of Britain's agricultural past.[50] We may question whether the Industrial Revolution had really cut so deeply "into the physical, social, and cultural terrain" of early nineteenth-century

Britain as to have had such an impact.[51] Furthermore, this backward-looking emphasis seems to underplay the pervasively progressive nature of Philip's opinions. His hopes for facilitating the formation of an independent African agricultural class probably derived much from influences such as the Scottish Society for the Promotion of Christian Knowledge's program for the evangelizing and civilizing of the Scottish Highlands.[52] Far from viewing the socioeconomic developments of his youth as the engines of the destruction of an idyllic English past, Philip saw them as an integral part of his own social and intellectual advancement. Through his proposed reforms Philip sought to bring the Khoi gains that he associated with his own life story, and he projected a vision that emphasized southern Africa's future rather than an obsession with a mythical British past.

This is not to say that Philip ignored Britain's history in his consideration of British rule at the Cape. Indeed, he looked back well beyond the eighteenth century for illustrations of the efficacy of sound colonial policy. Richard Hingley has recently suggested that the idea of the civilizing influence of the Roman Empire significantly shaped late nineteenth-century British attitudes toward imperialism.[53] However, already in 1828 Philip filtered his analysis of Britain's colonial administration through an idealized version of Rome's imperial past. Roman colonial governance, and its impact upon ancient Britain, also served as a model against which he could contrast his portrait of British colonialism in the Cape. Philip was especially critical of the British administration's failure to prevent its colonial officers from establishing commercial or financial interests within the colony and believed that in South Africa this led administrators to collude with the colonists to the disadvantage of the African population. Having praised the strict prohibitions against Roman colonial governors holding such property, he remarked that "nothing [could] be more dissimilar than the practice which originated with the Romans . . . and that followed by the British colonial government of the Cape of Good Hope."[54]

More significantly Philip looked to Britain's ancient past as an example of how sound colonial policy could lead to the advancement and civilization of a so-called barbarous people. The British public needed only look to its own nation's ancient history to see what might be accomplished in Africa. Philip suggested that as "the Romans might have found an image of their own ancestors in the representations they gave of ours . . . we may see what our ancestors were at the time Julius Caesar invaded Britain, by the present condition of the tribes of South Africa." He then linked the Roman, the Briton, and the African in a long continuum of colonial history and the progress of civilization. "It is here we see, as in a mirror," he continued, "the features of our progenitors, and, by our own history, we may learn the pitch to which such tribes may be elevated, by means favourable to their improvement."[55]

For the remedy to the unacceptable condition of the Africans in the colony Philip turned to a principle strongly connected to his own nonconformist roots, civil liberty. "Of all the causes which tend to generate prudential habits among the lower classes of society," he quoted from Malthus, "the most essential is, unquestionably, civil liberty."[56] Philip repeated throughout both volumes of the *Researches* his primary objective that "the same civil rights enjoyed" by white subjects of the Crown "should be extended to the coloured population in every part of the colony."[57] His call for the full civil equality of the African population was an unquestionably radical proposition, and yet one not without powerful analogies in the religious and political life of Britain in the 1820s.

That decade saw the issue of the repeal of the Test and Corporation Acts return to the forefront of dissenting politics. The resurgence of agitation over the issue was tied to important socioeconomic and religious changes within Britain: to the rapid growth of evangelical Dissent, to the growing material prosperity of many Dissenters, and to the growing political clout of the evangelical lobby on issues such as religious liberty and antislavery. The spirit of Philip's arguments in the *Researches* appeared, as well, in the observations of the United Committee upon the evils of the Test Acts. In 1827 the United Committee argued that although the "honours of a higher class" from which Dissenters were barred might be attained by only a few, "honours, though ultimately obtainable by but a few, are the objects of ambition, and stimulants to exertion, of all."[58] Dissenters smarting under the social and religious prejudice symbolized by the Test Acts demanded recognition of their newly influential status within British society. In the words of one respected historian of the subject, "What the Dissenters called for was not only religious liberty, but social mobility."[59]

The freedom to achieve such "social mobility," and to prove their usefulness to the colony, was exactly what Philip demanded for the Africans of the Cape. The *Researches in South Africa*, like the abolitionist movement, must also be understood within this context of the reshaping of the religious and political structure of early nineteenth-century Britain that gave rise to the dissenting politics of civil and religious equality.[60] The evidence suggests that it was no mere coincidence that Philip returned to Britain to advocate the rights of Africans at the very same time that nonconformists were preparing to enjoy their final triumph over religious discrimination and as the campaign to abolish slavery was reaching a fever pitch. The intensity of these issues gave a keen edge to nonconformist politics in the period, and the missionary movement participated with shared personnel as well as sympathies in transmitting the ideas and enthusiasm to a wider British world.

Thus, Philip's campaign illustrates the political resources available to missionaries concerned with native rights in the Cape Colony. John Comaroff characterized the missionaries as "the least potent whites in [the] colonial theater of southern Africa," subordinate to "the authority of the . . . government on the one hand," and without the "social and material resources" of the colonists on the other.[61] Philip's activities suggest the need to revise such an emphasis. The mission in South Africa was clearly not without support outside or influence in the colony. The few sympathetic colonial officials, such as Andries Stockenstrom, proved especially important allies to Philip and his colleagues. More significantly, by the 1820s the mission could appeal to the powerful evangelical lobby in Britain. Ultimate authority over colonial policy still resided in Westminster, and there can be little doubt of the evangelical Dissenters' skill at using public opinion to sway government policy.[62]

The Ordinance 50 Campaign

While in Britain Philip took full advantage of these connections and enlisted not only supporters of the missions but the full weight of the Anti-Slavery Society and its parliamentary leadership behind his cause. When examined in the broader context of both the colonial and metropolitan politics of the 1820s, it is fair to say that Philip enjoyed the upper hand over his colonial rivals. Neither does Philip's case sustain the claim that because of their "anti-establishment" sentiments the missionaries "did not welcome the presence of a colonial government."[63] Philip directed his criticisms toward the policies of the Cape government, not toward its existence. Colonial government played an essential role in his plans for South Africa as the guarantor of civil, religious, and economic freedoms to all persons within the colony, black or white. His vision for southern Africa combined a strong belief in the equality and humanity of the Africans, faith in the benefits of the free market, and a deep sense of the social implications of the gospel into a coherent argument for the advance together of Christianity, commercial prosperity, and civilization. Secure for the Africans a better situation, through civil and economic freedom, and their improvement would follow in due course. The

Researches in South Africa exemplifies those progressive early nineteenth-century attitudes toward Africa which Philip Curtin has called "conversionism,"[64] and the work certainly influenced the thinking of other leading figures in the missionary movement, including Buxton, Henry Venn, and David Livingstone. Christianity, commerce, and civilization were to become the catchwords of mid-nineteenth-century imperial and missionary activity.

A shrewd lobbyist, Philip succeeded in pressing his concerns upon the government, even in the tumultuous political year of 1827, which saw the departure of Liverpool and the short-lived administrations of Canning and Goderich. By the end of that year the new Colonial Secretary, Huskisson, agreed to direct the governor of the Cape, Bourke, to examine the condition of the free Africans.[65] Bourke assigned the task to Andries Stockenstrom, commissioner general for the eastern districts and one of the few allies of the missions within the colonial government. In London, the publication of the *Researches* in early 1828 was, Philip wrote to James Kitchingman, "almost instantaneously followed by a general conviction that I must carry my point."[66] Attracting enthusiastic public support, and with the backing of the Anti-Slavery Society, Philip won the passage, in 1828, of a motion to "secure to all natives of South Africa, the same freedom and protection . . . enjoyed by other free people of that colony."[67] While Philip celebrated the "great deliverance which the Lord has been pleased to grant to the natives of South Africa"[68] in Parliament, at the Cape, Stockenstrom, who had kept in close communication with Philip on the question of African rights, presented his report to Bourke. Influenced by communications with representatives of the LMS prior to his departure for the Cape, accepting Stockenstrom's recommendations, and telling the Colonial Secretary that the "necessity for such a measure has been apparent to me from a very early period after my arrival," Bourke granted the Africans civil equality.[69]

Known as Ordinance 50, the declaration fulfilled almost all of Philip's demands for the reform of colonial policy toward the Khoi. The statute ended the system of pass laws and all forms of compulsory labor, it abolished the apprenticeship of Khoi children without parental consent, it specified the process for the registration of written labor contracts, and it confirmed the right of free Africans to own land.[70] Missionaries of the LMS in South Africa welcomed Ordinance 50, the culmination of their struggle on behalf of the Khoi, with great rejoicing. Kitchingman hailed it "the Magna Charta of the natives," and John Melvill termed it "the greatest civil blessing the Hottentot nation ever received."[71] James Read welcomed its proclamation as a crucial first step on the path to establishing a free and prosperous community of Khoi within the colony. "The ordinance for the Hottentots is a great work, and a great point gained," he wrote to Kitchingman; "altho' the Hottentots will not be without oppression, yet there is now a basis to work upon."[72] In London, Philip recognized that parliamentary backing of the ordinance was essential for the reforms to have a positive effect at the Cape. Before returning to Cape Town from Britain in 1829, he and his allies convinced the government to reinforce, by an Order-in-Council, the protections granted to the Africans in Ordinance 50. The rights and privileges of the Khoi enshrined in Ordinance 50 could not be revoked by the Cape government without the consent of the King and his Council.[73]

Philip returned to the Cape in 1829 and encountered the wrath of colonists who vilified him for his role in the enactment of Ordinance 50, which they deemed "the work of the devil."[74] His persistent advocacy of the equality of the Khoi had slowly eroded his standing in the eyes of the majority of the white community, and his agitation on behalf of the Africans in Britain had turned white suspicion of the missions to outright hostility. Afrikaners resented Philip's leadership of the movement they held responsible for the steady deterioration of their authority and socioeconomic status. Growing numbers of British settlers also found his humanitarianism distasteful. Colonial publications, such as the Cape Town–based *De Zuid Afrikan* and *South African Tydschrift* and the English-language *Grahamstown Journal*, gave voice to white dissatisfaction with the new ordinance and their complaints about the increase in vagrancy and crime that they believed it fostered. As one Grahamstonian wrote in late 1829, "[T]he Ordinance was too sudden. It led the Hottentot astray. He did not know his bounds . . . he could not be checked . . . and he ran riot."[75] To most colonists, the overthrow of the existing racial and economic order of the colony seemed imminent.

Illustrative of white antagonism toward Philip was the libel suit brought against the missionary leader by William Mackay, the Deputy Landdrost of Somerset East. Mackay charged Philip with libel for having, in the *Researches*, alleged that he had abused his authority in his treatment of Khoi laborers in the district. The great interest caused by the suit reflected the intensity of the feeling against Philip, and Mackay without question enjoyed the "overwhelming sympathy" of the majority of colonists.[76] Freshly returned from several years in Britain, Philip seemed taken aback by the hostility within the colony directed toward him and his campaign. He had always felt that in his efforts to reform colonial policy at the Cape he "had the interest of the colonists as much as that of the Hottentots" in mind.[77] Missionaries in the field, on the other hand, were more prepared for the extent of the white opposition to Philip's cause. "A man who does anything for the natives here may expect to be hated for it," Kitchingman wrote in his journal at Bethelsdorp. "A most bitter spirit exists against Dr. Philip among many here. They seem to hate everything which has a tendency to raise the slaves and free people," he concluded.[78] Echoing the animosity of colonial opinion toward Philip, the judges ruled in favor of Mackay and ordered the missionary to pay damages and costs in total of £1,100.

Indicative, however, of Philip's substantial popularity with the religious public in Britain, the LMS organized a subscription campaign that easily collected the full amount of his legal costs. And Philip returned to Bethelsdorp in triumph to the adulation of the missionaries and the mission Khoi "as a prince entering the capital of his kingdom." The community sang hymns, giving thanks to God and to Philip, "whom God had used to procure their liberty," and even sang "God Save the King" in honor of George IV, who had granted it to them. They held a feast in Philip's honor, serving meats, vegetables, and deserts "prepared as in Europe" by the mission Khoi, who attended the banquet in waistcoats and ties while the women "wore dresses of printed Calico, with white stockings and small black shoes." Several leaders of the Khoi community gave speeches acknowledging the mission's role in alleviating their "misery and sufferings," and Philip urged the mission community to redouble its efforts to continue to spread Christianity and civilization under the new liberty granted by Ordinance 50. The event exemplified what Robert Ross has described as a "conjunction between Christianity, respectability, loyalty to Great Britain and political advance that was never repeated."[79]

Yet in 1829 the missionaries' hopes for the advancement of a prosperous, civilized, and christianized class of Khoi were never higher. Most of these hopes relied upon the prospects of the new government-sponsored settlement in the Kat River valley. Established in 1829 at the instigation of Stockenstrom, the settlement marked not only an effort to "benefit the forlorn remnants of the former possessors of South Africa," but another attempt to secure the eastern border of the colony. Stockenstrom convinced the governor, Sir Lowry Cole, that a settlement of numerous Khoi of "respectable character and industrious habits" might provide the best protection against intrusions by the Xhosa and contribute to the greater prosperity of the colony.[80] The idea had been entertained by Stockenstrom, Philip, and others concerned with African rights at least since 1823, when Thomas Pringle had written a plan for "Defending the Eastern Frontier of the Colony by a

Settlement of Hottentots."[81] The plan also seemed ideally suited to put into effect the rights of Khoi and other free Africans to own land as guaranteed by Ordinance 50. Many of the most successful of the mission Khoi from the LMS stations availed themselves of the opportunity to settle in the Kat River valley and requested permission from Philip to call James Read to establish a congregation among them.[82] The chapel at Kat River was the first predominantly African Independent congregation in southern Africa, and its first minister, Read, best summarized the hopes and aspirations of the missionary community for the endeavor.

> I cannot help embracing this opportunity of expressing my feeling of gratification at the present prospects of the Hottentots, a scene I have long been . . . working for for 28 years, and I must say my wishes, my prayers are answered and my feeble endeavours fully rewarded. . . . 'Tis an act of humanity, of wise policy, and of justice. The Hottentots certainly had a claim, a great one; they have been great losers and have received nothing in way of compensation. Government will find it is helping itself and the country at large and forwarding the great plan of general improvement and civilization.[83]

Over the next two decades, Read's aspirations for the Khoi and the colony proved far more difficult to achieve than he or his colleagues had hoped. The obstacles in the way of the missionaries' dreams not only stemmed from the resistance of the colonists to building a color-blind society but also were connected to important changes in evangelical Dissent taking place in Britain. We now turn to the character and the context of those transformations in the next chapter.

5

Church, State, and Dissenting Politics in the Age of Reform

The constitutional sea change of the reform era produced the next dramatic shift in the scope and character of evangelical dissenting politics. The repeal of the Test Acts, parliamentary reform, and the reconstruction of municipal governments made participation in the political life of the nation accessible to Dissenters in unprecedented numbers. Celebrating the passing of the Reform Bill, the nonconformist weekly the *Patriot* noted that Dissenters would no longer be forced to select between candidates "whose political sentiments were dramatically opposed to their own," the Tories, and the Whigs, who although allies in the fight for religious liberty held religious beliefs of which "they could not approve." In the future, Dissenters could elect "whom they please[d]" to represent them in Parliament.[1]

All the same, the revolution in Britain's constitution between 1828 and 1835 created concerns for numerous evangelical Dissenters who were reluctant to take up the title of "political dissenters." Dissenting publications, institutions, and prominent ministers all expressed concerns, lest the increase in "political spirit" should injure "the vitality of Christian ministration."[2] In the years following the agitation against Sidmouth's bill, evangelical Dissenters had conducted their political activity primarily upon the basis of defending religious liberty and advancing civil equality through parliamentary petitions and organizations like the Protestant Society for the Protection of Religious Liberty. Scripture provided evidence to justify these positions in both domestic and colonial politics, as John Philip noted in the preface to the *Researches in South Africa*.

> If it is the duty of Englishmen to claim the protection of the laws of their country; if the Apostle Paul was in the exercise of his duty when he claimed the privileges of a Roman citizen, and appealed from the judgement of Festus to the tribunal of Caesar,—it is to be hoped that the friends of humanity and of religion in England, will see it to be their duty to petition the British throne and the British parliament, that the natives of South Africa may have those rights secured to them, which have become necessary to the preservation and extension of religion among them.[3]

The robust political activity of evangelical Dissenters in the 1810s and 1820s was concentrated upon the principled assertion and defense of their rights against infringements by the established church or the state, and thus somewhat defensive in character.

Christian Citizenship and the Politics of Disestablishment

The changed landscape of postreform British politics necessitated some reconfiguration of the political dissenting ideology, partly in response to the increased accusations by Anglicans of Dissenters' worldly political interests and failure to respect "the powers . . . ordained of God."[4] One central feature of this process was the sacrilizing of political activity through the reinterpretation of the apostle Paul and his identity as a Roman citizen. Leading ministers, such as the Congregationalist John D. Harris, recast the apostle, who had admonished his followers to pray "for kings, and for all that are in authority,"[5] into an active and Christian citizen. These ideas expanded upon the conception of Paul as a citizen defending his rights— see the example of Philip's assertion above—formulating a new model of the apostle used to justify more earnest participation in politics. Paul, according to Harris, was a Roman citizen "who gloried in the distinction" and whose patriotism informed his life as an active Christian. From this, Harris encouraged Dissenters to become "Christian Citizens" themselves, with a concern for the social and spiritual improvement of the nation. "The golden law of love commands us, by legitimate means," he asserted, "to break the fetters of the slave, to watch over the interests of the social body, and to act as the anointed guardians of truth and freedom." True Christianity, Harris concluded, "accompanies the tradesman to the place of business, takes its seat by the judge, and to the Christian patriot it says daily, 'Be the citizen, in a manner worthy of the gospel of Christ.'"[6] During the 1830s these sentiments, combined with the increased access of Dissenters to political office, helped to give birth to a new and more militant style of dissenting politics.[7]

In 1830 John Wilks, secretary of the Protestant Society, encouraged nonconformists to take up the struggle against the remaining "grievances" that continued to mark their unequal status relative to the established church. These included the frequent denial of the right of burial in parish graveyards, the refusal of courts to recognize dissenting baptismal records and marriages conducted outside of the established church, the collections of poor rates from Dissenting chapels, and the requirement of Dissenters to pay church rates for the maintenance of the local parish church.[8] Wilks' demand for parliamentary action against the hardships faced by Dissenters led to the formation, in 1833, of a United Committee of delegates from the Protestant Society, the Dissenting Deputies, and the General Body of Dissenting Ministers to press the nonconformists' case in the public and political arenas. The United Committee set itself the task of securing for all Protestant nonconformists full equality with the members of the church.

The political goals of the United Committee received a sharper edge from the appearance of explicit calls, by dissenting ministers and layman, for the disestablishment of the Anglican Church. Most famously, the Rev. Thomas Binney of the King's Weigh House chapel made a stinging criticism of the unwarranted moral and spiritual authority exercised by the church in a sermon before his congregation in 1833.[9] In the appendix to a published edition of the address, Binney raised the stakes even further. "It is with me," he wrote,

> a matter of deep, serious, religious conviction, that the Established Church is a great national evil; that it is an obstacle to the progress of truth and godliness in the land; that it destroys more souls than it saves; and that, therefore, its end is most devoutly to be wished by every lover of God and man.[10]

Provocative as his words were, Binney was hardly a lone voice crying in the wilderness. His views represented a more militant and public expression of the voluntarism that had long provided the fundamental basis for dissent from the established church. During the 1830s nonconformists, in growing numbers, vocally upheld their commitment to this doctrine and the implicit criticism of the state church that it entailed. The participants at an 1834 meeting of the Protestant Society, for example, decisively resolved to

> proclaim their conviction that religion will most beneficially flourish where it receives only voluntary support; and that all compulsory and

> extorted contributions rather stint its growth, deform its loveliness, and
> embitter its fruit, than assist a blessing essential to social happiness.

Their denominations, the resolution continued, had no "design or desire
to obtain for themselves the exclusive privileges or state revenues of existing establishments," and "if proffered," they would "reject [them] with dis-
dain."[11] The United Committee itself, designed to advance the interests of
Dissent, was not immune to the intensifying politics of disestablishment. In
1834, two Unitarian members of the committee resigned following a dispute
over their involvement in the distribution of the *Regium Donum*, an annual
government grant of funds to support impoverished dissenting ministers.

The sentiments of Binney and the Protestant Society outraged Anglicans, and not a few evangelicals, for their candid expression of an outright
desire "to have the Church separated from the state."[12] Moderating voices
among the Dissenters, such as the editor of the *Patriot*, Josiah Conder, and
Edward Baines of the *Leeds Mercury*, expressed fears that calls for disestablishment might delay the accomplishment of more practical gains on issues
like the church rates. Whig politicians, such as Lord Durham, also cautioned that "the very agitation of the question" would "raise fears prejudices,
and such a bitter hostility" as to prevent the "redress of those acknowledged
grievances of which nothing but your own willful impudence can prevent
the settlement."[13]

Dissenters in Scotland also took up the call for disestablishment,
mounting a challenge to the established Presbyterian Kirk. Andrew Mar-
shall, a minister of the secessionist church, was denouncing the corruptive
influences of state interference in religion and praising the purity of voluntary Christianity as early as 1829. During the 1830s voluntary church
associations surfaced in cities and towns throughout Scotland, agitating for
disestablishment. Dissenters in Edinburgh coordinated a successful movement to refuse payment of church rates, "which created serious financial
difficulties for the established Church."[14]

In the heat of the controversy over the relationship between church and
state, some evangelical ministers continued to warn Dissenters away from
politics. John Clayton, a former director of the London Missionary Society (LMS), publicly disapproved of "the adoption of all violent measures"
to address the "admitted grievances" of Dissenters. Speaking on behalf of
what he claimed were "a considerable number" dissenting ministers, Clayton rejected the employment of "vituperation, invective, and biting sar-
casm as the means of effecting the most legitimate ends," and censured the
"noisy boasters, who are fond of telling us how little we have done for the

Dissenting interest." The reform of the established Church "must be the gradual work of time," Clayton concluded, and it was well for "ministers of the gospel of peace to abstain from political intermeddlings."[15] However, if the submissions to Dissenting publications and the numerous memorials to government advocating separation of church and state are any indication of nonconformist sentiment, ministers such as Clayton seemed to be swimming against the tide.

The Protestant Society, nonetheless, vowed not to let agitation over the establishment "engross their exclusive attention," and they encouraged "all members" to "exert their parliamentary influence" on a variety of prominent issues. Those singled out by the committee in 1834 included the provision "to the hundreds of thousands of emancipated negroes the blessings of education and . . . religious knowledge."[16] Ironically, the British government's determination to include the foreign missionary societies in its scheme to assist the education and improvement of the emancipated slaves was to interject the debate over state sponsorship of religion into the colonial arena.

Emancipation and the Government Grants Controversy

The Emancipation Act of 1833 had directed the government to take up the task of "aiding . . . local legislatures in proceeding upon liberal and comprehensive principles for the religious and moral education of the negro population to be emancipated."[17] To meet this responsibility the government made provisions for a £30,000 annual grant to assist the establishment of elementary education for the emancipated slaves and their children. Since the missionary societies had been supplying educational opportunities for slaves for decades, the government approached the religious institutions to include them in plans for developing the educational system. Sir George Grey, Undersecretary of State for the Colonies, invited representatives from the various missionary organizations to a conference in 1835, where he presented the government's proposal. Grey had determined "to aid the Societies at present engaged in the religious instruction of the Negroes, rather than originate a new and distinct system of Education."[18]

Basing government plans on the participation of the missions was bound to create controversy within the colonial society and among supporters of the West Indian interest. Aberdeen, the Colonial Secretary, recognized the intense animosity the former slave owners had for the educational work of the missions, but he determined that supporting the existing mission schools would be the most efficient use of government funds. The Colonial

Secretary admitted to members of the House of Lords "that a prejudice existed against the Missionaries" in the colonies, but he "looked for their most useful and active co-operation in effecting that which he considered indispensable." If the government did not "exert vigorous efforts" to educate the ex-slaves, "instead of a blessing their freedom would be a curse." The missionaries had a crucial role to play in the effort, and "he should be most happy" to give the Lords "such an assurance as would tranquilize all doubts" on the propriety of their conduct.[19]

The Colonial Office designed the plan upon the model of Henry Brougham's 1833 bill, which provided government support for the national and British and foreign school societies at home. Under this system the state provided funds to assist the construction of school buildings rather than direct aid for religious education itself. Aberdeen offered to give the missionary societies two-thirds of the cost of constructing new schools for emancipated slaves, leaving it to the societies to provide the remaining one-third from their own funds. Many friends of the missionary endeavor celebrated the state's support for what the Methodist Missionary Society called "communicating to the Negro the instruction necessary to prepare them for the new state of things . . . [and] . . . to make the boon of civil freedom a real and everlasting blessing."[20] Beyond the support for the construction of school buildings, the plan stressed that the schools should provide a "liberal and comprehensive" education founded upon reading, writing, and nonsectarian religious instruction. The government further stipulated that a system of state inspectors would supervise the schools during the first five years of the plan.[21]

Reactions of the several religious denominations to the government grants were mixed. The 1836 report of the Wesleyan Methodist Missionary Society praised the government's role in assisting the construction of "19 school-houses" during the first year.[22] More conservative elements within the established church, however, expressed reservations about the participation of nonconformist and evangelical Anglican missionaries in the scheme. These protests indicated the establishment's fear of the potentially destabilizing influences of their "schismatical and enthusiastic proceedings" among the emancipated slaves.[23] The most vocal controversy over the government grants, however, broke out within the ranks of the supporters and missionaries of the predominantly Congregationalist LMS. This debate over the propriety of a dissenting institution accepting government subsidies reflected important changes taking place within the Society and the denominational and political identity of Congregational dissent itself.

While the LMS had been born during an age of pan-evangelical zeal embodied by the Society's fundamental principle, in reality, the institution had always relied primarily upon the growing body of evangelical Congregationalists for its support and personnel. By the 1830s, this Congregational identity took on a new prominence, and was nowhere more evident than in the response of many of the Society's supporters and missionaries to the government's decision to grant funds to the LMS to support the education of the emancipated slaves. As was often the case in dissenting and missionary politics, the most intense feelings on matters of dissenting principle came from outside of London.

In the practical manner that governed most of their decisions with regard to budgetary and financial concerns, the Society's directors welcomed the idea of the government grants. Given that the money would be used exclusively for school buildings, they saw nothing in the plan that fatally compromised the Society's voluntary principles.[24] Yet for many of the Society's supporters, swayed by the increasingly vocal Congregationalist concern over the relationship between church and state, the directors' actions seemed an unmistakable violation of the most fundamental tenets of their religious tradition. Throughout 1835 and 1836 John Arundel, the Society's secretary, received a flood of letters from auxiliaries and concerned supporters warning against the "dangerous, not to say ruinous effect of receiving the support of government funds."[25]

Ministers and lay supporters of the Society protested against the government grants on a variety of grounds. The prominent Birmingham minister John Agnell James wrote of his concerns that the Society would open itself to critics' charges of "inconsistency . . . as advocates of the dissenting principle" should it accept state money "for the spread of religion."[26] William Gregory of Clifton called the plan "subversive of the voluntary nature of the society" and feared that receiving the funds would be "followed by the most deplorable consequences to the society itself."[27] One of the most forceful objections came from the committee of the Bristol Auxiliary Society. Having "heard that it [was] the intention of the Directors . . . to accept a grant of money from the government," the Bristol auxiliary submitted a formal admonition against "the propriety" of accepting the grants on the grounds that it was "inconsistent with the principle of a voluntary society to promote its objects by means received from compulsory exactions levied on the country at large."[28] In spite of the ecumenical pretensions of the Society's origin, it is clear that by the 1830s it had fully assumed the character of a dissenting institution.

The "Bristol Remonstrance," as it came to be known, galvanized considerable opposition to the grants among auxiliary societies across the country. Gregory noted that throughout "the north of England and Wales . . . the almost unanimous opinion" of friends of the Society was that "the grant ought to be rejected."[29] Quite common was the concern of Robert Ashton of Warminster that taking government grants would adversely affect the Society's support among the nonconformist public.

> The Bristol "Remonstrance" is making an impact in this quarter. I hope no injury to the Soc'y will ensue. Better far that the Soc'y should sacrifice a few hundred pounds from government, than that suspicions, jealousies and separaters [sic] should be felt and follow; when your losses should be far greater to the general cause, than the Parliamentary grant and besides might involve a principle whose influence on religion at home might be of the most pernicious character.[30]

Dissenters, such as Ashton, caught up in domestic debates over the relations among church, state, and education rightly feared the potentially "pernicious" influence at home of a decision to accept government grants to mission schools in the colonies.

In early nineteenth-century Britain, education was "inextricably mixed" with issues of religion and politics. The rapid and sustained population growth in Britain had illustrated the insufficiency of the educational provisions available to British children, and magnified calls for significant reforms. Religious divisions, however, routinely complicated the creation of a new educational system. In 1807 the House of Lords rejected Samuel Whitbread's proposal to use the poor rates to furnish education for indigent children, on the grounds that the schools were not to be under the authority of the established church. The objections of Dissenters brought about the defeat of Henry Brougham's education bill in 1820, which stipulated that schoolmasters be Anglican communicants. Nonconformists' protests against the bill reckoned it, along with Sidmouth's bill, as one of the most harmful assaults upon religious liberty in more than a century. Brougham's 1833 bill granting £20,000 of government funds to support the construction of school buildings also drew the criticism of many Dissenters as more than half of its funds went to support schools of the Anglican-controlled National Society. Given this background, the government's decision to provide state support for mission schools was bound to be controversial.[31]

Fearing the both domestic and colonial implications of the Society's accepting government funds, many Dissenters threatened to pull their support from the LMS should it recognize "the principle of taxing the public for the support of our missions in the West India Colonies."[32] William Gregory related the objection of a gentleman who had "subscribed . . . for many years £50 a year," who had "withdrawn his support, with the declaration that, if the grant is received he will never subscribe another farthing."[33] Should the directors "receive any part of the money levied on the Nation in the form of taxes," wrote David Derry of the Plymouth Auxiliary, "it will tend to paralize [*sic*] the efforts of the subscribers—produce disunion . . . and thus very seriously prejudice its true interests."[34] To many, the recourse to government aid not only contradicted the voluntary principle of the Society, it reflected the directors' lack of confidence in the generosity of the religious public. S. S. Wilson of Frome related to Arundel the conviction of his auxiliary that if the directors had wanted to raise "£2,000 or 5,000 . . . for the education of the guardian slaves," they needed "only to make it known" to their committed supporters who would surely respond with favor.[35] In the minds of many, government grants were not only objectionable on principle, but in light of the generosity of the Society's supporters they were wholly unnecessary.

Many of the protests, in fact, revealed a strong dissatisfaction with the directors' apparent decision to act upon the government grant without first consulting the auxiliary societies, or "making any very public or explicit declaration of the precise object to which any sum, if received, . . . would be applied."[36] H. T. Roper of the Devon Congregational Union deemed it especially "improper . . . for the Directors to contemplate such an alteration in the principle of this society without consulting the country constituency." Moreover, Roper emphasized, "the present ignorance of the country friends leaves them open to all the uncomfortable uncertainty which floating, and . . . incorrect, reports are calculated to produce."[37] In an effort to quell the controversy, the directors sent the Society's Foreign Secretary, William Ellis, to make a tour of the country in order to clearly communicate their intentions and the nature of the government grants. Ellis met with auxiliary societies and concerned ministers to explain that state funds would be used exclusively for building schools and would in no way be connected to the direct support of religious instruction. By clearing up this confusion over the purpose of the state aid Ellis did much to calm the "troubled waters" of the government grant controversy.[38]

Response from the Mission Field

The debate nonetheless continued, as the Colonial Office considered expanding the scope of the grant to assist the payment of teachers' salaries as well. Missionaries in the field now joined the dispute over the government grants, and among the most vocal opponents was Charles Rattray of Demerara. Declaring himself a conscientious Dissenter, he expressed his "great aversion to anything *Regium-Donum* like," as he perceived the grants to be. "I wish you could explain," he wrote to Ellis, "whether the prospective aid from Government does not come under that (as I would say) unscriptural mode of promoting and supporting Christianity." Rattray further expressed his concerns over the system of government inspections and the connection the grants established between the mission and the state. "In what relation will the Missionaries stand to these schools?" he asked. "Will not the Government support and inspection render them *bona fide* Government and not Mission schools? if not—What is the nature and what the real subject of the inspection?" Elaborating on his anxiety over the potential interference of government inspectors, "of whose principles and character we know nothing," he wrote,

> I seriously object to the principle of such inspectors. I do so not on my own account solely, for the stipendiary magistrate in this District appears to be more friendly than many of them. . . . It is uncertain, however, how soon we might be placed under the inspection of another.

The concern about the use of arbitrary government authority to interfere with the progress of evangelization came forth once again.

All the same, Rattray's opposition ultimately hinged upon his own commitment to the principles of Dissent. "I am one of those who seriously believe that Government, as such, should have no connection with the extension and establishment of Christ's kingdom," he declared; "I am from principle a Dissenter, and I repudiate the idea of being taken under the wing, and pensioned from the bounty of the state." As a missionary of the LMS he assured the directors that theywould always "have a right to demand an account of his stewardship." But as to the government, "or any other official inspectors," he could yield "no respect." He could not "serve two masters."[39]

The missionaries' anxiety over the potential appointment of state inspectors was well founded, given the intense hostility of the colonists for the missions. The editor of a memoir of the "Demerara Martyr," John Smith, observed that "the Missionaries will always be obnoxious to the . . . *higher classes* of their fellow Colonists, because of their efforts to protect the emancipated people from gross injustice." Long after the emancipation of the slaves, the colonial press continued to pour "vile abuse" upon the missionaries.[40] James Scott, another Demerara missionary, made principled objections to state support that would make mission teachers "salaried by government, . . . nothing more than mere government agents." However, Scott also came to the practical point in protesting against inspectors "on the grounds that . . . persons appointed by government . . . living among our enemies, would view us with prejudice." Relying upon local taxes to provide the government assistance, he noted, "would expose us to a greater share of odium than ever."[41]

Having learned their lesson, the directors of the LMS declined to take any further action on the grants "without first appealing to the Auxiliaries of the society generally."[42] The auxiliary at Darwen expressed its "apprehensions" over the Society "accepting another grant of money from the national treasury." They questioned whether the Society would "be found guilty of not a temporary swerving from its established course but of a determined and evident departure from it," and whether the LMS intended to forsake the "principle . . . [for] which our spiritual forefathers suffered the loss of all things and many of ourselves have endured the sacrifice of much."[43] The directors responded to the protests against the grants by appealing to the moral responsibility of the Society to provide education for the emancipated slaves, and "the strong and imperative claims of the youthful generation."[44] They argued that the limited acceptance of government support for such an important, and one might add expensive, undertaking did not compromise the Society's principles.

Members of the dissenting public, however, continued to express their opposition to the directors' logic. In early 1837, the *Evangelical Magazine*, having received a "mass of communications . . . for some months, on the subject of the L.M.S. receiving government grants," solicited contributions for a "free and full discussion" of the issue. The first contribution, from a pair of "highly respected gentlemen . . . warmly attached to the L.M.S.," made a detailed and principled refutation of the policy. The authors raised numerous objections to the initial grant and the pending "sums towards defraying the salaries of teachers." They "utterly repudiate[d]" the use of public money for the support of religious instruction, or any recognition of the notion that it was "the duty of government to provide RELIGIOUS instruction for the destitute." This argument not only renounced the provision of government grants for mission schools, it responded directly to the persistent claims of Whig politicians that they could not concede to Dissenters' sweeping demands for disestablishment because of the state's obligation to provide religious instruction for the poor. "The spread of religious truth," the authors maintained, was "the *exclusive* prerogative of the church," an explicit claim to the independence of the church from any and all ties to the state. "We cannot sanction," they asserted, "the taxation of the community in aid EVEN of evangelical truth."[45]

The continued, or increased, reliance upon state funds to support the work of the Society threatened to "destroy the independence of the institution." Not surprisingly, for a society so closely associated with the Congregationalist denomination, this theme of independence resonated throughout the protests against the government grants. Thomas Jackson of Bristol had written to Arundel of "how long the Society [had] prospered without any kind of *patronage* from persons in high places." The "simplicity of its principles, and perfect freedom from any connection with state policy," was "one reason why the Great Head of the Church ha[d] so signally owned its labors." The society's "simplicity," Jackson asserted, was its "greatest glory."[46] Such sentiments provided a subtle yet powerful contrast to the corruptive influence of the state upon what Dissenters were more loudly calling an illegitimate established church.

The LMS, Politics, and the Congregationalist Interest

Questions of patronage and the independence of church institutions from state interference were a prevailing concern of religious and political debates in Britain during the 1830s and 1840s. As nonconformists called for the disestablishment of the church, the conservative Anglican clergymen behind the Oxford movement claimed that the only means of defending it lay in preserving its independence from state interference. Controversies over the relationship between church and state in Scotland ultimately split the established Presbyterian Church. The contest between church patronage and the right of congregants to have a voice in the selection of their pastors lay at the center of the dispute. During the early nineteenth century an Evangelical Party, lead by the famous social reformer Thomas Chalmers, revitalized the movement to end the system by which church patrons (including the Crown, landowners, and corporations) appointed clergy to church livings without the consent of the congregation. As a series of civil court decisions in the late 1830s defended the rights of patrons, the Evangelical Party intensified its claims for and defense of the "independence of the church in matters of doctrine and ecclesiastical discipline." The controversy came to a head in 1843 when the Evangelicals, protesting "attacks made on the traditional liberties of the Scottish Church by the civil authorities in the British parliamentary state," walked out of the annual meeting of the General Assembly of the Kirk. Following this opening act of the "Great Disruption" of 1843,

more than one-third of the clergy of the Church of Scotland left to constitute new congregations of the "Free Church," based upon the principles of
voluntarism and the right of the congregation to choose its own minister.[47]

The government grants controversy underscored the difficulties faced
by the LMS, an institution founded on pan-evangelical and nonpolitical
principles, as its primary supporters became some of the most politically
active and vocal participants in British politics. The growth of the missionary movement, as well as the emergence of evangelical dissenting politics,
during the early nineteenth century helped to effect important changes in
the character of Protestant Dissent, and Congregationalism in particular.
Institutions established to carry out the task of evangelization, at home or
abroad, and societies founded to defend the religious liberties of Dissenters
increased the organization and centralization of the loosely affiliated congregations of nineteenth-century Dissent. The result was "a subtle change
in the meaning and usage of the word denomination itself," which did not
merely identify a set of principles or beliefs but assumed the existence of an
"organized entity" called the Baptist, or Congregationalist, or Methodist
denomination.[48] This change proved especially significant among Congregationalists, whose principles and traditions were most closely tied to the
concept of the independent congregation.

Throughout the 1830s contributors to Congregationalist publications
repeatedly called for greater unity in advancing the interests of the denomination and the spread of "true Christianity" throughout Britain. The progress of Congregationalist unity was in fact almost always closely connected
to the extension of home missionary efforts. "The reason why more is not
done in this way by our respected Christian brethren, of the same faith and
order," explained the *Home Missionary Magazine* in 1831, "is . . . because we
have not yet an efficient principle of adhesion in our ecclesiastical relations."
The magazine went on to praise the formation of the new General Congregational Union, calling it a great step on the path toward "the entire and
effectual demolition of Satan's kingdom in our land."[49]

Appeals for greater unity among Congregationalists also explicitly challenged the rising numbers of middle-class, or prosperous, members of the
denomination to do more for the cause. "It is, therefore, in my humble opinion," asserted one such article, "high time that [Congregationalists] acted
as a united body to do something to benefit and bless our country." "How
is it," asked Charles Hyatt in *Home Missionary Magazine*, "that all other
denominations have their denominational societies for Home Missionary
efforts, while the Independents have not theirs?" Hyatt argued that British

Congregationalists had both the resources and "the zeal for this good work." He celebrated what he saw as the growing interest within his denomination for joining together to promote evangelization.

> I take courage for the future, in the signs of the times in a denomination to which I have the honour to belong, and whose principles I conscientiously believe to be Scriptural; and which, of all others, appears best adapted for Home Missionary efforts. Brethren, union is the order of the day in the Congregational body; and God forbid you should not unite for the most glorious object . . . for the extension of "pure and undefiled religion" in our own beloved country.[50]

Congregationalists had, of course, since the 1790s been among the most active participants in this cause. The changes taking place during the 1830s, however, meant that greater numbers of them now did so openly claiming to represent the Congregational interest.

Typical of this transition was the alliance of the Home Missionary Society (HMS) with the Congregational Union in 1840–1841. John Agnell James, who had been instrumental in the creation of the Congregational Union, lobbied strongly for the incorporation of the HMS into the Congregational Union.

> The Society is now not only of the Congregational Body, but for it. Not that I mean to say Congregationalism is the ultimate object, but it is the spread of the kingdom . . . by means of the Congregational Churches, and in connection with their system of ecclesiastical polity.

The joining of the HMS with the Congregational Union, James argued, would only strengthen the churches' sense of obligation to support the cause. "The churches of our order would have the Institution as their own," he wrote, "and they are now bound in justice, in honor, and in truth to support it."[51] Denominational institutions had come fully to the fore in leading the cause of evangelization.

The identity of the LMS was also developing, in the eyes of many of its supporters, a more open and honest connection to the Congregational denomination. Greater numbers of protests against the observed Congregationalist predominance in the LMS emerged during the 1830s. When, in 1835, the Society turned down the application of a young Welshman named O. J. Rowlands, the decision provoked a minor crisis among its Welsh Calvinist Methodist supporters. William Griffith, a Congregationalist minister in Holyhead, wrote to the directors entreating for an explanation to "conciliate" those who felt "extremely sore on account of the young man's rejection." The Welsh Methodists were "already prone to be a little jealous of us Independents," he cautioned, "and on the present occasion think they have been unjustly" treated.[52] According to David Davies of Cardigan, the Welsh Methodist "Ministers and Elders" believed that Rowlands had been "treated in a very undeserving and improper manner," and protested that it was "not the first time a young man belonging to their Connexion has been refused on equally inadequate grounds."[53]

The numerous complaints of the Welsh Methodists all revealed a concern that the LMS was being taken over by the Congregationalists. "We are afraid that the Society is departing from its fundamental principle," wrote John Elias, "and that no candidate is very acceptable but from the Independents." He continued, in a decidedly pessimistic tone, "[O]ur friends Dr. Haweis, Dr. Waugh, Rev. R. Hill are no more . . . and we do not know whether there are many partakers of their excellent spirit among the present directors."[54]

Representatives of the LMS also came up against the hostility of the members of rival denominations, who resented or objected to the political views professed by many of its Congregationalist advocates. "I am in the North of Ireland," George Gogerly reported to the directors in 1837, "and never did I meet with such coldness and even direct opposition in my life." Episcopalian and Presbyterian ministers in Ulster refused their pulpits to the "Deputation of the L.M.S.," on account of Irish Congregationalists' attacks "upon [those] two Bodies . . . in a manner that was never attempted before." Gogerly "endeavoured," with considerable difficulty, to reaffirm the Society's nondenominational credentials and to disavow any direct connection to Congregationalism. "In a few cases I have succeeded . . . but in many cases I have not," he lamented. Dissenting politics, in this instance, worked decidedly against the interests of the Society's cause. "The strong political feeling which prevails has helped to produce this opposition to the Independents," Gogerly judged, "but particularly the Petition presented to the Government against the *Regium Donum*, as all the Presbyterians in Ireland receive it." He reluctantly concluded that "my stay in Ireland . . . will not be so long as I expected."[55]

In other instances the growth of dissenting political participation made it more difficult for the Society to maintain its profession of political neutrality or to escape from political controversy. This is nicely illustrated in the following response to the events surrounding the involvement of John Pye Smith, a distinguished Congregationalist divine and director of the

Homerton Academy, in the Middlesex election of 1837. In the days before
the 31 July ballot, Smith gave a speech in favor of the leading radical Joseph
Hume and against the Conservative candidate Henry Pownall. Following a
lengthy remonstrance against Pownall and the Conservative cause, Smith
offered the following praise for the radical Hume:

> Suppose that I see a man whom I have the pain of apprehending to fall
> short of what I deem important views in religion, but a man of honour-
> able character, in domestic life exemplary, a firm supporter of the rights
> of conscience—the greatest Protestant principle that a man must judge
> for himself in matters of religion—who during a long course of life has
> shown himself the friend of civil and religious freedom; and of justice
> and economy in the administration of affairs. . . . I find myself bound on
> every ground of reason and religion to do all that I can by fair and can-
> did argument to promote his return to Parliament. Such a man I believe
> Mr. Hume to be.[56]

The publication of the speech prompted a strong letter to the directors of the LMS from John Campbell. Campbell was an Anglican who had
"always taken a lively and somewhat active interest" in the Society's success,
"notwithstanding the difficulties which the present unhappy warfare with
the Dissenters raises up to embarrass . . . members of the Establishment."
Noting that several applicants for missionary work with the LMS studied at
Homerton Academy under Smith's tutelage, Campbell wrote to the Society
to inquire whether Smith's unmistakably provocative political comments
had been "approved or reprobated" by the directors, or "any steps taken to
place the students under a Tutor of more scriptural views than Dr. Smith
seems now to entertain and promulgate."

Campbell did not "quarrel" with the right of Smith, or any minister, to
participate in electoral politics, although he did question the appropriate-
ness of making a speech at a political rally. He indicated his great alarm at
Smith's rather indifferent attitude toward Hume's rationalist and heterodox
theological opinions, noting his disapproval that a tutor of the Society's missionaries should see "Mr. Hume's infidelity and profanity as merely a few
rash expressions." The correspondent also took issue with the political tone
of the speech, and Smith's vituperative attack upon the Conservative candidate Pownall.

> [Smith's] concentrated influence was used to persuade the population
> of Middlesex that Mr. Pownall . . . must be lamentably destitute of the
> knowledge and principles requisite for legislation and the conduct of

national affairs, "because he is a Conservative," a term which the Rev.
Doctor regards as meaning "conservative of evil"—as indicating principles which would make "injustice rampant"—would "poison the land
with intolerance and exclusion"—would "weaken Great Britain" and
throw Ireland into rebellion.

A Conservative himself, Campbell condemned the "heavy charges so reck-
lessly put forth" by Smith against Pownall and "the sound doctrine [of]
all who would maintain inviolate our glorious Constitution in Church and
State." Campbell concluded the letter expressing "unfeigned sorrow" that
"from what I have observed lately among some of my dissenting friends here
I am not confident that Dr. Smith's sentiments may not be sanctioned."[57]

This chapter has examined the difficulties presented to the LMS by
the changing character of dissenting politics during the reform era. The
transformed political landscape of the 1830s gave a sharper focus to dissenting politics and especially its criticisms of the established church. The
growing militancy of nonconformist attitudes toward the establishment,
coupled with the strengthening sense of denominational identity among
Congregationalists, posed new and complex challenges to the Society's traditional apolitical and nondenominational positions. Controversy over the
use of government funds to support mission schools for the emancipated
slaves represented more than a dispute over education or mission policy. The
government grants controversy gave Dissenters, especially those outside of
London, another means to articulate their general arguments for the separation of church and state. Religious conflict defined many of the most significant political and social issues in Britain during the 1830s, influencing
the development of domestic and colonial policy. Arguments over matters
of ecclesiastical authority and the independence of congregations gave shape
to dissenting politics in England and gave rise to the split in the Scottish
Church. As we shall see in the next chapter, they also played a significant
role in shaping the missionaries' participation in the fervent debates over the
status and power of colonists and Africans during one of the most turbulent
periods in the history of the Cape Colony.

6

Church, Race, and Conflict in the Cape Missions

In 1836 John Philip returned to Britain to testify before the parliamentary committee investigating the condition of the aboriginal peoples of the British Empire. Nearly a decade after his successful campaign to ensure the civil equality of the colonial Khoi, and as conflicts intensified on the eastern frontier, Philip had come again to press for the reform of colonial policy in southern Africa. He brought with him two African converts, Andries Stoeffels, a deacon in the independent congregation at Kat River, and Jan Tshatshu, a Xhosa chief. On 10 August 1836, members of the religious public of London filled Exeter Hall to hear addresses from Philip and the two Africans. As Stoeffels and Tshatshu stood before the assembly in Western attire, epitomes of the paternalist and benevolent ideals of the missionary movement, their speeches must have greatly satisfied those in attendance. "I Thank the English nation for what we have received at your hands," said Tshatshu, "you are our friends, we are your children." Stoeffels declared, "[W]e are tame men now; . . . you who have put your money into the plates. . . . I stand before you as the fruits of your exertions." Yet at the heart of each man's comments also lay a forceful demand for justice against the continued abuses of the colonial system in southern Africa. "If we are children of England, and of one with yourselves," Tshatshu challenged, "let us enjoy the privileges of Britons."[1]

According to the evangelical press, the Africans showed no "uneasiness or want of self-possession" before the parliamentary committee or at Exeter Hall. Their public appearances "aroused much interest" and provided excellent publicity for the London Missionary Society (LMS).[2] Stoeffels and Tshatshu were, however, much more than mere trophies of missionary success, and their presence with Philip had a deeply serious political purpose. Their testimony before Parliament constituted a crucial component of Philip's long campaign against the colonial government's policies in South Africa. Their manner and appearance testified to the benefits religious freedom, civil equality, and commercial opportunity offered to Britons and Africans alike. The onset of legal equality for the colonial Khoi had set the foundation for the great experiment of the Kat River settlement and the building of a prosperous and productive colony based upon the principles of equality and freedom of opportunity. Robert Ross has emphasized the strong appeal to Africans of this "combination of Christianity and respectability" associated with the missions in the Cape Colony during the 1830s and 1840s. It offered an "arena" within which Africans could assert their political rights, show pride in their Khoi ancestry, and celebrate their material improvement on an equal basis with the white colonial population.[3]

At the same time, Philip's return to Britain reflected the difficulties of bringing that humanitarian ideal to reality in the years since the emancipation of the Khoi in 1828. While missionary publications emphasized only the most successful and prosperous examples of African "civilization" and "improvement," alcoholism, depression, and poverty remained serious social problems among those Khoi less fortunate in their efforts to take advantage of the educational and economic opportunities offered at the missions. Large numbers of Khoi also remained landless, and although free to sell their labor, many remained subject to the potential exploitation of white employers.[4] James Read disclosed to the directors in 1834, "Altho' there [were] prospects of improvement" at Kat River, "yet the generality of the people [were] very poor and many of the children [were] obliged to appear in school either nearly or altogether naked."[5] Nevertheless, when Philip visited the settlement in 1834 he found considerable evidence of the "prospects of improvement" of which Read had written. After five years the settlers at Kat River numbered two thousand, possessed 624 horses, 5,406 head of cattle, and 8,925 sheep and goats, and had constructed fifty-five irrigation canals to water fields of wheat, barley, oats, and corn.[6]

Governor Cole had hoped that government sponsorship of the Kat River settlement would effectively reduce the influence of the LMS missionaries and avoid the political controversy that surrounded the missionary stations at Bethelsdorp and Theopolis. Cole had assigned W. R. Thompson, a former government agent to the Xhosa, to tend to the spiritual needs of the Kat

River settlement. A number of settlers of mixed white and African descent, known as "Bastards," welcomed Thompson and happily attended his Dutch Reformed congregation. However, he did not suit the substantial number of Khoi who had relocated to Kat River from the LMS missions. These Khoi settlers, who comprised nearly three-quarters of the settlement's population by the early 1830s, called for James Read to come up from Bethelsdorp to minister to their congregation. Read wrote to William Orme of the LMS that "the Hottentots . . . are very anxious that I should follow them" to Kat River. On Philip's first visit to the settlement he met with a "unanimous" desire on the part of the Khoi to have Read as their minister.[7] Aware of the controversy his appointment was likely to cause, Read assured Stockenstrom that he intended to "confine myself as much as possible to . . . spiritual concerns," and to avoid political entanglements.[8] By that time, however, the Kat River Khoi had begun to develop their own political voice, and increasingly became a rival political faction to the "Bastard" settlers under the pastorship of Thompson.

Cape Politics Following Ordinance 50

Read's move to Kat River, however, was only one of numerous concerns voiced by the colonists in the years after Ordinance 50. In early 1830 Philip recognized that "[f]inding that there was no possibility of succeeding in getting [Ordinance 50] wholly cancelled," the colonists became "clamorous for a Vagrant Act" to control so-called idlers and criminals. These categories were tacitly defined in racial terms, and it remained "to be proved," Philip contended, "that the aggregate of crime over the whole Colony" had increased since the enactment of the ordinance.[9] The missionaries of the LMS quickly attributed "the real object" of the demands for vagrancy legislation to the desire "to have the Hottentots again in the farmers' powers on what terms they might please to hold them." William Anderson wrote to Kitchingman of his fears that if a vagrancy act were "passed into law" it would "bear heavily" upon the Khoi. Anderson warned that the "advantages proposed by the 50th ordinance will be but trifling, and there will be no free labourers among the Hottentots."[10] The threat to reestablish control over the movement and labor of the Khoi struck at the very heart of the mission's hopes for the economic and spiritual advancement of the colony.

White settlers appealed with petitions and memorials to the colonial government for the institution of new legislation. Receptive to the complaints of the colonists, Governor Cole expressed his belief that the very act which rescued the Hottentots from oppression [Ordinance 50] made no provision for that wholesome degree of restraint by which a great proportion of them can alone be induced or made to labour for their maintenance and cease to be a scourge upon their neighbours.[11]

The interest of the colonists, and the Colony's Legislative Council, in passing a vagrancy law gained further momentum from the impending abolition of slavery in 1833. Colonel Wade, the governor's Colonial Secretary, took it upon himself to reassure white "Proprietors" that before the end of the apprenticeship of the emancipated slaves "other laws will be enacted . . . for . . . the punishment of vagrancy . . . and for securing a sufficiency of labourers to the Colony."[12] Such statements merely confirmed the suspicions of missionaries and the mission Khoi that vagrancy laws represented nothing less than "a betrayal of the essential principles of civilized policy."[13]

The Legislative Council's decision in 1834 to reinstate a vagrancy law, which empowered local officials to arrest any individuals unable to prove their means of subsistence for the previous three days, again ignited a political controversy. The proposed law attempted to circumvent the provisions of Ordinance 50 by applying the vagrancy measure to whites as well as blacks. Philip likened this ploy to passing a law "to prohibit Natives of the interior as well as those at the coast from fishing in the sea."[14] The missionary leader's nonconformist aversion to the arbitrary and restrictive use of authority continued to shape his criticism of colonial policy. He identified "[a]rbitrary control" as one of "the strongest passions in the human mind and the last species of authority which men are disposed to part with" and condemned the measure through which the Khoi would once again "fall into the hands of the magistrate, to be disposed of by him at his pleasure."[15]

Intense debate broke out in the press, pitting colonists supporting the measure in the *Grahamstown Journal* against their opponents in John Fairbairn's *Commercial Advertiser*. Both sides mobilized variations on the "standard 'liberal' arguments of the day" to defend their positions in the contest. Robert Godlonton, a leading figure among the Grahamstown settlers, stressed the necessity of legislation to "curb that propensity to Vagrancy" attributed to all Africans by the colonists. The *Journal* emphasized the importance of stimulating the Khoi "to habits of order and industry" against the dangers of the "unrestrained liberty" granted by Ordinance 50. Furthermore, the colonists asserted that the growth of crime deriving from vagrant Khoi infringed upon their security, their property, and the "undistributed enjoyment of legal rights . . . derived from the efficient protection of civil government." In this sense, vagrancy legislation was to operate as a civilizing measure, necessary, in Godlonton's words, to teach the Khoi "to understand the value of the social compact" while protecting the rights and property of colonists.[16]

Humanitarian opponents of the legislation drew upon those aspects of liberal political economy that had provided the foundation of their objections to slavery and the Hottentot Codes. A fundamental principle behind the missionaries' support for Ordinance 50 and the Kat River settlement was the idea that free labor and economic self-improvement, accompanied by Christianity, provided the surest path to civilization. As Philip had argued in the *Researches*, force and coercion in matters of labor and commerce "must have a depressing influence on the industry and morals of all ranks of the inhabitants" in the colony.[17] The missionaries and the Khoi orchestrated their own extensive petition campaign to oppose the Vagrancy Act and to force the Colonial Office in London to reject it. The contest over vagrancy legislation played out in a fashion similar to the petitionary politics that had flourished in Britain over the previous decade and a half. Petitions from colonists to the Legislative Council complaining of the rise of criminality had influenced its decision to approve the vagrancy law in 1834. In return, the Khoi and the missionaries petitioned colonial officials in the colony and in London to protest the arbitrary and harmful nature of the law and urged them to overturn it.

In August 1834 Philip urged Kitchingman to "fight to the teeth" against the vagrancy law. He further instructed him to prepare a memorial against the law "to be signed by all who can write on the institution" and those "who cannot with their marks."[18] Khoi at the missions and at Kat River responded overwhelmingly to the call to defend their rights under Ordinance 50. Nearly four hundred Kat River inhabitants signed a petition to the governor protesting the repressive nature of the law and organized political meetings to express their opposition. These public protests by the Khoi against the measure reflected the contributions of mission Christianity and humanitarian ideals in shaping a new sense of Khoi identity and political consciousness. The missionary George Barker called it "a new era in the politics of the colony, the Hottentots as a nation petitioning for their Civil Rights."[19] Assertions of the rights of the "Hottentot nation" filled the speeches of the Khoi at meetings in 1834. "I stand here my nation to advocate your cause," Philip Campher told the Kat River Khoi, "and if it should be that I must die for my nation, I could almost do it, provided that would secure your liberty." At Philipton, Andries Stoeffels celebrated the "first day . . . first time and . . . first place" for him to advance the freedom of his nation.[20]

The opposition of the Khoi to the measure also caused them to give voice to their concerns over the issues of land, labor, and liberty in colonial politics. Mission Khoi recognized and defended the significance of the protections enacted by Ordinance 50. "Every nation has its screen," Platje Jonker remarked at Bethelsdorp; "the white men have a screen, the colour of their skin . . . the 50th ordinance is our screen."[21] The Khoi protests closely linked their freedom to the confirmation of their right to own land and manifested a strong sense of the indignity of forced labor. "Better slaves at once than a man should compel me to work," declared Hendrik Heyn, "for there is no midway between slavery and freedom."[22] Like their missionary allies, the Khoi recognized the desire to control black labor that motivated the colonists' support for the new vagrancy legislation. The "vagrant law is for black men," protested a member of the Theopolis mission. Valentyn Jacobs of Kat River declared that the Khoi "must oppose this act . . . for if it passes every man will set his own price on our labour."[23] The protection of personal liberty, freedom of movement, and free labor lay at the heart of the Khoi's opposition to the law. Hendrik Heyn summed up the sentiment of their protests when he asked of the meeting at Philipton, "What is a nation without freedom?"[24]

At the center of the LMS' contributions to this emergence of "Hottentot nationalism" and political consciousness stood the figure of James Read. Born in 1777, Read worked as a carpenter in his native Essex before applying to become a missionary at the end of the eighteenth century. After landing at Cape Town in 1800, Read proved instrumental in assisting van der Kemp in the establishment of the first mission station at Bethelsdorp. Sharing van der Kemp's egalitarianism, Read also demonstrated himself quickly the close friend and ally of the Khoi. Although suspended as a missionary in the wake of his adultery by the Thom Synod of 1817, Read continued his active involvement with the Khoi as a carpenter and a resident of the Bethelsdorp station. From 1821 onward, he became Philip's most trusted partner in the crusade to secure the civil rights of the Khoi and to reform colonial policy in South Africa. Although, like many early missionaries, he lacked formal schooling, Read emphasized education as a central feature of the missions' program of improvement. Read and his son, James Read Jr., self-proclaimed liberals and radicals, supervised the education of the most politically active Khoi at Kat River and Bethelsdorp. These men, many of whom worked as traders, teachers, transport riders, and evangelists, did much in turn to promote the ideals of humanitarianism and mission Christianity among the colonial Khoi and among African communities beyond the border.[25]

In a letter to the directors written in 1834, Read described the results of this program of education and improvement.

> Our Hottentots have just been having a meeting to propose a . . . memo-
> rial to the Governor-in-Council against the Vagrant Act. They have writ-
> ten several letters in the public papers against it, so that they can now
> begin to defend their own cause. If they have a press of their own they
> could do it with better effect. This I hope will one day take place. We
> have some fine young men among [them?] that promise well to assist
> to carry on the work of God and espouse and defend the cause of their
> fathers.[26]

Read's testimony to the ability of the Khoi to contend with their European rivals "on their own terms" suggests the extent to which the mission Khoi were prepared to participate in colonial political debates and how much they drew upon the support of their "political patron[s]" among the missions to shape a language of opposition to the abuses of colonial policy.

The pressures exerted by the Khoi and the missionaries ultimately suc-ceeded in preventing the implementation of the Vagrancy Act. Throughout the struggle, Philip remained keenly aware of the power of public opin-ion and the influence of evangelical leaders in London. In the aftermath of emancipation, Buxton and the evangelical lobby in Britain forcefully opposed the threat of vagrancy laws in former slave colonies that might "per-petualise slavery under another name" and pressured the Colonial Office to do likewise.[27] Philip kept Buxton carefully informed of developments in the colony, seeking to draw on his influence with the Colonial Office. The missions took care to conduct their campaign so as to maximize its appeal to the religious public in Britain. Philip set aside the date of 18 August 1834 "as a day of humiliation and prayer before God, for the averting of the ordinance." This display of "vital religion," he assured Kitchingman, would "make a great impression" in Britain, and he advised the missionar-ies to "write down anything connected with the feeling and sentiments of the people," so that it might "be sent home."[28] When news of the vagrant law reached Britain it "produced a strong sensation" and considerable public sentiment in support of the Khoi and their protests. Philip fostered the case against the vagrancy legislation further by sending Buxton numerous letters and memorials, which the latter passed on to Spring-Rice, the Colonial Sec-retary. Although the law was approved by the colony's Legislative Council, the Colonial Office in London rapidly overturned it as contradictory to the spirit of the rights granted by Ordinance 50. "[I]t shall not pass into law!" rejoiced Philip in a letter to Kitchingman at the end of 1834.[29]

The development and progress of the Khoi in the eastern Cape took on greater significance when situated within the broader contexts of imperial politics and the relationship between the missions and the antislavery movement in particular. The fortunes of the Kat River settlers from 1829 onward promised to provide vital evidence to support abolitionists' claims of the benefits of free labor and the viability of emancipation. The creation of a community of economically successful and civilized free Khoi furnished a model for the transition from slavery to freedom and proof of the capabilities of Africans (or freed slaves) "when the door of manly ambition was flung open to them."[30] At the peak of its political influence, the humanitarian movement looked to the Kat River for evidence of the potential for the incorporation of civilized and christianized blacks into a new social and economic colonial order. As Andries Stoffels asserted to his sympathetic audience at Exeter Hall, "[W]e are coming on; we are improving; we will soon be one."[31] Yet in undertaking this endeavor, Philip, Read, and the Khoi were to come face to face with the challenges and difficulties of the colony's eastern frontier.

Violence and Conflict in the Eastern Cape

The intrinsic instability of the situation in the eastern Cape repeatedly frustrated the ambitious expectations for the Khoi settled at Kat River. Colonists, generally speaking, refused to accept arguments about the beneficial consequences for the colony of a settlement of prosperous and free Africans on its eastern border. They rather viewed the Khoi settlers with suspicion and coveted the fertile lands of the Kat River valley. Rumors, in late 1830, that veterans of the Cape Corps dwelling at Kat River intended to join the Xhosa in rebellion convinced colonists and local officials to send out a commando against the settlement. Henry Somerset, military commander on the frontier, intervened to prevent an actual assault on the Khoi community.[32] The rights and liberties granted to the Khoi by Ordinance 50, furthermore, proved difficult to enforce effectively on a vast frontier populated by white colonists who resented the socioeconomic advancement of the African population. Certain of the justice of the 1834 Vagrancy Act, for example, many field cornets and other local officers "immediately took action on the mere Draft" of the law (before it had been presented to the Colonial Office). They began requiring Khoi to once again obtain passes to move freely about the territory. The new colonial governor, Sir Benjamin D'Urban, was forced to remove several field cornets from office for having committed such acts in contradiction to Ordinance 50.[33] The precarious status of the rights of the Khoi remained a persistent problem on the frontier throughout the decade.

The often stormy and violent relations with African peoples across the colonial border further complicated frontier politics. The tensions between the Xhosa and white ranchers on the eastern frontier dated back to the late eighteenth century. The recurrent struggle over the control of land and cattle unsettled the border region and thwarted the ability of colonial governments to control the relations between the white and Xhosa communities. Colonists exploited rivalries between opposing African chiefs to seize cattle and encroach eastward into Xhosa territory, and the Xhosa made reprisals by launching raids across the inadequately defended border. The military conquest, in 1818–1819, of the lands between the Fish and Keiskamma rivers and the subsequent removal of the Xhosa to make room for the failed 1820 settlement scheme only exacerbated the bitterness on both sides. So, in addition, was the relationship between the government and the Xhosa complicated by the expulsion of Chief Maqoma, and his people, from parts of the same territories in 1828 to enable the founding of the Kat River settlement.[34]

An increased colonial military presence during the late 1820s and early 1830s allowed the government to maintain an upper hand, but failed to prevent continued conflict on the frontier. At the core of the hostility between colonists and Xhosa was the haphazard application of the patrol system used to settle disputes over cattle theft. During the late 1820s and 1830s, colonial policy allowed ranchers to form patrols to follow the spoor of stolen cattle to Xhosa villages to demand the return of livestock or some form of compensation. If the exact village could not be determined, patrols had the right to take retribution from those Xhosa "deemed most likely to be guilty." Such an expandable license, devoid of proper oversight, not surprisingly often "shaded into utter lawlessness."[35] The Xhosa repeatedly complained that arbitrary application of the spoor law allowed colonists to take their cattle, which merely presaged taking their land. These practices sparked periodic violent reprisals from the Xhosa and bore considerable responsibility for the outbreak of the frontier wars of 1835 and 1846–1847.

Both Philip and Andries Stockenstrom bitterly protested abuses of the patrol system, again reserving their primary criticism for flaws in the colonial administration that perpetuated the situation. "There is but a small section interested in the disturbance on the Frontier, and the acquisition of the cattle of the natives," Stockenstrom wrote, "but mismanagement makes the good suffer with the bad, and embitters the feeling of all." He blamed all of "the disturbances on the frontier of late years," on the patrol system, and on the failure to improve the functioning of the frontier government.[36] As commissioner general of the eastern Cape between 1828 and 1833, Stockenstrom attempted to stabilize the frontier through the creation of a treaty system between the government and Xhosa chiefs. Both Philip and Thomas Fairbairn supported this plan to establish mutual responsibility for maintaining order on the colonial border. Fairbairn's *Commercial Advertiser* argued that the Xhosa should in "every respect . . . be treated as a nation having a regular government . . . responsible to us, and we to them in every case."[37] Stability on the frontier depended not only upon stopping the colonists' efforts to deprive the Xhosa of their property but also upon changing the policies that made the abuses of the patrol system possible. Philip observed in 1836 that the "crisis is arrived at with regard to the system, and there must be an end put to it." He further warned that if "the present system be continued, ten thousand troops will not be sufficient to defend the extended frontiers of the colony."[38]

Connections to the Xhosa, dating from van der Kemp's abortive efforts to establish a mission among them in 1799, drew the LMS missions into the middle of the controversies in the eastern Cape. Over the first decades of the nineteenth century, the contact between the LMS and the Xhosa increased due to the development of an extensive network of legitimate trade across the border. Mission Khoi transported goods from Bethelsdorp for trade with Xhosa chiefs, such as Ngqika and Maqoma, and their people. The missions and the Kat River settlement even participated in a growing arms trade with the Xhosa as the disturbances on the frontier intensified. Andries Stoeffels, deacon at the Kat River chapel and a close associate of Read, was among those widely reputed to engage in the gun trade.[39] Although such trade was technically illegal, mission Khoi often justified the dealing of European weapons beyond the colonial border on the grounds of providing the Xhosa with the means to defend themselves against rapacious colonists.

Competition in the mission field also emerged as a complicating factor in the politics of the eastern Cape during the 1820s. Wesleyan Methodist missionaries appeared as a rival influence to the LMS, especially among the Xhosa beyond the colonial border. Many of the Methodist society's most prominent missionaries, such as their leader William Shaw, had been British settlers before taking up missionary work. Under the leadership of

Shaw, the Methodists expanded their presence, establishing six mission stations across the border during their first decade of operations. Methodist missionaries vied with the LMS for influence among the Xhosa chiefs, but their close connections to the British settlers led them to take a decidedly less activist stance on matters of colonial policy and indigenous rights. By the early 1830s powerful Xhosa chiefs, such as Maqoma, Bhotomame, and Thyali, had increasingly looked to Philip and the LMS as aides in their cause against the colonists and the government. Philip's part in the successful campaign against the Vagrancy Act further raised him in the estimation of Africans on both sides of the frontier. His actions in the wake of the 1835 war further established him as a defender of the Xhosa against the policies of colonial expansion.[40]

Under the administration of Sir Benjamin D'Urban, in 1834 Philip had promoted the expansion of the treaty system, acting as an informal emissary carrying communications between the Xhosa chiefs and Cape Town on his numerous tours of the missions. These attempts to further the system failed amid the perpetual struggles over stolen cattle, which were escalated by a severe drought that forced both colonists and Xhosa to range far and wide in search of grazing lands for their herds. Sporadic conflicts erupted into full-fledged war in December 1834. Colonial forces, composed of white colonists and a considerable number of Khoi, ultimately repulsed the Xhosa's assault upon the white farms and cattle. Under the command of Sir Henry Smith the colonial military pushed the Xhosa out of the colony and then advanced beyond the Kei River to force the surrender of the senior Xhosa chief, Hintsa. After making peace with the last of the warring chiefs, Governor D'Urban determined to consolidate the newly occupied territories east of the colonial border under British control. Calling the new lands Queen Adelaide Province, he proposed settling a portion of the lands with Africans from among the Mfengu and the Xhosa now brought under the colonial administration. The rest of the new territory would be left open to additional white settlement. The governor justified his actions on the grounds that the war had been an act of "unprovoked aggression" by the Xhosa, whom he vilified as "treacherous and irreclaimable savages."[41]

D'Urban's appropriation of the Queen Adelaide Province and his castigation of the Xhosa raised a storm of complaints from humanitarians and from within the Colonial Office in London. The LMS missionaries flooded the directors and Buxton with their protests, all asserting that the war had resulted, in fact, from the sustained abuse of the Xhosa under the flawed policies of the colonial frontier. Lord Glenelg, the Colonial Secretary and a staunch evangelical, was more sympathetic to the reports from the South African missions passed on to him by his close associate Buxton. Influenced by a combination of the objections of the LMS missions and the strong desire of the government to avoid the potential costs and difficulties of the acquisition of new colonial territories, Glenelg ordered D'Urban to abandon the new Queen Adelaide Province. The Colonial Secretary further directed the governor to return the colony to its 1834 boundaries and to begin negotiating treaties with the Xhosa chiefs to promote a peaceful solution to the troubles on the frontier.

John Philip Returns to Britain

The war of 1835 thus sparked a new concern for the welfare of the Africans beyond the colonial border among the evangelical lobby in Britain. The government had appointed Buxton chair of a Select Committee of the House of Commons to investigate the conditions of the aboriginal peoples of the British Empire. Charged to consider the most appropriate policies to pursue "in order to secure . . . the due observance of justice" for the indigenous populations, the committee made the recent conflict on the eastern Cape frontier a centerpiece of its investigation.[42] Philip came to London in 1836, with Stoeffels, Tshatshu, and the James Reads, senior and junior, to testify before the committee and to counter accusations that the war had been the result of unprovoked Xhosa aggression. The missionary leader as well as the African converts made a strong impression upon the committee members, many of whom had close connections to humanitarian and missionary institutions. In addition, the elder James Read made a comprehensive tour of the country, speaking before auxiliary societies and stirring up support for the missionary cause. Ever aware of the importance of public opinion, Philip had resolved to put Read to good use in the cause of African rights. He wrote explicitly to William Ellis of his wish for Read, the victim of some of the colonists' harshest attacks, "to appear . . . as a persecuted man and as the representative of a persecuted community."[43]

Stoeffels and Tshatshu created considerable excitement in London wherever they appeared, and their stories filled the pages of evangelical publications. Buxton arranged for the party to attend a session of Parliament for a debate on the Irish tithe bill, where they aroused "great interest" according to Read.[44] At Exeter Hall, Edward Baines, MP, a Congregationalist member of the parliamentary committee, and publisher of the *Leeds Mercury*, spoke of his observations of the Africans seated in the gallery of the House of

Commons on that evening. They were "evidently contemplating the scene with profound attention, and with mingled sensations of wonder and admiration," he said, "reflecting that the interests and the happiness of their own country were often involved in the deliberations of the assembly now before them." Stoeffels and Tshatshu had shown a proper reverence for the institutions of British liberty that testified to their suitability for receiving the full rights of British subjects.[45]

Baines also praised the Africans for having, through their own testimony before Parliament, taught Britain "a great lesson in political economy." In a remarkable commentary on the compatibility of just policies, Christianity, commerce, and civilization, he remarked,

> What was the lesson the chief [Tshatshu] had taught us? . . . that by doing justice to the people of Africa, we should introduce them to become our customers and friends—to take our wares and merchandise—that on visiting their coast, we might receive from them freight for our shipping, while they received from us articles that would advance their progress in comfort and civilisation, and in all the useful arts; and that thus we might receive and render mutual benefits.[46]

Such a forceful and comprehensive declaration of the missionary agenda had not been made in Britain since the publication of Philip's *Researches*.

The testimony of Philip, Stoeffels, and Tshatshu had seemingly carried the day with the committee and with the "pious and most friendly" Lord Glenelg and Sir George Grey of the Colonial Office.[47] Read exulted over the discomfiture of the Methodist missionaries, like William James Shrewsbury, who had given testimony in support of the colonists' view that the Xhosa bore sole responsibility for the war. The Colonial Office decided that it could not assign "the slightest value" to Shrewsbury's prosettler views on colonial policy, and the directors of the Wesleyan Missionary Society publicly expressed their "deepest regret and disapprobation" at the judgment of their missionary. "The poor Wesleyans are in the mire," Read wrote; "Lord Glenelg has exposed poor Shrewsbury, and 'tis said his society are obliged to disown him."[48] Baines revealed a remarkable confidence that the humanitarians had at last ushered in "a new era in our colonial history." He predicted "that from this day forward there never would be heard complaints of the driving of the native inhabitants from one river to another, of usurping and seizing their cattle, and of appropriating their territory."[49] Little did Read or Baines know just how difficult achieving justice and peace on the eastern frontier would prove to be.

Upon his return to the colony from Britain, Philip manifested a far more pessimistic view of the situation in southern Africa. In a letter to James Kitchingman he confided that "my views were never so gloomy with respect to the colony as they have been since my late return to it. We have through mercy gained victory after victory, and we seem at this moment as far from the end of our warfare as we were."[50] Philip's doubts concerning the future of South Africa arose out of his perception of the growing vehemence of the colonists' hostility toward Africans and their missionary champions in the wake of the 1835 war. He also feared the consequences of the expansion of white settlement beyond the borders of the colony set in motion by the commencement of the Great Trek.[51] The war against the Xhosa had hardened the antipathy of the white population, especially the British settlers, against the ideas of African progress that the missions espoused. The settlers understood the war as the result of the "unpredictable savagery" of the Xhosa, an argument put forth most forcefully in Robert Godlonton's tract on *The Irruption of the Kaffir Hordes*.[52] White colonists bitterly resented the government's abandonment of Queen Adelaide Province and took great offense at Glenelg's appointment of the old missionary ally, Andries Stockenstrom, to the post of lieutenant governor for the eastern regions. Stockenstrom instigated a heated confrontation with the governor, D'Urban, by attempting a complete overhaul of frontier policies. Stockenstrom also faced steady and bitter opposition from the settlers, who vilified him for having testified against them before Buxton's parliamentary committee and frustrated his every attempt at reform.

Such being the case, Philip's pessimism upon his return to the colony was more than justifiable. The growing hostility of the British settlers toward the Xhosa, coupled with the migration of the trekkers, posed serious obstacles to the realization of Philip's vision for the future of southern Africa. In spite of his severe criticisms of British colonial policies, Philip remained a fervent believer in the potential benefits of British imperialism. From the beginning to the end of his long career, the missionary leader never wavered in his faith that the enactment of lawful policies and the protection of British justice provided the best opportunity for the advancement of Christianity and civilization in Africa. Philip was, in fact, an imperial expansionist, albeit of a very different sort from most in South Africa. He supported the extension of British authority and justice to secure for African communities protection against what he saw as the sinister effects of the expansion of white settlement into the territories beyond the colonial border.

Philip made his views clear in a letter to James Read Jr. in which he contemplated the likely fate of the Xhosa in the absence of colonial reforms.

> On the subject of it being desirable that the Caffres should be retained as British subjects, I have long made up my mind. . . . [They] cannot otherwise be saved from annihilation. Were the Colony surrounded by belts of Native Tribes under British Government, nations would get time to form beyond us, but no Tribe will be allowed time to rise into civilisation and independence on our borders, if they are in immediate contact with our colonists.[53]

The converted Xhosa chief Jan Tshatshu echoed these sentiments in a letter to the LMS that supported the efforts of Stockenstrom to reform frontier policies in 1837. "The Kat River settlement, and the protection the Griquas have rendered to the colonies and to the tribes beyond them," Tshatshu argued, "show the great advantage . . . derived from having tribes of civilised men of color between the white Colonists and the barbarous tribes beyond the colony."[54]

Divisions within the LMS

Along with the escalating tensions of the colonial frontier, the mission communities of the LMS were not immune to controversy either. Throughout the 1830s and 1840s missionaries debated questions of church government and authority, the relationship between ministers and congregations, and the role of the missionary superintendent, Philip. While in one sense these contests mirrored the religious and political controversies under way in early Victorian Britain, they also incorporated genuine differences in attitudes toward race and the status of Africans in the mission churches that were specific to the colonial context. The conflict in the South African mission pitted Philip and his allies, especially the Reads, against the legendary Robert Moffat and a group of young missionaries on the eastern frontier led by Henry Calderwood.

Moffat had arrived in southern Africa in 1817 and had established his reputation at the Kuruman mission among the Tswana far to the north of the colonial border.[55] Moffat's relationship with Philip was marked by the clash of their strong personalities and by disputes over the social and political role of the missionary in the colonial arena. Far removed form the center of Cape society and government, Moffat was fiercely independent and expressed a strong distaste for Philip's and Read's involvement in the political controversies over the status of the colonial Khoi. While Moffat condemned the superintendent's politicking from Kuruman, Philip complained of what he saw as the missionary's arrogant and self-serving attitude. Moffat "would lay destitute the whole country," Philip wrote to William Ellis, "rather than it should bear a plant not of his own watering." James Read was even less charitable, calling Moffat an "ambitious, arbitrary, self-important narrowminded man."[56] The latter's participation in the Thom Synod of 1817, which had condemned Read for his sexual misconduct and his advocacy of Khoi rights, had embittered the relationship between the two missionaries throughout their long careers in South Africa.

During the 1820s and 1830s Philip and Moffat especially quarreled over the relationship between the LMS and the Griqua, who lived between the northern border of the colony and Moffat's outpost among the Tswana at Kuruman. A collection of predominantly mixed-race Africans, organized under the leadership of powerful "captains" such as Adam Kok, Barend Barends, and Andries Waterboer, the Griqua were important political and economic actors on the colony's northern frontier. The Griqua accepted mission Christianity as a means of shaping a cultural identity among their diverse communities and welcomed LMS missionaries as mediators between themselves and the colonial authorities. In the Griqua, Philip saw another example of the civilizing influence of Christianity at work in the formation of independent African communities. Following his return from London in 1829, he sought to secure the position of the Griqua against the expansion of white settlement through either incorporation into the colony or the establishment of a protectorate. In 1834 Governor D'Urban concluded a treaty with Andries Waterboer of Griquatown recognizing the status of the Griqua and promising protection against "intrusive white settlers."[57]

This did not suit Moffat, whose assessment of the Griqua differed significantly from that of Philip. Among the most significant consequences of the development of the Griqua communities was their promotion of Christianity north of the Orange River through an extensive network of native evangelists. Griqua captains also expected this missionary work to extend their political power within the region, but Moffat saw this expansion as a threat to his work among the southern Tswana. The Griqua, in turn, feared Moffat's interference in their affairs, and on one occasion even attempted to have him suspended by the LMS on allegations of adultery. In such circumstances, Moffat viewed Philip's championing of the Griqua as unwarranted meddling that endangered the interests of his own mission.[58]

In an effort to counter Philip's influence in the colony and over the missions, Moffat advocated the creation of a district committee system, whereby councils of ordained missionaries would oversee and govern the missions in place of a single superintendent. In 1839 he left for an extensive tour of Britain and spent part of his time there trying to convince the Society's directors to adopt the system. Moffat's proposal, at least, would have emasculated Philip's power. Read supposed, with some reason, that Moffat intended to convince the Society to remove Philip as its superintendent. "You are aware that Moffat is doing everything in his power in England to injure Dr. Philip," he wrote to Kitchingman, "calling him a tyrant, and trampling the missionaries under his feet, and trying to get him removed." Read continued that he feared there was "a majority of our Brethren here who are of the same feelings and who would rejoice to see [Philip] home tomorrow." From his perspective, the mission could not afford to lose Philip, "for he is a check to those who would willingly enslave the Hottentots again, and other coloured peoples."[59]

Upon his return from Britain, Moffat did find supporters for the committee system among a group of new missionaries on the eastern frontier led by Henry Calderwood. A Scotsman, Calderwood set sail for South Africa in 1838. Having met Calderwood prior to his departure from Britain, Read described him as "a fine man . . . a Presbyterian, but an excellent man, almost a radical."[60] As missionary to the Xhosa at Blinkwater, near the Kat River settlement, Calderwood was to prove something less than a radical. He and Read found themselves quickly at odds over their attitudes toward the Africans and their views on church governance. The two men became central figures in a bitter dispute that nearly split the LMS mission in two.

Shortly after his return from Britain in 1843, Moffat assisted Calderwood in establishing a committee of missionaries for the eastern district, before returning to Kuruman and organizing a second committee for the northern region. Conflict over the purpose of the committees, and their authority, ensued almost immediately following their formation. Read saw in Moffat's plans for the committee system a desire to gain control over the northern missions and to limit the influence of Griqua evangelists among the southern Tswana. From the beginning, he denounced the committees as nothing more than tools for restricting the participation of Africans in the mission churches and the influence of their strongest advocate, Philip.

In 1843 the LMS-supported congregation at Grahamstown, "the spiritual home of the British 1820 settlers," became the center of a dispute over the authority of African congregations to choose their own ministers.[61] The town contained an auxiliary missionary society that had sponsored the construction of a chapel in which both mission Khoi and white nonconformist settlers worshiped. Over more than a decade John Monro, the first LMS agent in Grahamstown, had built up the congregation paying special attention to the education and improvement of the Khoi. In 1838 the LMS approved the appointment of the Rev. John Locke as Monro's successor, and Locke established a very different relationship with the Grahamstown congregation. According to James Read Jr., Locke's "ideas of the [Khoi] were begotten and matured in Graham's Town society," and he devoted the majority of his attention to the white parishioners.[62] The spiritual needs of the Khoi fell primarily to Nicholas Smit, the mission's young schoolteacher. Smit worked enthusiastically with the Khoi community, but his relationship with Locke soured following Smit's ordination as a full missionary in 1842. A power struggle ensued, and within a year Smit decided to leave Grahamstown. In 1843 he moved to Kat River, where he began work with the Reads as a printer.

This was hardly the end of the matter, however, as a significant portion of the Grahamstown Khoi (about one hundred) refused to accept Locke and seceded from the church. "[S]ince Mr. Monro left, Mr. Smit was our schoolmaster and our preacher," their representatives protested in a letter to the Society's directors, "and since Mr. Lock began to build his church for the English people we began to talk together that we will have Mr. Smit for our minister for then we will have a church for ourselves."[63] The Grahamstown Khois' claim to the traditional Congregationalist right to call their own minister incited a heated debate between rival factions emerging within the LMS.

Moffat and Calderwood convened a meeting of the eastern district committee, which defended Locke and the status and authority of ordained ministers against the interference of their congregation. "If these people, through unreasonable and wicked opposition, had succeeded in their object," Locke contended, "would it not have furnished a precedent for others to follow when any dispute may occur between them and their missionaries?"[64] Moffat, Calderwood, and Locke all saw the machinations of the Reads behind the complaints of the Grahamstown Khoi. Locke insisted to the directors that the influence of Smit and "other parties" (almost certainly a reference to the Reads) had worked upon the Grahamstown Khoi, cultivating in them "the manifestation of a most improper spirit towards me and their fellow members."[65]

James Read, and his son, did weigh in on the controversy as the most vocal defenders of Smit's supporters. Read rejoiced in the initial protests of the Grahamstown Khoi as "the commencement of voluntaryism among the Hottentots . . . in this country and of independency or congregational-ism."[66] He had no doubts on the propriety of the Africans' claims, or of their desire to select their own pastor. "It certainly is a right," Read argued, "as much as they have a right to choose their own elders and deacons." His opponents claimed that the Grahamstown Khoi had no right to call their own minister unless possessed of the resources "to pay him." This argument Read dismissed out of hand.

> [The] white people gave Mr. Locke a call and he accepted it without a word about salary, but now that the coloured people give Smith a call they are told it cannot be, that they [cannot?] have a choice without they can pay him, and they are abused and called everything . . . because they dare prefer Smith to Locke.[67]

Read stood firm on his own religious and egalitarian principles. At the outset of the controversy he had confessed to Kitchingman that although he had "never [taken] any party" to that point, he would now "declare [him-self] to be an Independent or Congregationalist." He clearly recognized the racial outlook of his adversaries and concluded that their object was "not to have native agents or native churches to have a voice in anything."[68] Remarking that William Thompson had been welcomed by a meeting of the Dutch Reformed ministers at Graaf Reinet with one of his "black elders," Read expressed his fears that the LMS would fall "behind the Dutch church [because] our Brethren say they will not have a black or Native Agent to present at our meetings!!"[69]

In the midst of the Grahamstown controversy, the proponents of the committee system also intensified their criticisms of Philip, and the office of superintendent. Philip had expressed to the directors his serious reserva-tions about the committee system, which had drawn a harsh reply from missionaries on the eastern frontier under Calderwood's direction. For their part, Moffat and Calderwood argued that decisions made by a majority of ordained missionaries in committee would be more democratic than the potentially arbitrary or tyrannical decisions of an individual superinten-dent. Calderwood went so far as to compare superintendents (like Philip) to "Bishops or mock-bishops" and to suggest that for "congregational Dis-senters" (like the Reads) to prefer them to "an association of brethren" was "something new under the Sun." Another primary complaint was a concern that the superintendent might be unduly influenced by information "from improper sources."[70] This clearly reflected an objection, on the part of the Calderwood party, to the close relationship between Philip and the Reads, and Philip's reliance on them as his primary source of intelligence from the mission field. The controversy over the committee system ultimately came down to a struggle over the control of the missions and the ability to influence mission policy.

Calderwood's circle also pressed the directors to dismiss the Reads, senior and junior, on the grounds that they had sought to undermine the position and authority of the Society's missionaries. As evidence, they pointed to a series of letters, discussing the recent controversies, between the Reads and two Khoi deacons at Calderwood's Blinkwater congregation. At bottom, Calderwood's complaint was that the Reads chose to put trust in and to side with the interests of the Africans against his missionary brethren. This subject loomed large in Calderwood's charges against them to the directors.

> It should . . . be here considered that there is an important difference between Missionaries conversing however freely among themselves . . . and this kind of intercourse which the Messrs Read have with the Native people. To speak or write of his Brethren secretly, in this manner to any one even the most intelligent Europeans would be highly dishonourable, . . . but to do so to the Natives is cruel to them & unfairness towards his Brethren in no common degree. . . . [W]hile Mr. J.R. speaks with the greatest disrespect & affected scorn & . . . in the lowest terms of the Missionaries, he speaks to & of the people in terms of marked respect and affection.[71]

Proponents of maintaining an appropriate social distance between the white missionaries and their African congregations, Calderwood's faction objected strongly to the familiarity of the Reads' relationships with the mission Khoi. The theological and ideological influences that accorded Africans a fundamental humanity and equality in the missionary thinking of the early nineteenth century, personified by Read and Philip, was fading in the generation of Calderwood and Locke.

In a long letter to Kitchingman, Read condemned the committee system's implications for the mission and the progress of African participation in the Church. "'Tis a sorry affair," he lamented, "it strikes at the very root of the fundamental principle of our Society. It is establishing Presbyterianism." This was a true enough charge, for Calderwood was, of course, a

Scottish Presbyterian. Read argued further that the committee system was "worse than Presbyterianism" because it made no provisions for lay representation. "In the system proposed the churches are entirely at the mercy of the reverends." Read kept himself well abreast of events in Britain and recognized the parallels between the controversies over the rights of congregations there and the strife within the Cape mission. "To force a pastor upon a church without in any way to consider its judgement would be to hand over God's heritage," he stated. "This has given rise to the struggle in the Scotch Church that has proved to [be] fatal."[72] The struggles between the missionaries of the LMS reflected those over churches and authority driving the religious controversies in Britain itself. On a more fundamental level, however, in the contest over control of the missions differences in ecclesiastical loyalties reflected deeper divisions in attitudes toward race and the status of Africans in colonial society.

The End of John Philip's Career

In the midst of all this strife, Philip began to think of "leaving Africa altogether," especially as the directors had given their approval to the committee system. Tiring of the incessant conflict between his missionaries, and tired from his long struggle against the abuses of the colonial system, Philip tendered his resignation to the directors in 1843. He was forthright in defending the Reads against the charges of Calderwood and the eastern committee and expressed his deep sadness at the sight of missionaries of the LMS turning against one another. He pointedly advised the directors to recall that James Read and his son were "more popular with the natives . . . than those who oppose them" and formed "the only party among our missionaries in whom the chiefs have confidence." He warned of dire consequences for the Xhosa should the Reads be dismissed and expressed frustration at his seemingly diminished influence at the Mission House in London. The respect recently given to his opinions by the directors "has been in the inverse ratio of the opportunities I have had of forming sound conclusions on every subject connected with our missions," he wrote with a profound sense of bitterness.[73]

The intensely independent Read had bristled at times over conduct by Philip that might have infringed upon his autonomy. He believed that the Society's fundamental principle granted the missionaries considerable freedom from the interference of the superintendent. "Here I am a little independent of the Doctor," he wrote from Kat River in 1839, with a considerable sense of pride. "We have our own plans and we execute them. If the Doctor will give us any assistance we take it, otherwise we get on without it as well as we can."[74] Yet for nearly two decades Read and Philip had always seen eye to eye on the struggle to secure the rights of indigenous peoples. Both men perceived the importance of the other as the primary advocates for the African cause. "We could spare [Philip] as superintendent," wrote Read upon hearing of Philip's possible resignation, "but not as a friend of the aborigines and coloured people generally." Defending Philip's tactics, and his own, Read dismissed those, like Moffat and Calderwood, who would call "trying to prevent ill treatment, bloodshed and war, meddling with politics."[75]

The directors ultimately refused Philip's resignation, and despite his sorrow at the abiding conflict between his missionaries, he continued to defend his egalitarian convictions. Both Philip and Read recognized that the logic of Calderwood and the others regarding church government in the mission ultimately stemmed from a greater antipathy toward the African population. This new generation desired "not to have Native agents or Native churches to have a voice in anything." Read had expressed his anxieties about the racial attitudes of the new missionaries to Kitchingman as early as 1840.

> Few of the brethren think as we do respecting Native Agency in any way, and I fear the feeling respecting colour is retrograding. With us we are pushing on to raise the people in the scale of society; others are for leaving them behind or pushing them back.[76]

Attempting to explain to the Society's directors the source of the dispute between Read and Calderwood, Philip plainly identified their respective attitudes toward race as the heart of the matter.

> The parties never can be brought to act together and the only thing we can do with them is to keep them from threatening each other and from open war. They are entirely different men and represent two different classes of missionary. What is esteemed and practiced as a virtue by the one is viewed as a crime in the eyes of the other. You will find the key to this secret in the following passage in Calderwood's letter. . . . "We object to the kind of intercourse which [Read] has with the coloured people.". . . Both parties would do the coloured people good but in different ways. In order to raise the people James Read would treat them as brethren and to this Mr. Calderwood says "We object."[77]

The tone of the passage leaves little doubt as to which approach Philip believed to be the most suitable to the progress of the Khoi and the colony as a whole.[78]

During the 1840s the egalitarian beliefs of Philip and Read were slowly losing ground to the advance of new and more racist attitudes within British society, as well as among the new generation of missionaries. At the same time, the influence and effectiveness of the evangelical, humanitarian lobby in Britain were waning. In 1841 Buxton, with the support of the Anti-Slavery Society, had sponsored the launch of an expedition to promote the advance of Christianity and legitimate commerce on the Niger River. Disease and death contributed to the ruin of the expedition and led many Britons to begin to question the promise of the missionary enterprise to bring Christianity and civilization to the African continent. "Hope gave way to disillusion, enthusiasm to apathy," Howard Temperley has written. "Africa was an awful place. Why should the British take it upon themselves to redeem her?" Buxton himself had left Parliament, and died in 1845, severely weakening the humanitarian lobby's ability to influence colonial policies. The tide seemed to be turning against the ideas of Philip and Read, as a growing share of the public began to question the propriety of aspiring to make Africans "culturally indistinguishable from Europeans."[79]

In southern Africa, the interests and the aims of the white settlers began to gain new ground. As divisions within the LMS mission deepened throughout the 1840s, the colonists found, in John Mitford Bowker, an advocate who possessed a propagandistic flair equal to that shown by Philip in the *Researches*. Bowker, the eldest son of a successful British settler family, despised Philip and the LMS missionaries for their constant "blackening and belying" of the colonists and for "representing them at home as the oppressors and destroyers of the aborigines of the colony." Bowker articulated the fundamental tenets of settler frontier ideology and dismissed what he believed to be the erroneous and harmful policies of the humanitarian lobby. The missionaries, in compelling the Colonial Office to abandon the acquisition of the Queen Adelaide Province, had kept potentially productive land in the possession of irredeemable savages. "Is it just," he asked a meeting of white settlers in 1844, "that a few thousands of ruthless, worthless savages are to sit like a nightmare upon a land that would support millions of civilized men happily?" The answer was, manifestly, no. "Heaven forbids it," Bowker declared. He further suggested that it was the misguided humanitarian ideals of the missionaries, and their influence over colonial policy, that bore primary responsibility for the failure to civilize the African population. In contrast to Philip's vision of civilization flowering from the combination of Christianity and economic freedom, Bowker asserted that "savage nations must be taught to fear and respect, to stand in awe of a nation whose manners and customs, whose religion it is beneficial and desirable for them to adopt." Subjugation rather than emancipation provided the key to civilization, and this should be achieved by conquest "if no milder means are effective."

The settler interest thus placed the blame for the instability of the colonial frontier squarely upon the doorstep of the their missionary rivals. "The cant of the day is leading well-intentioned people astray from the promotion of civilization in Africa," Bowker insisted. "Niger Expeditions, Aborigines Protection Societies, Anti-Slavery Societies, Mission Institutions, as at present conducted, are things of naught." Turning the tables on Philip's idealization of Roman colonization, he noted that while "Roman manners and customs were rapidly adopted by conquered Britons," he was "not aware that Agricola had become patron to an Ancient Briton Civilization Society!" Far from abetting the progress of civilization, Bowker argued, "[c]olonization has been fettered with the wild theories of pseudo-philanthropists, whose cant and folly has been foisted into the very laws of the colonies."[80]

More alarming, from the standpoint of the mission and the Khoi, was that these ideas seemed to be gaining ground within government and other influential circles. The early 1840s saw the introduction of increasingly coercive vagrancy laws in the West Indian colonies in an attempt to revive shrinking levels of sugar production. The Cape Legislative Council passed its own Masters and Servants Law in 1839. The law received the approval of the Colonial Secretary, Lord John Russell, in 1841 after it had been rewritten to remove all specific references to race. As the law made no allusion to whites or "coloureds," some celebrated it as the end of racial legislation in southern Africa. However, even as it granted laborers continued protection from abusive employers, much of the law was clearly contrived to secure more reliable sources of black labor within the colony. As enforced throughout the 1840s, it increasingly subordinated the interests of African laborers to those of their primarily white masters.[81] A succession of colonial governors in the latter part of the decade, Sir Peregrine Maitland, Sir Henry Pottinger, and Sir Henry Smith, all criticized what they perceived to be the "unjustifiably privileged" status of the Khoi in colonial law.[82] They appointed several prominent opponents of the missions, including Bowker and John Montagu, to positions of authority in the colony.[83] James Read became increasingly alarmed at the retreat from humanitarian policies. The developing consensus among colonists and government, he observed, was that "the black men should not possess property in the soil, but rather become the slaves of, or disappear before, the White Man."[84]

Evidence for the spread of these opinions also exists in the reactions of the metropolitan press to the recurrent violence on the colonial frontier between 1847 and 1851. *The Times* took a decidedly hostile view toward the Xhosa, and their humanitarian allies, in its assessment of the frontier conflict. The paper compared the British government's policy in the Cape unfavorably with that of the U.S. government toward Native Americans in its western territories.

> The red tribes have rarely troubled the Government of America, for the simple reason that the whites were allowed to have their way with them. Had there been Aborigines Protection Societies as strong in New York as in London, we should see a reflection of our Cape troubles in every western State; but there philanthropy was powerless against local policy. The rifle did its work, and the savages disappeared.

The article concluded that the contest on the Cape frontier came down to a choice between "the sacrifice of the settlers, or the extermination of the Caffres."[85]

The African communities of the Kat River and the LMS mission stations showed a growing sense of desperation in response to the "profound contempt of colour, and lofty pride of caste" progressing within colonial society.[86] The victories of the humanitarian cause, Ordinance 50, the abolition of slavery, and the defeat of the 1834 vagrancy law, seemed to have failed in creating a new social and economic order at the Cape. In 1846, an aging and despondent Philip observed that the return of war to the frontier would "fall with a peculiar and destructive weight" upon the mission Khoi.[87] The disastrous consequences of the frontier wars, the persistence of racial discrimination, and the growing demands of white farmers for more land led many Khoi to question the ability of the LMS missions to deliver on their promises. Willem Uithaalder of Kat River expressed the degree of their frustrations when he remarked to W. R. Thompson,

> Sir, you and Mr. Read were both young men when you came among us and you are now both old, . . . yet these oppressions won't cease. The Missionaries have for years written, and their writings won't help. We are now going to stand up for our own affairs. We shall show the settlers that we too are men.[88]

When, in 1851, the Xhosa again invaded the colony, Uithaalder and several of the Kat River Khoi joined them in the fight. The participation of this minority of the Khoi in the so-called "Hottentot Rebellion" of 1851 was a disaster for the people of the Kat River. The government broke up the settlement, as well as the LMS mission station at Theopolis, transferring most of the land and property into the hands of white settlers. A prominent member of the Kat River community, Andries Botha, was tried and convicted of treason.

In the spring of 1850, on the eve of the recurrence of the frontier wars, Robert Godlonton's *Grahamstown Journal* offered the following assessment of Cape politics during the first half of the nineteenth century.

> On the eastern frontier a contest between stern justice and mistaken philanthropy has been raging upwards of thirty years. . . . The British people . . . influenced by certain powerful, presumably religious associations, have given their voices against their fellow-countrymen. There has, however, never been so important a crisis as now at hand. . . . The voice of every colonist must be loud in demanding, that every Institution, where a number of the coloured races are, or can be drawn together, shall be broken up. . . . If we destroy, or prevent the building of the nest, we shall not be liable to the incursion of the brood.[89]

By the middle of the century the voices of the colonists appeared to have at last gained the ear of the British public and the British government. In the midst of the 1851 uprising and its aftermath, the two champions of the African's cause, John Philip and James Read, died. For three decades, they had waged a constant struggle to secure the civil and legal equality of the indigenous peoples of southern Africa. Out of this "landless proletariat," they had labored to build "a Christian elite, able to compete on equal terms with whites."[90] At the end of their lives, all that they hoped for seemed to have come to naught, defeated by the obstacles of incessant warfare, emergent racism, and religious divisions within the mission. And yet the voices of the humanitarian movement would not be fully silenced or be denied their legacy.

Epilogue

What the Cape system offered was a new method of political adjustment. . . .
Here was an important precedent, not some vague theory, but a practical
example of the non-racial principle enshrined in legislation.

—Peter Walshe
Black Nationalism in South Africa

As the members of the London Missionary Society (LMS) community at
Hankey carried the body of John Philip to his grave in late August 1851,
the prospects for the LMS missions' political and economic agenda looked
bleak. The humanitarian lobby had lost much of its considerable influence
in London, and the wars on the eastern frontier had made the opposition
of the colonial government and the white population to African advancement more resolved. In the wake of the "Hottentot Rebellion" of 1851 the
British authorities were to dismantle the Kat River settlement, which Philip
and others saw as the most promising enterprise for building their desired
independent African middle class. Little could the mission community have
imagined that one of the more important legacies of the movement's goals
would come via the enactment of a policy that John Philip had actively
resisted throughout his career.

   During his years in the Cape Colony Philip had persistently opposed
proposals for the transfer of power from London to Cape Town. His efforts

on behalf of the colonial Khoi had depended upon the missions' ability to influence the government in Westminster, and Philip had always looked to the Colonial Office to protect against the most severe injustices committed by white settlers and government officials in the colony. Without guarantees of African participation, he believed that self-government in the Cape "spelt doom" for the Africans both within and beyond the colonial border. Local government, under the control of the colonists, could not be relied upon to render justice to the African communities, or to effectively counter the expansion of white settlement.[1]

During the early 1850s, however, the demand for representative government gained new momentum. Earl Grey, who took the office of Colonial Secretary in 1846, supported the notion of expanding self-government in the colonies through elected legislatures. The immediate source of the new agitation, however, was the Colonial Office's proposal to settle a shipload of Irish convicts at the Cape. The almost universal opposition to this plan forced the Colony's governor, Smith, to institute an election to seat a new Legislative Council. The four leading contestants in the poll included the prominent Afrikaners Christoffel Brand and F. W. Reitz and the liberal/ humanitarians Fairbairn and Stockenstrom. The governor sought to balance the various interests of colonial society by appointing to the new Council Robert Godlonton of the Grahamstown settlers, who had finished well down the list in the election results. United in their opposition to the influence of the British settlers, the other four refused to take their seats on the Council alongside Godlonton. They called, instead, for the beginning of negotiations to create an elected parliament.

Fairbairn had backed the goal of self-government since his days as a leading voice against Somerset during the 1820s. While he had focused his attention upon the struggle for African rights during the 1830s and 1840s, he now took on the cause of representative government with new enthusiasm. Given the obliging attitude of the Colonial Secretary, Grey, toward colonial self-rule, the question of if the colony would be granted a parliament was quickly settled. The real debate in the negotiations centered on the matter of who would be eligible to vote. The inclusion of Fairbairn and Stockenstrom in the process ensured that the interests of the Africans would receive full consideration in the debates over the franchise. Joined by the representatives of the Afrikaners, who had their own reasons for seeking to limit the power of the British settlers in the new legislature, Fairbairn and Stockenstrom pressed strongly for the inclusion of the Africans in the political process.

So it was that the 1853 constitution of the Cape Colony established a nonracial franchise, based upon a low property qualification that ensured African participation in the electorate. This participation was, admittedly, limited. A half-century later, African men still made up only about 5 percent of the voting rolls in the Cape as compared to 10 percent for coloureds, and 85 percent for whites. Still, African and coloured voters formed a significant enough element of the electorate in certain districts to ensure that their votes mattered to candidates of all parties.[2] There is little question that in principle, and in practice, the Cape constitution was one of the most liberal anywhere in the world during the second half of the nineteenth century. In effectively fixing an equal political right for the African subjects of the Colony, it was an accomplishment toward which the ideas and actions of Philip and the missionaries of the LMS had made a significant contribution.[3]

This book has situated the roots of this legacy within not only the influences of evangelical Christianity and the Enlightenment but also the specific context of early nineteenth-century British politics and the nonconformist struggle for civil and religious equality. I have argued that the social conscience of the dissenting missionaries of the LMS developed within their own experience of religious intolerance and social marginalization at home. This is not, necessarily, to equate the complaints of British Dissenters with the hardships faced by colonized peoples in the early nineteenth-century British Empire. Rather, the missionaries' demands for the equal rights of the colonized are more readily comprehensible and persuasive when interpreted through their own experiences of social and political inequality.

By the second half of the nineteenth century liberal ideas of the potential for racial equality seemed to be in full retreat in southern Africa. According to one historian, the persistent conflict on the eastern Cape frontier had brought missionaries and others to "a very different mental universe from the pioneering days of the 1830s." This "closing of the missionary mind" increasingly shifted blame for the failures of missionary policy away from the colonial government and directed it instead upon the Africans themselves.[4] Such changes were taking place throughout most of the Empire. The press, and leading cultural figures such as Thomas Carlyle, celebrated the Jamaican governor Edward John Eyre's use of military force to crush black rioters at Morant Bay, Jamaica, in 1865. Carlyle praised Eyre's actions for saving the lives of thousands of British men and women "from the murder and lust of black savages." In his accounts of the uprising, Eyre himself described the "feelings of race within the black man's breast impenetrable to those without." Britons could not know the genuine "character and tone of thinking" of the brutal and savage "negro population." Eyre, who as a young colonial officer in Australia had lauded the Aborigines' potential for civilization, now fully manifested the racialist doctrines of the mid-Victorian age.

And yet Eyre's conduct gave rise to a raging debate in Britain over the proper conduct of British colonial officials. Prominent liberals, such as John Stuart Mill, joined by a substantial number of Dissenters and abolitionists, denounced Eyre's recourse to martial law, and the resultant violation of the fundamental rights of British subjects. Although it may not have carried the public debate—upon Eyre's acquittal from civil prosecution *Punch* smugly observed, "We really cannot murder a man for saving a colony"— the liberal humanitarian ideology remained the most dogged rival to nineteenth-century colonial policies of violence and racial oppression.[5]

By the first decade of the twentieth century, a thorough reinterpretation of the early nineteenth-century humanitarian program of the LMS had taken place. Philip, Read, and their fellow missionaries were recast as misguided, if perhaps well-intentioned, figures in the history of racial politics in southern Africa. In 1911 the *Encyclopaedia Britannica's* account of their activities in the Cape Colony accurately represented the conventional wisdom on the subject.

> The zeal of the missionaries frequently outran their discretion . . . especially in the early day.s . . . [A]mong the Hottentots within the colony they instilled notions of antipathy to white farmers, and withdrew large numbers of them from agricultural pursuits. Their general attitude may be explained as a reaction against the abuses which they saw going on around them, and to a misconception of the Hottentot and Bantu races.

The article then proceeded to refute the early nineteenth-century missionary movement's agenda using the racial logic that had come to dominate British attitudes toward the colonized:

> A longer experience of all the African negroid races has led to a considerable modification in the views originally held in regard to them. The black man is not simply a morally and intellectually undeveloped European, and education, except in rare instances, does not put him on an equality with the European.[6]

At the same time the British government was engaged in the final stages of creating the Union of South Africa and adopting within its constitution the seeds of the ultimate elimination of the nonracial Cape franchise. In following the debates over the South Africa Act, it is not too difficult to find the champions of an alternative to a white-dominated South Africa. A resolution of the Aborigines Protection Society pressed upon the government the "grave importance of safeguarding the existing native franchise . . . and its extension to duly qualified natives."[7] In a letter to *The Times*, Charles Bruce protested against "the violation of that principle of equal opportunity, without distinction of race, colour, or creed, which was the faith of the Victorian era."[8] J. Tengo Jabavu, a member of the African deputation to the London conference on the South African constitution, warned that "what the Imperial Parliament is being asked to sanction will be used as a precedent in future legislation against all native advance, and that Parliament will be quoted for all time as having put its seal on discrimination."[9]

With the support of some influential Liberal politicians, such as Sir Charles Dilke and the Labour Party MPs led by Ramsay MacDonald, W. P. Schreiner, a former Prime Minister of the Cape Colony, took up the cause of removing the so-called color-bar provisions from the South Africa Act. "The coloured inhabitants," Schreiner protested, "are barred from the opportunity to rise and evolve naturally, which is the right of every free man in a free country." His party acted "upon the doctrine of the right to freedom of opportunity–equality of opportunity."[10] In Schreiner's words, and in those of the other protesters, one can hear the more than faint echo of John Philip, James Read, and the mission Khoi of the early nineteenth century.

As this study has shown, missionaries were more than simply agents in the process of the expansion of British culture, British values, and British power around the globe. By way of their theological and political convictions, the Congregationalist missionaries of the LMS posed an alternative model of British imperialism, grounded upon an idea of the basic rights of religious, economic, and political freedom. In places like the West Indies and southern Africa these influences often facilitated the rise of languages of opposition to the policies of social and racial oppression. The enduring significance of these early nineteenth-century missionary ideals for the political struggles of the colonial, and postcolonial, worlds is explicit in the following commentary on the South African Prime Minister John Vorster, taken from a 1969 edition of *Sechaba*, the official publication of the African National Congress.

> John Vorster, we are told, is Prime Minister of Western Christian Civilization's bastion state in Africa. . . . But, Mr. Vorster it seems, can't get along with the Christians. . . . What are these attitudes that set the Christian Prime Minister to abuse Christian priests as though they were dangerous revolutionaries? . . . Racialist South Africa has a long history of

hating those Christians who were not prepared to limit their Christianity to a decent weekly attendance at Church, while the servants prepared the Sunday dinner. Vorster himself refers to the troubles of the voortrekkers with missionaries—their crime was to have fought to end the evil practice of slavery at the Cape. And the voortrekkers never forgave them for it. In recent years, we remember, how Father Trevor Huddleston and Bishop Reeves were hounded out of South Africa. Their crime was to have identified themselves with the struggles of the oppressed, and to have had the courage to speak out against apartheid. Funny, isn't it, that the crusaders of Western Christian civilisation just can't get on with the Christians.[11]

When assessing the role of the missionary movement within the social, political, and economic forces that shaped the racial order of the British Empire, we do well also to recognize those who helped to mold the voices of opposition.

Notes

Introduction

1 E. Halévy, *The Birth of Methodism in England*, ed. B. Semmel (Chicago: 1971), 1. See also Halévy, *A History of the English People in the 19th Century*, vol. 1, *England in 1815* (New York: 1961).

2 R. W. Davis, *Dissent in Politics, 1780–1830: The Political Life of William Smith, MP* (London: 1971), xiv.

3 T. Larsen, *Contested Christianity: The Political and Social Contexts of Victorian Theology* (Waco, Tex.: 2004), 145; see also Larsen, *Friends of Religious Equality: Nonconformist Politics in Mid-Victorian England* (Woodbridge, UK: 1999). For a broader range of the history of dissent and politics, also see J. E. Bradley, *Religion, Revolution and English Radicalism: Nonconformity in Eighteenth-Century Politics and Society* (Cambridge: 1990); R. Floyd, *Religious Dissent and Political Modernization: Church, Chapel and Party in Nineteenth Century England* (New York: 2007); G. I. T. Machin, *Politics and the Churches in Great Britain: 1832 to 1868* (Oxford: 1977).

4 See, e.g., L. Davidoff and C. Hall, *Family Fortunes: Men and Women of the English Middle Class, 1780–1850* (London: 1987); A. D. Gilbert, *Religion and Society in Industrial England, 1740–1914* (London: 1976); A. A. McLaren, *Religion and Social Class* (London: 1974); H. McLeod, *Piety and Poverty: Working Class Religion in Berlin, London, and New York, 1870–1914* (New York: 1996); D. Valenze, *Prophetic Sons and Daughters: Female Preaching and Popular Religion in Industrial England* (Princeton: 1985); J. Wolffe, *God and Greater Britain, 1843–1945* (London: 1994).

5 The classic example is E. P. Thompson's treatment of Methodism in *The Making of the English Working Class* (New York: 1963). See also R. Hole,

Pulpits, Politics and Public Order in England, 1760–1832 (Cambridge: 1989); T. W. Laqueur, *Religion and Respectability: Sunday Schools and English Working Class Culture, 1780–1850* (New Haven: 1976); R. Moore, *Pit-Men, Preachers and Politics* (Cambridge: 1974); and the work of J. Seed on English Unitarians, e.g., "Theologies of Power: Unitarianism and the Social Relations of Religious Discourse, 1800–50," in Morris, *Class, Power and Social Structure in British Nineteenth-Century Towns*, 107–56.

6   A. L. Stoler and F. Cooper, "Between Metropole and Colony: Rethinking a Research Agenda," in Cooper and Stoler, *Tensions of Empire*, 1–56.

7   C. Hall, *Civilising Subjects: Metropole and Colony in the English Imagination, 1830–1867* (Chicago: 2002); S. Thorne, *Congregational Missions and the Making of an Imperial Culture in Nineteenth-Century England* (Stanford: 1999). U. S. Mehta also argues that the rhetoric of nineteenth-century liberalism masked an exclusionary logic when applied by British liberals to colonized peoples. Mehta, *Liberalism and Empire: A Study in Nineteenth-Century British Liberal Thought* (Chicago: 1999).

8   M. Watts' monumental study of nineteenth-century Dissent provides ample evidence of the social diversity of nonconformist churches, especially his meticulous analysis of the religious census of 1851. See Watts, *The Dissenters*, vol. 2 (Oxford: 1995) esp. 22–30, 558–92, and appendices 1 and 2. For a challenge to assumptions about the links between urbanization and secularization, see H. McLeod, ed., *European Religion in the Age of Great Cities* (London: 1995), especially the chapters by C. G. Brown and S. Williams. D. Hempton's *The Religion of the People: Methodism and Popular Religion, c. 1750–1900* (London: 1996) also convincingly demonstrates the relevance and appeal of evangelical religion across a broad social spectrum in early nineteenth-century Britain.

9   This generalization, of course, oversimplifies a more complex array of historiographical interpretations. A first generation of postwar African historians, such as J. F. A. Ajayi and E. A. Ayandele, presented judicious accounts of the impact of the missionary movement, albeit from a decidedly non-European perspective. See Ajayi, *Christian Missions in Nigeria, 1841–1891* (London: 1965) and Ayandele, *The Missionary Impact on Modern Nigeria 1842–1914* (London: 1966). For examples of a more antagonistic assessment, strongly influenced by Marxist theory, see A. Dachs, "Christian Missionary Enterprise and Sotho-Tswana Societies in the Nineteenth Century," in Dachs, *Christianity South of the Zambezi*, vol. 1, 53–62; M. Legassick, "The Griqua, the Sotho-Tswana and the Missionaries" (Ph.D. diss., University of California, Los Angeles, 1969); A. Temu and B. Swai, *Historians and Africanist History: A Critique—Post-Colonialist Historiography Examined* (London: 1981); J. S. Dharmarah, *Colonialism and Christian Mission: Post-Colonial Reflections* (Delhi: 1993). For a defense of the liberal tradition, in the South African context, against the criticisms of Marxist and other scholars, see J. Butler, R. Elphick, and D. Welsh, eds., *Democratic Liberalism in South Africa: Its History and Prospect* (Middletown, Conn.: 1987).

10   This is the general tenor of the institutional histories of the missionary societies, such as R. Lovett's centennial *History of the London Missionary Society* (London: 1896). For a more contemporary work argued in a similar vein, see B. Stanley, *The Bible and the Flag: Protestant Missions and British Imperialism in the Nineteenth and Twentieth Centuries* (Leicester: 1990).

11   N. Etherington, ed., *Missions and Empire: Oxford History of the British Empire Companion Series* (Oxford: 2005); A. Porter, *Religion versus Empire? British Protestant Missionaries and Overseas Expansion, 1700–1914* (Manchester: 2004).

12   R. Anstey, *The Atlantic Slave Trade and British Abolition, 1760–1810* (London: 1975), and "Slavery and the Protestant Ethic," in Craton, *Roots and Branches*, 157–81.

13   J. and J. Comaroff, *Of Revelation and Revolution: Christianity, Colonialism, and Consciousness in South Africa*, vols. 1 and 2 (Chicago: 1991, 1997); see also J. Comaroff, "Images of Empire, Contests of Conscience: Models of Colonial Domination in South Africa," *American Ethnologist* 16 (1989): 661–85. Some key works that have helped to shape the historiography of southern Africa in the wake of the Comaroffs' study include P. Landau, *The Realm of the Word: Language, Gender and Christianity in a Southern African Kingdom* (London: 1995); R. Elphick and R. Davenport, eds., *Christianity in South Africa: A Political, Social, and Cultural History* (Berkeley: 1997); R. Ross, *Status and Respectability in the Cape Colony, 1750–1870* (Cambridge: 1999); E. Elbourne, *Blood Ground: Colonialism, Missions, and the Contest for Christianity in the Cape Colony and Britain, 1799–1853* (Montreal: 2002).

14   The Comaroffs' work is reflective of broader trends that have shifted the focus from the missionary's role as an agent of conquest, to examining the missionary as an agent of cultural imperialism. Many of these studies have also stressed the means by which the colonized embraced mission Christianity for their own reasons and for their own purposes. A common criticism of the Comaroffs' work is that they grant too much power to the ideologies and actions of the missionaries and fail to fully appreciate or account for the agency of the indigenous population. See J. D. Y. Peel, "For Who Hath Despised the God of Small Things? Missionary Narratives and Historical Anthropology," *Comparative Studies in Society and History* 37, no. 3 (1995): 581–607; E. Elbourne, "Word Made Flesh: Christianity, Modernity, and Cultural Colonialism in the Work of Jean and John Comaroff," *American Historical Review* 108, no. 3 (2003): 435–59.

15   See Comaroffs, *Of Revelation and Revolution*, chap. 4, and Comaroff, "Images of Empire."

16   *KP*, quoted in "Editor's Introduction," 26.

Chapter 1

1   M. Horne, *Letters on Missions* (London: 1784).

2   School of Oriental and African Studies Library: Council for World Missions/

London Missionary Society Archive (SOAS, CWM/LMS), Minutes of the
Board of Directors, 17 March and 22 September 1795.

3   The participants at the Baker's Coffeehouse meetings reflect the influence
of pan-evangelical sentiment present at the formation of the LMS: David
Bogue, Independent, Joseph Brooksbank, Independent, John Eyre, Anglican,
John Love, Church of Scotland, John Reynolds, Independent, James Steven,
Church of Scotland, and Matthew Wilks, Independent/Calvinist Methodist.

4   . Doddridge, *The Evil and Danger of Neglecting the Souls of Men*, quoted in
E. A. Payne, "Doddridge and the Missionary Enterprise," in Nuttall, *Philip
Doddridge*, 88.

5   W. Carey, *An Enquiry into the Obligations of Christians to Use Means for the
Conversion of the Heathen* (Leicester: 1792).

6   Watts, *Dissenters*, vol. 2, 6–7.

7   For a history of Carey's mission, see E. D. Potts, *British Baptist Missionaries in
India* (Cambridge: 1967).

8   Anonymous (David Bogue), *Evangelical Magazine* (*EM*), September 1793,
378–80, emphasis in original.

9   SOAS, CWM/LMS, Home Office, Personal/5, Unpublished Manuscript
History of the LMS by William Ellis.

10   *EM*, January 1795, preface.

11   Watts, *Dissenters*, vol. 2, 24. Fully detailed in appendices at the end of vol. 2.

12   J. Walsh, "'Methodism' and the Origins of the English-Speaking Evangelicalism," in Noll, Bebbington, and Rawlyk, *Evangelicalism*, 20.

13   Watts, *Dissenters*, vol. 1, 394.

14   G. Rupp, *Religion in England, 1688–1791* (Oxford: 1986); A. Walls, *The Missionary Movement in Christian History* (Edinburgh: 1996), chap. 18; Watts,
Dissenters, vol. 1, 421–28.

15   Cited in Rupp, *Religion in England*, 299.

16   Watts attaches primary significance to the contribution of the charity school
movement to the growth of eighteenth-century evangelicalism. See *Dissenters*, vol. 1, 423.

17   Hempton, *Religion of the People*, 51.

18   Watts, *Dissenters*, vol. 1, 426.

19   For a concise discussion of the theological differences between the two evangelists, see Watts, *Dissenters*, vol. 1, 428–34.

20   G. M. Ditchfield, *The Evangelical Revival* (London: 1998), 62–63.

21   See Watts, *Dissenters*, vol. 1, 399–401.

22   Walsh, "Methodism," 20–22.

23   Hempton, *Religion of the People*, 2.

24   Thompson, *Making of the English Working Class*. See Thompson's treatment
of Methodism in chap. 4.

25   See, e.g., A. Everitt, *The Pattern of Rural Dissent: The Nineteenth Century*
(Leicester: 1972).

26   See chap. 3 in Hempton, *Religion of the People*.

27 Hempton, *Religion of the People*, 6–7. On this theme, see the work of W. R. Ward, esp. *The Protestant Evangelical Awakening* (Cambridge: 1992) and *Faith and Faction* (London: 1993).

28 See Watts, *Dissenters*, vol. 1, 434–45.

29 J. Taylor, *The Apostles of Fylde Methodism* (London: 1885), 21–22.

30 D. Lovegrove, *Established Church, Sectarian People: Itinerancy and the Transformation of English Dissent, 1780–1830* (Cambridge: 1988).

31 B. Nightingale, *Lancashire Nonconformity; or, Sketches, Historical and Descriptive, of the Congregational and Old Presbyterian Churches in the County,* vol. 1 (Manchester: 1890), 174–75.

32 Nightingale, *Lancashire Nonconformity*, vol. 1, 9–16.

33 Watts, *Dissenters*, vol. 2, 136.

34 *EM*, 1799, 511.

35 Lovegrove, *Established Church*, chap. 4.

36 Nightingale, *Lancashire Nonconformity*, vol. 1, 115.

37 See M. Noll, *The Rise of Evangelicalism: The Age of Edwards, Whitefield and the Wesleys* (Leicester: 2004); G. Nuttall, "Continental Pietism and the Evangelical Movement in Britain," in *Pietismus and Reveil*, ed. J. Van Den Berg and J. P. Van Dooren (Leiden, Netherlands: 1978); Rupp, *Religion in England.*

38 S. Neill, *A History of Christian Missions* (New York: 1986), 192–93. Recent interpretations suggest that the idea of a transition from a hyper-Calvinism to a more moderate Calvinism is overly simplistic and misrepresents the range of theological views in eighteenth-century evangelicalism. Moreover, historians have tended to use the term *moderate Calvinism* in poorly defined and overly general ways. This view argues that a theological shift that took place during the revival was a shift away from excessive dogmatism, rather than a rejection of widespread hyper-Calvinist beliefs. See K. Stuart, *Restoring the Reformation: British Evangelism and the Francophone Reveil, 1816–1849* (Milton Keynes, UK: 2006), chap. 1.

39 Lovegrove, *Established Church*, 22.

40 Lovegrove, *Established Church*, 19; see also B. Stanley, *Bible and the Flag*, 61–63.

41 Cited in Walls, *Missionary Movement*, 246; see also Watts, *Dissenters*, vol. 2, 11.

42 D. Bogue, "Objections against a Mission to the Heathen, Stated and Considered," in *Sermons Preached in London at the Formation of the Missionary Society* (London: 1795), 126.

43 Stanley, *Bible and the Flag*, 67–70.

44 T. Grove, *The Evangelical Commission* (London: 1800), 91.

45 Quoted in Stanley, *Bible and the Flag*, 61.

46 Watts, *Dissenters*, vol. 2, 6–7.

47 SOAS, CWM/LMS, Home Office, "History of the LMS," author unknown, unpublished manuscript, [1845?].

48   J. Brewer, "The Certain Accomplishment of Divine Predictions," in *Sermons Preached at the Annual Meeting of the Missionary Society* (London: 1802), 104.

49   Anonymous (Bogue), *EM*, September 1793, 378.

50   SOAS, CWM/LMS, Home Office, "History of the LMS," author unknown, unpublished manuscript, [1845?].

51   Stanley, *Bible and the Flag*, 70–74. See also Stanley, "Commerce and Christianity: Providence Theory, the Missionary Movement, and the Imperialism of Free Trade, 1842–1860," *Historical Journal* 26, no. 1 (1983): 71–94.

52   A. Porter, "Commerce and Christianity: The Rise and Fall of a Nineteenth-Century Missionary Slogan," *Historical Journal* 28, no. 3 (1985): 597–621.

53   SOAS, CWM/LMS, Candidates Papers; SOAS, CWM/LMS, Home Office: Directors' Memorial to Government on East India Company, 20 April 1812.

54   J. Griffin, "The Signs of the Times Favourable to the Cause of Missions," in *Sermons Preached at the Annual Meeting of the Missionary Society* (London: 1807), 94.

55   *Parliamentary Register* 26 (1789), 150, quoted in Stanley, *Bible and the Flag*, 71.

56   Bogue, "Objections against a Mission," 146.

57   Nightingale, *Lancashire Nonconformity*, vol. 1, 16.

58   SOAS, CWM/LMS, Home Office: 1/6/A, Samuel Greatheed to John Eyre, 13 February 1798.

59   J. Jefferson, "The Diffusion of the Gospel," in *Sermons Preached at the Annual Meeting of the Missionary Society* (London: 1811), 40.

60   *The Home Missionary Magazine* (*HMM*), April 1835, 135.

61   Carey, *Enquiry*, 13.

62   Thorne, *Congregational Missions*, 44.

63   A. Mearns, *England for Christ: A Record of the Congregational Church and Home Missionary Society* (London: 1886), appendix.

64   Walls, *Missionary Movement*, 247.

65   Nightingale, *Lancashire Nonconformity*, vol. 1, 149.

66   Dr. Williams's Library (DWL), Proceedings and report of the North Bucks Association of Independent Churches and Ministers, 1819, 15.

67   Mearns, *England for Christ*, 22–24.

68   Mearns, *England for Christ*, 31.

69   *HMM*, September 1832, 339.

70   "Cry Aloud Spare Not," *Missionary Hymns, Composed and selected for the public services at the annual meeting of the Missionary Society in London; and for the monthly meetings for prayer in town and country* (London: 1812), 50.

Chapter 2

1   *Parl. Debs.*, vol. 19, col. 1128.

2   *Parl. Debs.*, vol. 19, col. 1131.

3   B. L. Manning, *The Protestant Dissenting Deputies* (Cambridge: 1952), 130–32.

4   *Parl. Debs.*, vol. 14, cols. 854–58.
5   Rev. J. Thomas, *Strictures on Subjects Chiefly relating to the Established Religion and the Clergy* (London: 1807), 2, 36.
6   As J. Clark has noted, "Dissent ultimately implied a gesture of defiance against the idea of a hierarchical, deferential Anglican society." *English Society, 1688–1832* (Cambridge: 1985), 379.
7   Bishop of Durham to Sidmouth, 11 July 1809, in G. Pellew, *The Life and Correspondence of the Right Honourable Henry Addington, First Viscount Sidmouth*, vol. 3 (London: 1847), 40–41.
8   Mr. Sparrow to Sidmouth no date, in Pellew, *Life*, 43–44.
9   Dr. Luke Booker to Sidmouth no date, in Pellew, *Life*, 43, emphasis in original.
10   *Gentlemen's Magazine* 1 (1790): 248–51.
11   Cited in Thorne, *Congregational Missions*, 45.
12   Halévy, *Birth of Methodism*, 1; see also Halévy, *History of the English People*. For Halévy, "Methodism" meant evangelical Dissent in general, not just the Wesleyan Methodists. Halévy's terminology, although consistent with the imprecise usage of the term during the early nineteenth century, has been a point of some confusion for modern historians, including E. Hobsbawm and E. Thompson, who focused their attention primarily upon the Wesleyans and the Primitive Methodists to the exclusion of other evangelical nonconformists.
13   E. J. Hobsbawm, *Labouring Men: Studies in the History of Labour* (London: 1964), 23–33. Thompson, *Making of the English Working Class*, 350–401.
14   B. Semmel, *The Methodist Revolution* (New York: 1973); A. D. Gilbert, "Religion and Political Stability in Early Industrial England," in O'Brien and Quinault, *The Industrial Revolution and British Society*, 79–99, 98. S. Piggin challenges Semmel's conclusions in "Halévy Revisited: The Origins of the Wesleyan Methodist Missionary Society: An Examination of Semmel's Thesis," *Journal of Imperial and Commonwealth History* 9 (1980): 17–37.
15   Piggin, "Halévy Revisited," 18.
16   Thorne, *Congregational Missions*, 46–47.
17   Bishop of Gloucester to Sidmouth no date, in Pellew, *Life*, 38–39.
18   Sidmouth to Hiley Addington, 9 May 1811, in Pellew, *Life*, 46, emphasis in original.
19   *Parl. Debs.*, vol. 20, col. 242.
20   Pellew, *Life*, 51.
21   *Parl. Debs.*, vol. 20, col. 241.
22   *Parl. Debs.*, vol. 19, col. 1130.
23   Guildhall Library (GL), Dissenting Deputies MS 3083, 4, Report of the Dissenting Deputies, 25 May 1810.
24   Thomas Coke to Sidmouth, 20 April 1811, in Pellew, *Life*, 47; Pellew, *Life*, 51.
25   *Parl. Debs.*, vol. 14, col. 855.
26   *Parl. Debs.*, vol. 19, col. 781.

27   D. Hempton, *Methodism and Politics in British Society, 1750–1850* (London: 1984), 99.

28   Mr. Thompson to Sidmouth, 14 May 1811, in Pellew, *Life*, 51.

29   GL, Dissenting Deputies MS 3083, 4, Dissenting Deputies, 13 May 1811.

30   DWL, 12.58 (12), John Gurney to Thomas Belsham, 28 June 1811.

31   Davis, *Dissent in Politics*, 155.

32   *EM*, vol. 19, 239–41.

33   Hempton, *Methodism and Politics*, 98. The Wesleyan leadership persisted in defending Methodists from government interference by claiming to be loyal members of the establishment. Sidmouth's bill shows that by 1811 such protestations had begun to wear thin upon the defenders of the church. However, it is significant to note the relative easiness with which the Wesleyans formed a tacit, if not formal, alliance with the Dissenters in the petition campaign against the bill.

34   *EM*, vol. 19, 242–44.

35   DWL, Gurney to Belsham, 28 June 1811.

36   John Rylands Library, Methodist Papers, Thomas Coke Correspondence, PLP/28/19/3, Coke to Rev. Richard Gower, 18 April 1811.

37   Hempton, *Methodism and Politics*, 101, 243; Davis, *Dissent in Politics*, 155.

38   *Parl. Debs.*, vol. 19, col. 1132; vol. 20, cols. 247–49.

39   *Parl. Debs.*, vol. 20, cols. 239–40.

40   *Parl. Debs.*, vol. 20, col. 250.

41   *Parl. Debs.*, vol. 20, col. 249.

42   *Parl. Debs.*, vol. 20, col. 233.

43   Davis, *Dissent in Politics*, 171. Protestant Dissenters and Roman Catholics were excluded from municipal government and national offices by the Corporation Act of 1661 and the Test Act of 1673, which gave both groups common cause to work for their repeal. However, their theological differences often kept the groups apart.

44   *Parl. Debs.*, vol. 20, col. 234.

45   *Parl. Debs.*, vol. 20, col. 250.

46   Thomas Belsham to Benjamin Hobhouse, June 1809, in J. Williams, *A Memoir of Rev. Thomas Belsham* (London: 1833).

47   Whitbread Collection, L.4341, Spencer Perceval to the Dissenting Deputies, 10 April 1812.

48   Piggin, "Halévy Revisited," 26; Davis, *Dissent in Politics*, 191–93.

49   British Library (BL), Liverpool Papers, Add. MS 38238, Letterbook, Liverpool to the Archbishop of Canterbury, 30 June 1812.

50   BL, Add. MS 58951, Holland to Lord Grey, 23 May 1813.

51   BL, Add. MS 58951, Holland to Grenville, 21 May 1811.

52   BL, Add. MS 58952, Holland to Grenville, 8 January 1813. It is important to clarify, again, that by "Methodists" Holland meant evangelical nonconformists in general and that his closest contacts were with evangelical Dissenters not Wesleyans.

53 The clauses removed restrictions in the Test Act of 1673 that applied to both English Catholics and Protestant Dissenters. The Test Act of 1678, which barred Roman Catholics from Parliament, was ostensibly the main target of the bill and remained so after the other clauses were deleted.

54 *Parl. Debs.*, vol. 25, cols. 1112–14; vol. 26, cols. 152–53, 276–77.

55 Durham University Library (DUL), Grey Papers, Grey to Holland, 18 May 1813.

56 BL, Dropmore 58952, Holland to Grenville, 8 January 1813. Rowland Hill received his education at Eton and St. John's, Cambridge, but was never ordained an Anglican priest. Hill spent much of his career as an itinerant preacher and minister of the Surrey Chapel. He served as a director of several important evangelical organizations, including the London Missionary Society and the Religious Tract Society. See R. H. Martin, *Evangelicals United: Ecumenical Stirrings in Pre-Victorian Britain, 1795–1830* (London: 1983), chaps. 3 and 8.

57 BL, Add. MS 51545, Holland to Grey, 19 May 1813.

58 The Test Act of 1673 did not apply to Catholics in Ireland, and therefore, as shown above, Holland and the Whigs intended the clauses to benefit Protestant Dissenters as much as the small population of English Catholics.

59 BL, Holland Papers 51576, Whitbread to Holland, 8 May 1813.

60 BL, Add. MS 51545, Holland to Grey, 23 May 1813.

61 DUL, Grey Papers, Grey to Holland, no date (c. 21 May 1813).

62 BL, Add. MS 51545, Holland to Grey, 23 May 1813.

63 BL, Holland Papers 51573, Smith to Holland, 14 July 1820.

64 Davis, *Dissent in Politics*, chap. 12; see esp. 222–30.

65 K. P. Sen Gupta, *The Christian Missionaries in Bengal, 1793–1883* (Calcutta: 1971), 17.

66 SOAS, CWM/LMS, Home Office: 2/4/B, J. Dyer to the Directors, 10 January 1809.

67 SOAS, CWM/LMS, Home Office: 2/6/A, Directors' Memorial to Government on East India Company, 20 April 1812.

68 SOAS, CWM/LMS, Home Office: 2/7/B, Wilberforce to Burder, 2 June 1812.

69 *EM*, vol. 21, 1813, preface.

70 *EM*, vol. 21, 1813, 282.

71 *EM*, vol. 21, 1813, 285; *Methodist Magazine*, vol. 26, 1813, 399.

72 *Parl. Debs.*, vol. 26, col. 1048. Marsh's accusation was not accurate; the measure did include provisions for the establishment of the first Anglican bishopric in India.

73 *Parl. Debs.*, vol. 26, col. 1018.

74 *EM*, vol. 21, 280, 321. P. Carson has argued that the amendment of the charter proved to be something less than an outright victory for the dissenting missions. Although missionaries could now obtain licenses, they remained under fairly strict controls from the Company authorities. This was certainly

true; however, evangelicals in 1813 clearly saw, and celebrated, the amendment of the charter as a great victory and a sign of their growing political influence. While the long-term consequences may have been a mixed bag for the missionaries, Carson herself admits that the amendment of the charter in 1813 "demonstrated that a major readjustment of Britain's political and economic priorities had taken place." Carson, "The British Raj and the Awakening of the Evangelical Conscience: The Ambiguities of Religious Establishment and Toleration, 1698–1833," in Stanley, *Christian Missions*, 67; see also Carson, "Soldiers of Christ: Evangelicals and India, 1784–1833" (Ph.D. diss., University of London, 1988).

75 Clark, *English Society*, esp. chaps. 5 and 6.

76 Rev. T. Haweis, "The Apostolic Commission," in *Sermons Preached at the Formation of the Missionary Society* (London: 1795), 7, emphasis in original. Haweis might best be described as an "irregular" evangelical churchman who was a chief trustee of the Countess of Huntingdon's connexion and frequented with evangelical Dissenters in support of pan-evangelical missionary projects like the LMS. See Martin, *Evangelicals United*, chap. 3.

77 See, e.g., Rev. H. B. Kendall, *Origin and History of the Primitive Methodist Church* (London: [1906?]), vol. 1, bk. 1, 7–156.

78 P. Jupp, *British Politics on the Eve of Reform: The Duke of Wellington's Administration, 1828–1830* (London: 1998), 445; also see 216–21.

79 R. W. Davis, ed., *Lords of Parliament* (Stanford: 1995), 102.

Chapter 3

1 *Parl. Debs.*, vol. 2, cols. 961–63.

2 J. Oldfield, *Popular Politics and British Anti-Slavery: The Mobilisation of Public Opinion against the Slave Trade, 1787–1807* (Manchester: 1995), 1–2.

3 E. Williams, *Capitalism and Slavery* (Chapel Hill, N.C.: 1944); T. Clarkson, *The History of the Rise, Progress, and Accomplishment of the Abolition of the African Slave-Trade by the British Parliament* (London: 1808).

4 S. Drescher, "Capitalism and Abolition: Values and Forces in Britain, 1783–1814," reprinted in *From Slavery to Freedom: Comparative Studies in the Rise and Fall of Atlantic Slavery* (New York: 1999), 6; *From Slavery to Freedom*, 2–3. For the critique of the Williams' thesis see Drescher, *Econocide: British Slavery in the Era of Abolition* (Pittsburgh: 1977). Drescher suggests that the abolition of the slave trade bore primary responsibility for the economic decline of West Indian slavery. Other works related to the debate include D. B. Davis, *The Problem of Slavery in Western Culture* (London: 1966); D. Eltis, *Economic Growth and the Ending of the Transatlantic Slave Trade* (Cambridge: 1987); and B. Solow and S. Engerman, eds., *British Capitalism and Caribbean Slavery: The Legacy of Eric Williams* (Cambridge: 1987).

5 D. Turley, *The Culture of Antislavery, 1780–1860* (London: 1991), 7.

6 Quoted in J. Pollock, *Wilberforce* (London: 1977), 236.

7   Anstey, "Slavery and the Protestant Ethic," 157–81.

8   Anstey, "Slavery and the Protestant Ethic," 162.

9   Rev. B. W. Mathias, *The Christian Duty of Promoting the Gospel* (London: 1813).

10   Anstey, "Slavery and the Protestant Ethic," 161. Pointing to the failure of the abolitionist movement among evangelicals in the American South, D. Matthews and others have questioned Anstey's conclusion that these theological trends provided the primary impulses to evangelicals' participation in the antislavery movement. See Matthews, "Religion and Slavery: The Case of the American South," in Bolt and Drescher, *Anti-Slavery, Religion, and Reform*, 207–32. Matthews plausibly suggests that it was a combination of evangelical influences with the ideas of artisan radicals that gave the British movement its particular impetus. In this chapter, I suggest that the significance of evangelicals' growing concern for the protection of religious freedom should be added to the mix. Anstey's argument, nonetheless, remains vitally important for emphasizing the role of "anti-slavery as a means of sanctifying, or . . . sacrilising the cause of social justice" among early nineteenth-century evangelicals. See the comments of D. B. Davis, in Craton, *Roots and Branches*, 179.

11   M. Turner, *Slaves and Missionaries: The Disintegration of Jamaican Slave Society, 1787–1834* (Urbana, Ill.: 1982), 7–8.

12   Lovett, *History of the LMS*, 319.

13   Baptist Missionary Society, Letter of Instructions; *A Statement of the Plan, Object and Effects of the Wesleyan Missions to the West Indies* (London: 1824), 8, quoted in Turner, *Slaves and Missionaries*, 9–10.

14   *Demerara. Further Papers, Copy of Documentary Evidence* (House of Commons: 1824), 27–29.

15   E. Viotti da Costa, *Crowns of Glory, Tears of Blood: The Demerara Slave Rebellion of 1823* (Oxford: 1994), 9–12.

16   W. A. Hankey, *A Letter to Thomas Wilson, Esq. Occasioned by the "Analysis" of His Evidence on the Subject of Slavery before the Committee of the House of Commons* (London: 1833), 73.

17   Turner, *Slaves and Missionaries*, 4.

18   See Turner's account of the ambiguities of the Jamaican laws in *Slaves and Missionaries*, 14–15.

19   An account of the law passed by the Corporation of Kingston in *EM*, October 1807, 471–72.

20   *EM*, October 1807.

21   da Costa, *Crowns of Glory*, 10–12; *Journal of the Assembly of Jamaica*, 1802–1807; Turner, *Slaves and Missionaries*, 16.

22   See the reports of the meetings of the Dissenting Deputies (GL, MS 3083, 4) for their persistent objections to the attempts of West Indian planters to restrict missionary activity during the years 1807–1809.

23   GL, MS 3083, 4, 334–37, Dissenting Deputies, 29 November 1811.

24   Lovett, *History of the LMS*, 320.

25   da Costa, *Crowns of Glory*, 113.

26   SOAS, CWM/LMS, Demerara: Wray to Board of Directors, 20 October 1808. The Dutch minister's hostility toward Wray's work stemmed largely from provisions in Dutch colonial law that provided for the manumission of baptized slaves.

27   SOAS, CWM/LMS, Demerara: Wray to Board of Directors, 20 October 1808.

28   da Costa, *Crowns of Glory*, 119; Lovett, *History of the LMS*, 321.

29   SOAS, CWM/LMS, Minutes of the Board of Directors, 19 August 1811.

30   Lovett, *History of the LMS*, 322–23.

31   C. Northcott, *Slavery's Martyr: John Smith of Demerara and the Emancipation Movement, 1817–1824* (London: 1976), 12–15; da Costa, *Crowns of Glory*, 128–29.

32   SOAS, CWM/LMS, Journal of John Smith, Journals: West Indies and British Guiana, 1807–1825 (hereafter Smith's Journal), 17 July 1818.

33   Smith Papers, CWM/LMS, quoted in Northcott, *Slavery's Martyr*, 30–31.

34   Smith's Journal, 30 April 1820.

35   Smith's Journal, 25 May 1823.

36   Smith's Journal, 2 August 1822.

37   Smith's Journal, 13 July 1823.

38   Wilberforce had, nonetheless, done his part to reactivate the movement through the publication of his 1823 (London) work, *An Appeal to the Justice, and Humanity of the Inhabitants of the British Empire, on behalf of the Negro Slaves of the West Indies*.

39   *Parl. Debs.*, vol. 9, cols. 256–360.

40   *Parl. Debs.*, vol. 9, cols. 256–360.

41   da Costa, *Crowns of Glory*, 177–78; Northcott, *Slavery's Martyr*, 54–55; Turner, *Slaves and Missionaries*, 104–5.

42   Smith's Journal, 25 May 1823.

43   M. G. Lewis, *Journal of a West India Proprietor, Kept during a Residence in the Island of Jamaica* (repr., New York: 1969), 22 and 26 March 1816. Lewis attributed his inclusion in the slaves' rumors to what the colonists considered "[his] overindulgence to [his] negroes."

44   da Costa, *Crowns of Glory*, 178.

45   da Costa gives a full and insightful account of the origination of the rumors within the slave communities in Demerara; *Crowns of Glory*, 171–97; Northcott, *Slavery's Martyr*, 52–55; Smith's Journal, 25 July and 8 August 1823.

46   da Costa, *Crowns of Glory*, 197–206.

47   da Costa, *Crowns of Glory*, chap. 6; Northcott, *Slavery's Martyr*, chaps. 6 and 7.

48   London Missionary Society, *Report of the Proceedings against the Late Rev. John Smith, of Demerara . . . Who Was Tried under Martial Law, and Condemned to Death, on a Charge of Aiding and Assisting in a Rebellion of the Negro Slaves* (repr., New York: 1969).

49   Turner, *Slaves and Missionaries*, 104–11; *BM*, July 1823, 278.

50   Huskisson to Keane, 22 September 1826, quoted in Turner, *Slaves and Missionaries*, 121.

51   Address from the Assembly, CO 137/165, quoted in Turner, *Slaves and Missionaries*, 122.

52   See Anstey, "The Pattern of British Abolitionism," in Bolt and Drescher, *Anti-Slavery*, 28; M. Brock, *The Great Reform Act* (London: 1973), 103–4; and E. Halévy, *Triumph of Reform* (New York: 1961), 4.

53   SOAS, CWM/LMS, Home Office: 5/7/B, Copy of the Board of Directors' Memorial to Viscount Goderick.

54   SOAS, CWM/LMS, Home Office: 5/7/B, Copy of the Board of Directors' Memorial to Viscount Goderick.

55   SOAS, CWM/LMS, William Ellis Letters: 1832–1839, Ellis to Buxton, 15 December 1832.

56   Hankey, *Letter*, 5.

57   Hankey, *Letter*, 3.

58   SOAS, CWM/LMS, Auxiliary Records: 1, Newcastle 1827–1935, Minutebook 1827–44, 14 September and 16 November 1831.

59   SOAS, CWM/LMS, Home Office: 5/7/A, Ebeneezer Juvenile Auxiliary Missionary Society to Board of Directors, no date, 1832.

60   SOAS, CWM/LMS, Minutes of the Board of Directors, 23 December 1831.

61   SOAS, CWM/LMS, Home Office: 5/7/A Hankey to Board of Directors, 24 November 1831, 11 and 13 February 1832.

62   SOAS, CWM/LMS, Minutes of the Board of Directors, 12 January 1832.

63   Minutes of Evidence, in Hankey, *Letter*, 47–82.

64   DWL, Minutes of the General Body of Dissenting Ministers, 25 April 1833, 272–73.

65   SOAS, CWM/LMS, Newcastle Auxiliary, 15 February 1832.

66   Drescher, "Capitalism and Abolition," 6.

67   See Oldfield, *Popular Politics*, chap. 2.

68   R. Robinson, *Slavery Inconsistent with the Spirit of Christianity* (London: 1788), 24–25.

69   Quoted in Anstey, "Pattern of British Abolitionism," 28.

70   Turley, *Culture of Antislavery*, 235–36.

71   T. Jackson, ed., *The Works of Richard Watson* (London: 1834), vol. 1, 502.

Chapter 4

1   CL/Wits, A. 65 f, Journal of James Kitchingman, 28 January and 2 March 1825; see also J. Philip, *Researches in South Africa* (London: 1828), vol. 1, 336–44.

2   Philip, *Researches*, vol. 1, 343–44.

3   N. Pityana, "What Is Black Consciousness?" in Moore, *Black Theology*, 59.

4   See Comaroff, "Images of Empire."

5   For more on the history of Dutch settlement and rule, see R. Elphick and

H. Giliomee, eds., *The Shaping of South African Society, 1652–1840*, 2nd ed. (Cape Town: 1989); T. Keegan, *Colonial South Africa and the Origins of the Racial Order* (London: 1996), chap. 2.

6   The exercise of categorizing the indigenous population of the Cape is extremely complex. While the terms *Khoi* and *San* refer to linguistic groups, scholars have generally differentiated them on the basis of their manner of subsistence, identifying the Khoi as pastoralists and the San as hunter-gatherers. The Africans involved in the mission politics considered in this chapter were primarily, but not exclusively, of Khoi background.

7   CL/Wits, A 569 f, R. J. V. D. Riet to J. H. Craig, 12 June 1796.

8   See Annual Reports of the London Missionary Society, 1799–1811; Lovett, *History of the LMS*, vol. 1; A. Ross, *John Philip, Missions, Race, and Politics in South Africa* (Aberdeen, UK: 1986), chap. 2.

9   Lovett, *History of the LMS*, vol. 1, 540–44; A. Ross, *John Philip*, 38–47. On van der Kemp, also see I. H. Enklaar, *Life and Work of J. Th. van der Kemp, 1747–1811: Missionary Pioneer and Protagonist of Racial Equality in South Africa* (Cape Town: 1988), as well as E. Elbourne, "Concerning Missionaries: The Case of Dr. Van der Kemp," *Journal of South African Studies* 17 (1991): 153–64. Elbourne and R. Ross brand van der Kemp a militant premillenarian to account for his uncompromising advocacy of the rights of colonial Africans. The missionary was certainly eccentric, but I have seen little evidence to suggest that his theology was significantly different from the providentialist, postmillenarian views of the mainstream of the missionary movement. See E. Elbourne and R. Ross, "Combating Spiritual and Social Bondage: Early Missions in the Cape Colony," in Elphick and Davenport, *Christianity in South Africa*, 37.

10   Van der Kemp to the Dutch Missionary Society, 23 April 1803, in *Transactions of the Missionary Society*, vol. 2 (London: 1803–1806), 94.

11   *Memoir of the Rev. J. T. VanderKemp, M.D., Late Missionary in South Africa, Printed by Order of the Directors of the Missionary Society* (London: 1813), 31.

12   Keegan, *Colonial South Africa*, 84; R. Ross, *Status and Respectability*, 95.

13   Lovett, *History of the LMS*, 534–36; W. M. Macmillan, *The Cape Colour Question: A Historical Survey* (London: 1927), 92–94; A. Ross, *John Philip*, 48–51.

14   Macmillan, *Cape Colour Question*, 101–3; A. Ross, *John Philip*, 74–76.

15   See A. L. Drummond and J. Bulloch, *The Scottish Church, 1688–1843* (Edinburgh: 1973); H. Escott, *A History of Scottish Congregationalism* (Glasgow: 1960).

16   Lovett, *History of the LMS*, vol. 1, 541. For a more thorough biographical sketch of Philip's Scottish background, see A. Ross, *John Philip*, chap. 3.

17   Keegan, *Colonial South Africa*, 63–65.

18   *The Cambridge History of the British Empire* (Cambridge: 1936), vol. 8, 252, cited in A. Ross, *John Philip*, 87.

19   Cited in A. K. Millar, *Plantagenet in South Africa: Lord Charles Somerset* (Cape Town: 1965), 196.

20 A full account of Philip's disputes with Somerset is given by Macmillan in *Cape Colour Question*, chap. 14.

21 Philip, *Researches*, vol. 1, 213.

22 SOAS, CWM/LMS, Africa Odds: Philip Papers, 3/5, John Philip, "A Narrative Written for Buxton."

23 *The Missionary Herald*, Boston, vol. 29, 1833, 414.

24 A. Ross, *John Philip*, 100–101.

25 SOAS, CWM/LMS, Home Office: 4/2/A, William Wilberforce to George Burder, 26 March 1823.

26 *KP*, John Philip to James Kitchingman, 24 October 1823.

27 CL/Wits, *SACA*, no. 10, 10 March 1824.

28 CL/Wits, *SACA*, no. 11, 17 March 1824.

29 Keegan, *Colonial South Africa*, 94.

30 John Philip to Board of Directors, 27 June 1823, quoted in Macmillan, *Cape Colour Question*, 187.

31 Macmillan, *Cape Colour Question*, 203. The government commissioners did ultimately, in 1828, publish their report which substantiated many of the mission's criticisms of colonial policy toward the African population.

32 John Philip to T. F. Buxton, 4 May 1827, quoted in Macmillan, *Cape Colour Question*, 217.

33 For Philip's dealings with Buxton, see Macmillan, *Cape Colour Question*, 217.

34 Philip, *Researches*, vol. 1, 395.

35 Lovett, *History of the LMS*, vol. 1, 548; see also Philip, *Researches*, vol. 1, 200–220.

36 Philip, *Researches*, vol. 2, 361–62.

37 Philip, *Researches*, vol. 1, 395.

38 Philip, *Researches*, vol. 1, 369.

39 Philip, *Researches*, vol. 1, 374.

40 Keegan, *Colonial South Africa*, 91.

41 Philip, *Researches*, vol. 1, 377.

42 Philip, *Researches*, vol. 1, 383.

43 Philip, *Researches*, vol. 1, 381.

44 Keegan, *Colonial South Africa*, 91. The question of the relationship between the missionary movement and the Enlightenment is explored more generally in B. Stanley, ed., *Christian Missions and the Enlightenment* (Grand Rapids: 2001).

45 Philip, *Researches*, vol. 1, 387.

46 D. Stuart has noted the significance of this idea in evangelical discourse during the early nineteenth century. "Unlike the discourse of 'scientific' racism in the later nineteenth century, where racial categories were seen as fixed and unalterable, in this discourse of cultural absolutism the barriers between the 'civilized' and the 'savage' were easily permeated. Whilst this meant that (some) savages could be saved and could achieve equality, it also meant the civilized themselves could 'fall' or degenerate." Stuart makes much of Philip's report on the condition of the colonial Africans to the society's directors

shortly after his arrival in the Cape and its use of a "coherent" language of
racial domination that suggested Africans "were criminals and dissidents in
need of magisterial control, children in need of a father, servants in need of a
master and, only after all of these, sinners in need of a saviour." The implication is that the missionary's humanitarian rhetoric covered for a program of
racial and cultural dominance. While I would not discount the significance
of cultural chauvinism within missionary ideology, this seems to discredit
too much the egalitarian sentiment common to many of the early LMS missionaries in southern Africa. Furthermore, it fails to account for the ways that
Philip's thinking about the Africans and their condition clearly changed over
the course of his first decade in the colony. As is evident in *Researches*, Philip
increasingly associated the moral and cultural flaws of both Africans and the
Boers with the influence of the inequitable legal system in the colony. His
remedy was the establishment of legal and civil equality for the free African
population. Stuart, "Converts or Convicts? The Gospel of Liberation and
Subordination in Early Nineteenth-Century South Africa," in Hansen and
Twaddle, *Christian Missionaries and the State*, 66–75.

47   Philip, *Researches*, vol. 1, xiii.
48   Philip, *Researches*, vol. 1, 365.
49   As D. Turley has argued in his study of the antislavery movement, the "abo-
     litionist prospectus was one in which everybody gained and nobody lost."
     Philip's design for the future of southern Africa can be understood in the
     same way. Turley, *Culture of Antislavery*, 37.
50   Comaroff, "Images of Empire," 667–68. See also Comaroffs, *Of Revelation
     and Revolution*, vol. 1, chap. 2.
51   Comaroff, "Images of Empire," 663.
52   See B. Stanley, "Christianity and Civilization in English Evangelical Mission
     Thought, 1792–1857," in Stanley, *Christian Missions*, 180–82.
53   R. Hingley, *Roman Officers and English Gentlemen: The Imperial origins of
     Roman Archeology* (London: 2000).
54   Philip, *Researches*, vol. 1, 359.
55   Philip, *Researches*, vol. 2, 317.
56   Philip, *Researches*, vol. 1, 373. Civil liberty is a principle not often associated
     with Malthus, but the reference suggests something of Philip's familiarity
     with contemporary thinkers and their works. For another account of Mal-
     thus' influence upon early nineteenth-century evangelicals, see B. Hilton,
     *The Age of Atonement: The Influence of Evangelicalism on Social and Economic
     Thought, 1785–1865* (Oxford: 1988).
57   Philip, *Researches*, vol. 2, 308–9.
58   *Statement of the Case of the Protestant Dissenters under the Corporation and Test
     Acts* (London: 1827), 12.
59   Davis, *Dissent in Politics*, 213.
60   See chapter 3 above, and Turley, *Culture of Antislavery*, 235–36.
61   Comaroff, "Images of Empire," 675.

62 See chapter 2 above, and Jupp, *British Politics on the Eve of Reform.*

63 Comaroff, "Images of Empire," 669.

64 P. Curtin, *The Image of Africa* (Madison, Wis.: 1964), 259–61 and 414–16.

65 Macmillan, *Cape Colour Question,* chap. 15.

66 *KP*, John Philip to James Kitchingman, 18 July 1828.

67 *Parl. Debs.*, vol. 19, cols. 1693–94.

68 Philip to Kitchingman, 18 July 1828.

69 Macmillan, *Cape Colour Question,* 214. In 1825 Bourke had written to the directors of the LMS that he was "extremely anxious for the improvement of the Hottentots, and without inquiry into the particular notions of Christianity inculcated, I shall, wherever it may be in my power, afford assistance to those missionaries who labour to raise the unhappy natives in the scale of civilized beings." Note also the tolerant character of Bourke's reference to the dissenting missions as compared to the suspicious and antagonistic attitude of his predecessor Somerset.

70 See Elbourne, "Freedom at Issue: Vagrancy Legislations and the Meaning of Freedom in Britain and the Cape Colony, 1799–1842," *Slavery & Abolition* 15, no. 2 (1994): 127–33; Keegan, *Colonial South Africa,* 103–6; and A. Ross, *John Philip,* 102–11.

71 CL/Wits, Journal of James Kitchingman, 27 October 1828.

72 *KP*, James Read to James Kitchingman, 26 August 1828.

73 Upon hearing news of the proclamation of Ordinance 50 in London, Philip wrote that "there was nothing wanted but the Seal of the King in Council, without which Ministers must be aware it would be of no value in the Colony, as it might otherwise be set aside by new enactments and leave us where we were." Quoted in Macmillan, *Cape Colour Question,* 218–19.

74 Keegan, *Colonial South Africa,* 105.

75 Fragment of a letter to George Grieg, a Cape Town printer, November 1829, quoted in Macmillan, *Cape Colour Question,* 222.

76 Macmillan, *Cape Colour Question,* 225.

77 *KP*, John Philip to James Kitchingman, 10 June 1830, 101.

78 CL/Wits, Journal of James Kitchingman, 12 August 1830.

79 This account of the celebration comes from the French missionary, Samuel Rolland, who attended Bethelsdorp with Philip; in R. Ross, *Status and Respectability,* 118–19.

80 C. W. Hutton, ed., *Autobiography of the Late Sir Andries Stockenstrom* (Cape Town: 1964), vol. 2, 358; *KP*, 130.

81 *KP*, 129–30.

82 SOAS, CWM/LMS, South Africa: 11/3/D, James Read to William Orme, 30 July 1829; SOAS, CWM/LMS, South Africa: 12/1/D, John Philip to W. A. Hankey, 18 December 1830.

83 *KP*, James Read to Andries Stockenstrom, 16 June 1829.

Chapter 5

1   *Patriot*, 13 June 1832, 168.

2   *CM*, July 1831, 408 and 406.

3   Philip, *Researches*, vol. 1, xxix.

4   Rom 13:1-3 KJV.

5   Cited in *CM*, January 1835, 58.

6   J. D. Harris, *The Christian Citizen: A Sermon Preached in Aid of the London City Mission, at the Poultry Chapel, December 6, 1836* (London: 1837), 6, 8.

7   For this explanation of the sacrilization of dissenting politics I am indebted to Christopher Pepus for several conversations examining the subject during our doctoral research at Washington University. For an opposing view, which claims this was a period of the desacrilizing of dissenting politics, see J. Ellens, *Religious Routes to Gladstonian Liberalism: The Church Rate Conflict in England and Wales, 1832–1868* (University Park, Pa.: 1994).

8   *CM*, 1830, 437–43.

9   T. Binney, *An Address Delivered on Laying the First Stone of the New King's Weigh House* (London: 1834).

10 Binney, *Address Delivered on Lating*, 34.

11 *BM*, June 1834, 244.

12 J. Pratt, *Memoir of Josiah Pratt* (London: 1849), 292, cited in Martin, *Evangelicals United*, 197–98.

13 *BM*, June 1834, 247.

14 S. J. Brown and M. Fry, *Scotland in the Age of Disruption* (Edinburgh: 1993), chap. 1. A tradition of secession from the Scottish Church on the grounds of opposition to state interference and patronage dated to the 1730s. See J. R. McIntosh, *Church and Theology in Enlightenment Scotland: The Popular Party, 1740–1800* (East Lothian, UK: 1998).

15 *The Times*, 20 February 1835.

16 *BM*, June 1834, 245.

17 *Parl. Debs.*, vol. 17, 14 May 1833.

18 SOAS, CWM/LMS, Minutes of the Board of Directors, 13 July 1835.

19 *Parl. Debs.*, vol. 26, 27 February 1835, cols. 417–23.

20 *Report of the Wesleyan Methodist Missionary Society* (London: 1836), 55–56.

21 Public Record Office, CO 318:122, 80–82, cited in P. T. Rooke, "A Scramble for Souls: The Impact of the Negro Education Grant on Evangelical Missionaries in the British West Indies," *History of Education Quarterly* 21, no. 4 (1981): 431.

22 *Report of the Wesleyan Methodist Missionary Society*, 55.

23 Sir Lionel Smith to Lord Glenelg, 8 August 1835, CO 318:122, 109, also cited in Rooke, "Scramble for Souls."

24 The decision was not made, however, without some controversy among the Board of Directors. The board minutes for 13 April 1835 make note of "three hours" of deliberation "during which several members of the board expressed their views" on the matter. Thomas Golding's letter (23 October 1835) to

John Arundel, secretary of the LMS, suggests that the resolution to accept the grant passed by a majority of only two.

25 SOAS, CWM/LMS, Home Office: 6/6/A, David Derry to John Arundel, 20 November 1835.
26 SOAS, CWM/LMS, Home Office: 6/6/A, J. A. James to Arundel, 10 April 1835.
27 SOAS, CWM/LMS, Home Office: 6/6/A, William Gregory to Arundel, 30 September 1835.
28 SOAS, CWM/LMS, Home Office: 6/6/A, John Davies to Arundel, 8 September 1835.
29 Gregory to Arundel, 30 September 1835.
30 SOAS, CWM/LMS, Home Office: 6/6/A, Robert Ashton to Arundel, 15 October 1835.
31 Watts, *Dissenters*, vol. 2, 535–57.
32 SOAS, CWM/LMS, Home Office: 6/6/A, Thomas Golding to Arundel, 23 October 1835.
33 Gregory to Arundel, 30 September 1835.
34 Derry to Arundel, 20 November 1835.
35 SOAS, CWM/LMS, Home Office: 6/6/A, S. S. Wilson to Arundel, 11 November 1835.
36 Derry to Arundel, 20 November 1835.
37 SOAS, CWM/LMS, Home Office: 6/6/A, H. T. Roper to Arundel, 11 July 1835.
38 Wilson to Arundel, 11 November 1835.
39 SOAS, CWM/LMS, British Guiana: 5, Charles Rattray to William Ellis, 14 March 1836, emphasis in original.
40 E. A. Wallbridge, *The Demerara Martyr: Memoirs of the Rev. John Smith, Missionary to Demerara* (repr. Santa Barbara, Calif.: 1970), 418.
41 SOAS, CWM/LMS, British Guiana: 5, James Scott to Ellis, 1 April 1836. The missionary societies succeeded in overcoming their missionaries' fears of the inspectors only by prevailing upon the government to allow inspectors to be appointed by the societies themselves.
42 SOAS, CWM/LMS, Minutes of the Board of Directors
43 SOAS, CWM/LMS, Home Office: 7/1/A, S. T. Porter to Arundel, 27 January 1837.
44 SOAS, CWM/LMS, Outgoing: 1835–37, Ellis to Robert Taylor, 31 October 1836.
45 *EM*, January 1837, 23–26, emphasis in original.
46 SOAS, CWM/LMS, Home Office: 6/6/A, Thomas Jackson to Arundel, 9 October 1835.
47 Brown and Fry, *Scotland in the Age of Disruption*, i and chap. 1.
48 D. M. Thompson, *Denominationalism and Dissent, 1795–1835: A Question of Identity* (London: 1985), 22–23.
49 *HMM*, January 1831, 29.

50   *HMM*, March 1840, 33–35.

51   *HMM*, September 1840, 157–58.

52   SOAS, CWM/LMS, Home Office: 6/4/A, William Griffith to Arundel, 8 June 1835.

53   SOAS, CWM/LMS, Home Office: 6/4/A, David Davies to Arundel, 15 August 1835.

54   SOAS, CWM/LMS, Home Office: 6/4/A, John Elias to Arundel, 12 September 1835.

55   SOAS, CWM/LMS, Home Office: 7/2/A, George Gogerly to Arundel, 21 August 1837.

56   Quoted in SOAS, CWM/LMS, Home Office: 7/2/A, John Campbell to Arundel, 12 and 28 August 1837.

57   SOAS, CWM/LMS, Home Office: 7/2/A, John Campbell to Arundel, 12 and 28 August 1837.

Chapter 6

1   *Missionary Magazine*, no. 4, September 1836, 56–58.

2   SOAS, CWM/LMS, Africa Odds: 9, *Jan Tzatzoe and the Africa Witnesses* (London: 1836).

3   R. Ross, *Status and Respectability*, 119.

4   For more on this, see E. Elbourne, "'To Colonize the Mind': Evangelical Missionaries in Britain and the Eastern Cape, 1790–1837" (Ph.D. diss., Oxford University, 1991).

5   SOAS, CWM/LMS, South Africa: 14/1/C, Read to Ellis, 3 July 1834.

6   *KP*, 132–33.

7   SOAS, CWM/LMS, South Africa: 11/3/D, Read to William Orme, 30 July 1829; 12/1/D, Philip to W. A. Hankey, 18 December 1830.

8   *KP*, 133, Read to Stockenstrom, 16 June 1829.

9   Philip, "Notes on a Journey into the Interior," 18 January 1830, quoted in Macmillan, *Cape Colour Question*, 223.

10   *KP*, 122, William Anderson to Kitchingman, 23 May 1830.

11   Cole to Goderich, 10 May 1831, quoted in Macmillan, *Cape Colour Question*, 234.

12   Circular of January 1834, quoted in Macmillan, *Cape Colour Question*, 234.

13   Philip, Memorial to the Governor, November 1834, quoted in Macmillan, *Cape Colour Question*, 238.

14   Macmillan, *Cape Colour Question*, 238.

15   *KP*, 122, Philip to Kitchingman, 1 August 1834.

16   *Grahamstown Journal*, 11 September 1834, 142; *Report form the Select Committee on Aborigines with the Minutes of Evidence, Appendix and Index* (Imperial Blue Books, 1836/1837), no. 7, 538, and no. 7, 425, 755–77, quoted in Elbourne, "Freedom at Issue," 137.

17   Philip, *Researches*, vol. 1, 367.

18   *KP*, 122, Philip to Kitchingman, 1 August 1834.

19   SOAS, CWM/LMS, South Africa: 14/2/A, George Barker to John Campbell, 2 October 1834.

20   SOAS, CWM/LMS, South Africa: 14/2/B, Barker to William Ellis, 6 October 1834; *SACA*, 3 September 1834. The concept of "Hottentot nationalism" was first put forward by S. Trapido in "The Emergence of Liberalism and the Making of 'Hottentot Nationalism,' 1815–1834," in *The Societies of Southern Africa in the 19th and 20th Centuries*, collected seminar papers of the Societies of Southern Africa Seminar, Institute of Commonwealth Studies, vol. 17 (London: 1992), 34–59.

21   Quoted in Barker to William Ellis, 6 October 1834.

22   CL/Wits, *SACA*, 6 September 1834.

23   Quoted in Barker to William Ellis, 6 October 1834.

24   CL/Wits, *SACA*, 6 September 1834.

25   On Read, see C. Saunders, "James Read: Towards a Reassessment," in *The Societies of Southern Africa in the 19th and 20th Centuries*, collected seminar papers of the Societies of Southern Africa Seminar, Institute of Commonwealth Studies, vol. 7 (London: 1992); also see Elbourne, "To Colonize the Mind," 308–10; Keegan, *Colonial South Africa*, 118.

26   Read to Ellis, 3 July 1834.

27   Thomas Fowell Buxton papers, Rhodes House, Oxford, vol. 13, 125–46, cited in Elbourne and R. Ross, "Combating Spiritual and Social Bondage," 43.

28   *KP*, 123, Philip to Kitchingman, 1 August 1834.

29   *KP*, 124, Philip to Kitchingman, 20 December 1834.

30   T. Pringle, *Narrative of a Residence in South Africa* (London: 1835), 279–80.

31   *Missionary Magazine*, no. 4, September 1836, 58.

32   See A. Ross, *John Philip*, 122.

33   Macmillan, *Cape Colour Question*, 244.

34   For an account of the turbulent events of the first two decades of the nineteenth century and the role of the LMS within them, see A. Ross, *John Philip*, chaps. 1 and 2. See also Keegan, *Colonial South Africa*, 127, on the material and economic interests driving the conflict on the eastern frontier. Keegan makes a provocative argument for the essentially materialist character of colonial developments in the early nineteenth-century Cape. I do, however, take issue with his conclusion that "[i]n the end, liberal humanitarianism turned out to be a shallow, tawdry, deceptive thing." This may be true, to an extent, in the long term. However, Keegan seems to discount too much the tangible legal, political, and economic benefits that did result from the humanitarian efforts of missionaries, and others, during the middle of the nineteenth century.

35   Keegan, *Colonial South Africa*, 136–37.

36   Stockenstrom, *Autobiography*, vol. 2, 12, quoted in A. Ross, *John Philip*, 130.

37   Quoted in Keegan, *Colonial South Africa*, 138; Keegan documents Fairbairn's

steady public support for the treaty system in the pages of *SACA* from 1832 onward.

38   *Missionary Magazine*, no. 4, September 1836, 61.

39   Keegan, *Colonial South Africa*, 135–36; J. Green, *The Kat River Settlement in 1851* (Grahamstown, South Africa: 1853); le Cordeur and Saunders note the accusations of James Read's involvement in supplying weapons to the Xhosa during the 1846–1847 war; *KP*, 146 and 156.

40   Keegan, *Colonial South Africa*, 132–34; A. Ross, *John Philip*, 176–77; Stanley, *The Bible and the Flag*, 94–95.

41   General Orders, 11 May 1835, quoted in A. Ross, *John Philip*, 138.

42   Quoted in *KP*, 161. Keegan asserts that the committee became "in practice . . . an inquisition into the iniquities of border policy towards African people on and beyond the eastern frontier of the Cape Colony." *Colonial South Africa*, 148–49.

43   SOAS, CWM/LMS, South Africa: 15/1/B, Philip to Ellis, 11 February 1836.

44   *KP*, 165, Read to Kitchingman, 2 August 1836.

45   *Missionary Magazine*, no. 4, September 1836, 67.

46   *Missionary Magazine*, no. 4, September 1836, 67.

47   Read to Kitchingman, 2 August 1836.

48   British Parliamentary Papers, 39 (279), 120; *KP*, 165n15; 164, Read to Kitchingman, [July?] 1836.

49   *Missionary Magazine*, no. 4, September 1836, 67.

50   *KP*, 200, Philip to Kitchingman, 25 May 1838.

51   From 1834 to 1840 approximately fifteen thousand Boers, under the leadership of men like Louis Tregardt, A. H. Potgieter, and Piet Retief, departed from the colony ostensibly in protest against the British Parliament's abolition of slavery. For an account of missionary responses to the northward migration of the trekkers, see A. Ross, *John Philip*, chap. 6.

52   A. Ross, *John Philip*, 135; R. Godlonton, *A Narrative of the Irruption of the Kaffir Hordes into the Eastern Province of the Cape of Good Hope, 1834–1835* (Grahamstown, South Africa: 1836).

53   SOAS, CWM/LMS, South Africa: 14/4 and 5; Philip to James Read, June and October 1835.

54   Jan Tshatshu and James Read to LMS, 24 November 1837, reprinted in *Missionary Magazine*, no. 20, January 1838, 7–8.

55   See C. Northcott, *Robert Moffat: Pioneer in Africa, 1817–1870* (London: 1961); J. S. Moffat, *The Lives of Robert and Mary Moffat* (London: 1886); R. Moffat, *Missionary Labours and Scenes in Southern Africa* (London: 1842).

56   SOAS, CWM/LMS, South Africa: 16/1/C, Philip to Ellis, 29 July 1838; *KP*, 206, Read to Kitchingman, 11 March 1839.

57   Keegan, *Colonial South Africa*, 180–82; A. Ross, *John Philip*, 156. For a more substantial treatment of the relations between the Griqua and the missionaries, see Legassick, "The Northern Frontier to c. 1840: The Rise and Decline of the Griqua People," in Elphick and Giliomee, *Shaping of South African*

Society, 358–420; and R. Ross, *Adam Kok's Griquas: A Study in the Development of Stratification in South Africa* (Cambridge: 1976).

58 Elbourne, "Freedom at Issue," 134–35; and A. Ross, *John Philip*, 44–45.

59 *KP*, 217, Read to Kitchingman, 2 December 1840.

60 *KP*, 196, Read to Kitchingman, 15 February 1838.

61 R. Ross, "Congregations, Missionaries and the Grahamstown Schism of 1842–43," in de Gruchy, *London Missionary Society in Southern Africa*, 120–31.

62 SOAS, CWM/LMS, South Africa: 19/3/A, Read Jr. to Philip, 17 July 1843; James Read Sr. seems to have been a rather poor judge of the attitudes of prospective missionaries. In a letter to Kitchingman (*KP*, 176, 11 April 1837) he refers to Locke as "one of our sort." Locke, like Calderwood, proved to be anything but. Ross attributes Locke's character to his origins in "the disciplinarian background of British Nonconformity," although it is not at all clear what he means by this ("Congregations, Missionaries," 126).

63 SOAS, CWM/LMS, South Africa: 19/1/C, Deacons and Subscribers, Graham's Town, to the Directors, 1843.

64 SOAS, CWM/LMS, South Africa: 19/3/A, Locke to Philip, 8 July 1843.

65 SOAS, CWM/LMS, South Africa: 19/3/A, Locke to Philip, 8 July 1843.

66 *KP*, 240, Read to Kitchingman, 11 December 1843. Philip openly supported Read's conviction that Africans should have a voice in choosing their missionaries. In a letter to Read, he noted the appearance of similar controversies among the missions in the West Indies. "'Tis rather singular," he observed, "that the subject here should be agitated at the same time" (*KP*, 236).

67 *KP*, 241, Read to Kitchingman, 22 January 1844.

68 *KP*, 236, Read to Kitchingman, 17 July 1843.

69 Read to Kitchingman, 11 December 1843.

70 SOAS, CWM/LMS, South Africa: 20/2/D, Brownlee, Kayser, Merrington, Locke, Birt, Calderwood and Gill to LMS, 10 October 1844.

71 SOAS, CWM/LMS, South Africa: 20/2/D, Calderwod and Birt to LMS, 26 September 1844.

72 Read to Kitchingman, 22 January 1844. Illustrative of how keenly missionaries kept informed of such developments at home, the representatives of the Glasgow Missionary Society in the colony voted in 1843 to join the Free Church of Scotland. E. Elbourne suggests that the "disputes over spiritual authority and its relationship to temporal authority were occurring in parallel in Scotland and the Cape Colony, both industrialising countries with an expanding potential electorate in which debates about political citizenship interacted with debates about the relationship of church and state" ("Whose Gospel? Conflict in the LMS in the Early 1840s," in J. W. de Gruchy, ed., *London Missionary Society in Southern Africa, 1799–1999* (Athens, Ohio: 2000), 132–15, 136). This seems a less than compelling statement given the rather uncertain basis upon which the early nineteenth-century Cape can be defined as an "industrializing" society. The fundamental issues at stake

in the disputes were clearly ecclesiastical, and in the case of the colony also racial.

73   *KP*, 194, Philip to Board of Directors, 1843.

74   *KP*, 206, Read to Kitchingman, 11 March 1839.

75   *KP*, 210, Read to Kitchingman, 24 June 1839.

76   *KP*, 218, Read to Kitchingman, 2 December 1840.

77   SOAS, CWM/LMS, South Africa: 22/1, Philip to Directors, 31 March 1846.

78   Calderwood ultimately left the service of the LMS and took up a position as a government agent in the Xhosa territories. In this capacity he became an influential advisor to successive governors on colonial policy during the late 1840s and 1850s.

79   H. Temperley, *White Dreams, Black Africa: The Antislavery Expedition to the River Niger, 1841–1842* (New Haven: 1991), 166; see also Curtin, *Image of Africa*, chap. 15.

80   J. M. Bowker, *Speeches, Letters, and Selections* (repr., Cape Town: 1962), 129, 131–32.

81   Keegan, *Colonial South Africa*, 125–27.

82   A. Ross, *John Philip*, 194–204.

83   Upon seeing the area surrounding the Kat River settlement, Montagu is reputed to have said, "It is a pity that such black Devils should have such a fine country." R. Ross, *Status and Respectability*, 157.

84   SOAS, CWM/LMS, South Africa: 23/3/C, Read to A. Tidman, 21 January 1848.

85   *The Times*, 21 June 1851.

86   William Porter, Attorney General of the Cape Colony, quoted in J. J. Freeman, *A Tour of South Africa* (London: 1851), 212–13.

87   SOAS, CWM/LMS, South Africa: 23/1, Philip to Tidman, 15 May 1846.

88   James Read Jr., *Kat River Settlement*, 47, quoted in Elbourne, "Conflict in the LMS," 154.

89   *Grahamstown Journal*, 16 March 1850.

90   *KP*, "Editor's Introduction," 28.

Epilogue

1   A. Ross, *John Philip*, 210.

2   L. M. Thompson, *The Unification of South Africa, 1902–1910* (Oxford: 1960), 110. During the late 1800s the number of Africans on the common voters roll remained at around twelve thousand. In the 1886 elections, Africans constituted 47 percent of the electorate in five eastern Cape districts. P. Walshe, *Black Nationalism in South Africa: A Short History* (Johannesburg: 1973), 5.

3   Walshe, *Black Nationalism*, 212–14.

4   R. Price, *Making Empire: Colonial Encounters and the Creation of Imperial Rule in Nineteenth-Century Africa* (Cambridge: 2008)., 147.

5   See C. Hall, "Imperial Man: Edward Eyre in Australia and the West Indies, 1833–66," in Schwartz, *Expansion of England*, 130–70. This is also a primary theme of Hall's *Civilising Subjects*, her larger work on the subject of missions and empire. For more on dissenting participation in the Eyre controversy, see Larsen, *Contested Christianity*, chap. 12.

6   *Encyclopaedia Britannica*, vol. 25 (11th ed.; Cambridge: 1911), 471.

7   *The Times*, 20 May 1909.

8   *The Times*, 26 July 1909.

9   *The Times*, 19 August 1909.

10   *The Times*, 5 July 1909.

11   "Vorster and the Christians," *Sechaba, Official Organ of the African National Congress of South Africa* 3, no. 1 (1969): 18.

Bibliography

Archival Sources

British Library: Additional Manuscripts, Dropmore Papers, Holland Papers.
Dr. Williams' Library: Early Nineteenth Century Periodicals, and Correspondence.
Durham University Library: Grey Papers.
Guildhall Library: Reports of the Dissenting Deputies.
John Rylands Library, University of Manchester: Methodist Archives.
School of Oriental and African Studies Library: Council for World Missions/London Missionary Society Archive: Minutes of the Board of Directors, Home Office Correspondence, South Africa Correspondence, West Indies Correspondence, Missionary Journals, Candidates Papers. Annual Reports of the London Missionary Society, 1799–1811.
Wesleyan Methodist Missionary Society Archive (Microfilm): Thomas Coke Correspondence.
Whitbread Collection
William Cullen Library, University of the Witwatersrand: Missionary Journals and Correspondence.

Periodical Literature and Newspapers

The Baptist Magazine
The Congregationalist Magazine
Evangelical Magazine

The Evangelical Magazine and Missionary Chronicle
The Home Missionary Magazine
The Methodist Magazine
The Missionary Magazine
The Patriot
The Times

Published and Secondary Sources

Ajayi, J. F. Ade. *Christian Missions in Nigeria, 1841–1891.* London: 1965.

Anstey, Roger. *The Atlantic Slave Trade and British Abolition, 1760–1810.* London: 1975.

———. "Slavery and the Protestant Ethic." In Craton, *Roots and Branches,* 157–81.

Ayandele, Emmanuel A. *The Missionary Impact on Modern Nigeria, 1842–1914.* London: 1966.

Baylay, Christopher A. *Imperial Meridian: The British Empire and the World, 1780–1830.* London: 1989.

Bebbington, David W. *Evangelicalism in Modern Britain: A History from the 1730s to the 1980s.* London: 1995.

Beck, Roger B. "Bibles and Beads: Missionaries as Traders in Southern Africa in the Early Nineteenth Century." *Journal of African History* 30, no. 2 (1989): 211–25.

Binney, Thomas. *An Address Delivered on Laying the First Stone of the New King's Weigh House.* London: 1834.

Boas, Jack. "The Activities of the London Missionary Society in South Africa, 1806–1836: An Assessment." *African Studies Review* 16, no. 3 (1973): 417–35.

Bogue, David. "Objections against a Mission to the Heathen, Stated and Considered." In *Sermons Preached in London at the Formation of the Missionary Society* (1795), 126.

Bolt, Catherine, and Seymour Drescher, eds. *Anti-Slavery, Religion, and Reform.* Folkestone, UK: 1980.

Bowker, John Mitford. *Speeches, Letters, and Selections.* 1864. Reprint, Cape Town: 1962.

Bradley, James E. *Religion, Revolution and English Radicalism: Nonconformity in Eighteenth-Century Politics and Society.* Cambridge: 1990.

Brewer, Jehoiada. "The Certain Accomplishment of Divine Predictions." In *Sermons Preached at the Annual Meeting of the Missionary Society* (1802), 104.

Brock, Michael. *The Great Reform Act*. London: 1973.

Brown, Stuart J., and Michael Fry. *Scotland in the Age of Disruption*. Edinburgh: 1993.

Butler, Jeffrey, Richard Elphick, and David Welsh, eds. *Democratic Liberalism in South Africa: Its History and Prospect*. Middletown, Conn.: 1987.

Cain, P. J., and A. G. Hopkins. *British Imperialism: Innovation and Expansion, 1688–1914*. London: 1993.

Carey, William. *An Enquiry into the Obligations of Christians to Use Means for the Conversion of the Heathen*. Leicester: 1792.

Carson, Penny. "The British Raj and the Awakening of the Evangelical Conscience: The Ambiguities of Religious Establishment and Toleration, 1698–1833." In Stanley, *Christian Missions*, 45–70.

———. "Soldiers of Christ: Evangelicals and India, 1784–1833." Ph.D. diss., University of London, 1988.

Clark, J. C. D. *English Society, 1688–1832*. Cambridge: 1985.

Clarkson, Thomas. *The History of the Rise, Progress, and Accomplishment of the Abolition of the African Slave-Trade by the British Parliament*. London: 1808.

Colley, Linda. *Britons: Forging the Nation, 1707–1837*. New Haven: 1992.

Comaroff, Jean. *Body of Power, Spirit of Resistance: The Culture and History of a South African People*. Chicago: 1985.

Comaroff, Jean, and John Comaroff. *Of Revelation and Revolution: Christianity, Colonialism, and Consciousness in South Africa*. Vol. 1. Chicago: 1991.

———. *Of Revelation and Revolution: Christianity, Colonialism, and Consciousness in South Africa*. Vol. 2. Chicago: 1997.

Comaroff, John. "Images of Empire, Contests of Conscience: Models of Colonial Domination in South Africa." *American Ethnologist* 16 (1989): 661–85.

Cooper, Frederick, and Ann Laura Stoler, eds. *Tensions of Empire: Colonial Cultures in a Bourgeois World*. Berkeley: 1997.

Costa, Emilia Viotti da. *Crowns of Glory, Tears of Blood: The Demerara Slave Rebellion of 1823*. Oxford: 1994.

Craton, Michael, ed. *Roots and Branches: Current Directions in Slave Studies*. New York: 1979.

Curtin, Philip. *The Image of Africa*. Madison, Wis.: 1964.

Dachs, Anthony, ed. *Christianity South of the Zambezi*. Vol. 1. Gwello, Zimbabwe: 1973.

Davidoff, Leonore, and Catherine Hall. *Family Fortunes: Men and Women of the English Middle Class, 1780–1850*. London: 1987.

Davis, David Brion. *The Problem of Slavery in the Age of Revolution, 1770–1823*. Ithaca, N.Y.: 1975.

———. *The Problem of Slavery in Western Culture*. London: 1966.

Davis, Richard W. *Dissent in Politics, 1780–1830: The Political Life of William Smith, MP*. London: 1971.

———, ed. *Lords of Parliament*. Stanford: 1995.

Dedering, Tilman. "Khoikhoi and Missionaries in Early Nineteenth-Century Southern Namibia: Social Change in a Frontier Zone." *Kleio* 22 (1990): 24–41.

de Gruchy, John, ed. *The London Missionary Society in Southern Africa, 1799–1999: Historical Essays in Celebration of the Bicentenary of the L.M.S. in Southern Africa*. Athens, Ohio: 2000.

Dharmarah, Jacob S. *Colonialism and Christian Mission: Post-Colonial Reflections*. Delhi: 1993.

Ditchfield, G. M. *The Evangelical Revival*. London: 1998.

Drescher, Seymour. *Econocide: British Slavery in the Era of Abolition*. Pittsburgh: 1977.

Drummond, Andrew L., and James Bulloch. *The Scottish Church, 1688–1843*. Edinburgh: 1973.

Elbourne, Elizabeth. *Blood Ground: Colonialism, Missions, and the Contest for Christianity in the Cape Colony and Britain, 1799–1853*. Montreal: 2002.

———. "Concerning Missionaries: The Case of Dr. Van der Kemp." *Journal of South African Studies* 17 (1991): 153–64.

———. "Freedom at Issue: Vagrancy Legislations and the Meaning of Freedom in Britain and the Cape Colony, 1799–1842." *Slavery & Abolition* 15, no. 2 (1994): 114–50.

———. "'To Colonize the Mind': Evangelical Missionaries in Britain and the Eastern Cape, 1790–1837." Ph.D. diss., Oxford University, 1991.

———. "Whose Gospel? Conflict in the LMS in the Early 1840s." In de Gruchy, *London Missionary Society in Southern Africa*, 132–55.

———. "Word Made Flesh: Christianity, Modernity, and Cultural Colonialism in the Work of Jean and John Comaroff." *American Historical Review* 108, no. 3 (2003): 435–59.

Elbourne, Elizabeth, and Robert Ross. "Combating Spiritual and Social Bondage: Early Missions in the Cape Colony." In Elphick and Davenport, *Christianity in South Africa*, 37.

Ellens, Jacob. *Religious Routes to Gladstonian Liberalism: The Church Rate Conflict in England and Wales, 1832–1868*. University Park, Pa.: 1994.

Elphick, Richard, and Rodney Davenport, eds. *Christianity in South Africa: A Political, Social, and Cultural History.* Berkeley: 1997.

Elphick, Richard, and Hermann Giliomee, eds. *The Shaping of South African Society, 1652–1840.* 2nd ed. Cape Town: 1989.

Eltis, David. *Economic Growth and the Ending of the Transatlantic Slave Trade.* Cambridge: 1987.

Enklaar, Ido H. *Life and Work of J. Th. van der Kemp, 1747–1811: Missionary Pioneer and Protagonist of Racial Equality in South Africa.* Cape Town: 1988.

Escott, Harry. *A History of Scottish Congregationalism.* Glasgow: 1960.

Etherington, Norman, ed. *Missions and Empire: Oxford History of the British Empire Companion Series.* Oxford: 2005.

Everitt, Alan. *The Pattern of Rural Dissent: The Nineteenth Century.* Leicester: 1972.

Floyd, Richard. *Church, Chapel and Party: Religious Dissent and Political Modernization: in Nineteenth-Century England.* New York: 2007.

Freeman, Joseph John. *A Tour of South Africa.* London: 1851.

Gilbert, Alan D. "Religion and Political Stability in Early Industrial England." In O'Brien and Quinault, *The Industrial Revolution and British Society,* 79–99.

———. *Religion and Society in Industrial England, 1740–1914.* London: 1976.

Godlonton, Robert. *A Narrative of the Irruption of the Kaffir Hordes into the Eastern Province of the Cape of Good Hope, 1834–1835.* Grahamstown, South Africa: 1836.

Green, John. *The Kat River Settlement in 1851.* Grahamstown, South Africa: 1853.

Griffin, John. "The Signs of the Times Favourable to the Cause of Missions." In *Sermons Preached at the Annual Meeting of the Missionary Society* (1807), 83–117.

Grove, Richard. "Scottish Missionaries, Evangelical Discourses and the Origins of Conservation Thinking in Southern Africa, 1820–1900." *Journal of Southern African Studies* 15, no. 2 (1989): 163–87.

Grove, Thomas. *The Evangelical Commission.* London: 1800.

Halévy, Elie. *The Birth of Methodism in England.* Edited by Bernard Semmel. Chicago: 1971.

———. *A History of the English People in the 19th Century.* Vol. 1, *England in 1815.* Translated by E. I. Watkin. New York: 1961.

———. *Triumph of Reform.* New York: 1961.

Hall, Catherine. *Civilising Subjects: Metropole and Colony in the English Imagination, 1830–1867.* Chicago: 2002.

———, ed. *Cultures of Empire: Colonisers in Britain and the Empire in the Nineteenth and Twentieth Centuries.* New York: 2000.

———. "Imperial Man: Edward Eyre in Australia and the West Indies, 1833–66." In Schwartz, *Expansion of England,* 130–70.

———. *White, Male, and Middle Class: Explorations in Feminism and History.* New York: 1992.

Hall, Catherine, and Sonya O. Rose, eds. *At Home with Empire: Metropolitan Culture and the Imperial World.* Cambridge: 2006.

Hankey, William Alers. *A Letter to Thomas Wilson, Esq. Occasioned by the "Analysis" of His Evidence on the Subject of Slavery before the Committee of the House of Commons.* London: 1833.

Hansen, Holger Bernt, and Michael Twaddle, eds. *Christian Missionaries and the State in the Third World.* Athens, Ohio: 2002.

Hansen, Karen Tranberg, ed. *African Encounters with Domesticity.* New Brunswick, N.J.: 1992.

Harris, John D. *The Christian Citizen: A Sermon Preached in Aid of the London City Mission, at the Poultry Chapel, December 6, 1836.* London: 1837.

Haweis, Rev. Thomas. "The Apostolic Commission." In *Sermons Preached at the Formation of the Missionary Society* (1795), 5–23.

Hempton, David. *Methodism and Politics in British Society, 1750–1850.* London: 1984.

———. *The Religion of the People: Methodism and Popular Religion, c. 1750–1900.* London: 1996.

Hilton, Boyd. *The Age of Atonement: The Influence of Evangelicalism on Social and Economic Thought, 1785–1865.* Oxford: 1988.

Hingley, Richard. *Roman Officers and English Gentlemen: The Imperial Origins of Roman Archaeology.* London: 2000.

Hobsbawm, Eric. *Industry and Empire.* New York: 1969.

———. *Labouring Men: Studies in the History of Labour.* London: 1964.

Hole, Robert. *Pulpits, Politics and Public Order in England, 1760–1832.* Cambridge: 1989.

Huber, Mary Taylor, and Nancy C. Lutkehaus. *Gendered Missions: Women and Men in Missionary Discourse and Practice.* Ann Arbor, Mich.: 1999.

Hutton, Charles William, ed. *Autobiography of the Late Sir Andries Stockenstrom.* Vol. 2. Cape Town: 1964.

Jackson, Thomas, ed. *The Works of Richard Watson.* London: 1834.

Jefferson, Joseph. "The Diffusion of the Gospel." In *Sermons Preached at the Annual Meeting of the Missionary Society* (1811), 40.

Jupp, Peter. *British Politics on the Eve of Reform: The Duke of Wellington's Administration, 1828–1830.* London: 1998.

Keegan, Timothy. *Colonial South Africa and the Origins of the Racial Order.* London: 1996.

Kendall, Rev. H. B. *Origin and History of the Primitive Methodist Church.* London: 1906(?).

Landau, Paul. *The Realm of the Word: Language, Gender and Christianity in a Southern African Kingdom.* London: 1995.

Laqueur, Thomas W. *Religion and Respectability: Sunday Schools and English Working Class Culture, 1780–1850.* New Haven: 1976.

Larsen, Timothy. *Contested Christianity: The Political and Social Contexts of Victorian Theology.* Waco, Tex.: 2004.

———. *Friends of Religious Equality: Nonconformist Politics in Mid-Victorian England.* Woodbridge, UK: 1999.

Lawson, Philip. *The East India Company: A History.* New York: 1993.

Le Cordeur, Basil, and Christopher Saunders. *The Kitchingman Papers: Missionary Journals, 1817–1848, from the Brenthurst Collection.* Johannesburg: 1976.

Legassick, Martin. "The Griqua, the Sotho-Tswana and the Missionaries." Ph.D. diss., University of California, Los Angeles, 1969.

———. "The Northern Frontier to c. 1840: The Rise and Decline of the Griqua People." In Elphick and Giliomee, *Shaping of South African Society*, 358–420.

Lewis, Matthew Gregory. *Journal of a West India Proprietor, Kept during a Residence in the Island of Jamaica.* 1834. Reprint, New York: 1969.

London Missionary Society. *Report of the Proceedings against the Late Rev. John Smith, of Demerara . . . Who Was Tried under Martial Law, and Condemned to Death, on a Charge of Aiding and Assisting in a Rebellion of the Negro Slaves.* 1824. Reprint, New York: 1969.

Lovegrove, Deryck. *Established Church, Sectarian People: Itinerancy and the Transformation of English Dissent, 1780–1830.* Cambridge: 1988.

Lovett, Richard. *History of the London Missionary Society.* London: 1896.

Machin, G. I. T. *Politics and the Churches in Great Britain: 1832 to 1868.* Oxford: 1977.

Macmillan, William Miller. *The Cape Colour Question: A Historical Survey.* London: 1927.

Manning, Bernard Lord. *The Protestant Dissenting Deputies.* Cambridge: 1952.

Martin, Roger H. *Evangelicals United: Ecumenical Stirrings in Pre-Victorian Britain, 1795–1830*. London: 1983.

———. "Missionary Competition between Evangelical Dissenters and Wesleyan Methodists in the Early Nineteenth Century: A Footnote to the Founding of the Methodist Missionary Society." *Proceedings of the Wesley Historical Society* 42, no. 3 (1979): 81–86.

Mathias, B. W., Rev. *The Christian Duty of Promoting the Gospel*. London: 1813.

Matthews, Donald. "Religion and Slavery: The Case of the American South." In Bolt and Drescher, *Anti-Slavery, Religion, and Reform*, 207–32.

McIntosh, John R. *Church and Theology in Enlightenment Scotland: The Popular Party, 1740–1800*. East Lothian, UK: 1998.

McLaren, A. Allan. *Religion and Social Class*. London: 1974.

McLeod, Hugh, ed. *European Religion in the Age of Great Cities*. London: 1995.

———. *Piety and Poverty: Working Class Religion in Berlin, London, and New York, 1870–1914*. New York: 1996.

Mearns, Andrew. *England for Christ: A Record of the Congregational Church and Home Missionary Society*. London: 1886.

Mehta, Uday Singh. *Liberalism and Empire: A Study in Nineteenth-Century British Liberal Thought*. Chicago: 1999.

Memoir of the Rev. J. T. VanderKemp, M.D., Late Missionary in South Africa, Printed by Order of the Directors of the Missionary Society. London: 1813.

Millar, Anthony Kendal. *Plantagenet in South Africa: Lord Charles Somerset*. Cape Town: 1965.

Moffat, John Smith. *The Lives of Robert and Mary Moffat*. London: 1886.

Moffat, Robert. *Missionary Labours and Scenes in Southern Africa*. London: 1842.

Moore, Basil, ed. *Black Theology: The South African Voice*. London: 1973.

Moore, Robert. *Pit-Men, Preachers and Politics*. Cambridge: 1974.

Morris, Robert J., ed. *Class, Power and Social Structure in British Nineteenth-Century Towns*. Leicester: 1986.

Neill, Stephen. *A History of Christian Missions*. New York: 1986.

Nightingale, Benjamin. *Lancashire Nonconformity; or, Sketches, Historical and Descriptive, of the Congregational and Old Presbyterian Churches in the County*. Vol. 1. Manchester: 1890.

Noll, Mark. *The Rise of Evangelicalism: The Age of Edwards, Whitefield and the Wesleys*. Leicester: 2004.

Noll, Mark A., David W. Bebbington, and George A. Rawlyk, eds. *Evangelicalism: Comparative Studies of Popular Protestantism in North America, the British Isles, and Beyond 1700–1900*. Oxford: 1994.

Northcott, Cecil. *Robert Moffat: Pioneer in Africa, 1817–1870*. London: 1961.

———. *Slavery's Martyr: John Smith of Demerara and the Emancipation Movement, 1817–1824*. London: 1976.

Nuttall, Geoffrey. "Continental Pietism and the Evangelical Movement in Britain." In *Pietismus and Reveil*, edited by J. Van Den Berg and J. P. Van Dooren. Leiden, Netherlands: 1978.

———, ed. *Philip Doddridge: His Contribution to English Religion*. London: 1951.

O'Brien, Patrick K., and Roland Quinault, eds. *The Industrial Revolution and British Society*. London: 1993.

Oldfield, James. *Popular Politics and British Anti-Slavery: The Mobilisation of Public Opinion against the Slave Trade, 1787–1807*. Manchester: 1995.

Orchard, Stephen. "The Origins of the Missionary Society." *Journal of the United Reformed Church History Society* 5, no. 8 (1996): 440–58.

Payne, E. A. "Doddridge and the Missionary Enterprise." In Nuttall, *Philip Doddridge*, 79–101.

Peel, John D. Y. "For Who Hath Despised the God of Small Things? Missionary Narratives and Historical Anthropology." *Comparative Studies in Society and History* 37, no. 3 (1995): 581–607.

Pellew, George. *The Life and Correspondence of the Right Honourable Henry Addington, First Viscount Sidmouth*. Vol. 3. London: 1847.

Philip, John. *Researches in South Africa*. Vols. 1 and 2. London: 1828.

Piggin, Stuart. "Halévy Revisited: The Origins of the Wesleyan Methodist Missionary Society: An Examination of Semmel's Thesis." *Journal of Imperial and Commonwealth History* 9 (1980): 17–37.

———. *Making Evangelical Missionaries, 1789–1858: The Social Background, Motives, and Training of British Missionaries to India*. Abingdon, UK: 1984.

Pityana, Nyameko. "What Is Black Consciousness?" In Moore, *Black Theology*, 58–63.

Pollock, John. *Wilberforce*. London: 1977.

Porter, Andrew. "Commerce and Christianity: The Rise and Fall of a Nineteenth-Century Missionary Slogan." *Historical Journal* 28, no. 3 (1985): 597–621.

———. *Religion versus Empire? British Protestant Missionaries and Overseas Expansion, 1700–1914*. Manchester: 2004.

Potts, E. Daniel. *British Baptist Missionaries in India*. Cambridge: 1967.

Price, Richard. *Making Empire: Colonial Encounters and the Creation of Imperial Rule in Nineteenth-Century Africa*. Cambridge: 2008.

Pringle, Thomas. *Narrative of a Residence in South Africa*. London: 1835.

Report of the Wesleyan Methodist Missionary Society. London: 1836.

Robinson, Robert. *Slavery Inconsistent with the Spirit of Christianity*. London: 1788.

Rooke, Patricia T. "Evangelical Missionary Rivalry in the British West Indies: A Study in Religious Altruism and Economic Reality." *Baptist Quarterly* 29, no. 8 (1982): 341–55.

———. "The Pedagogy of Conversion: Missionary Education to the Slaves in the British West Indies, 1800–1833." *Paedagogica Historica* 18, no. 2 (1978): 356–74.

———. "A Scramble for Souls: The Impact of the Negro Education Grant on Evangelical Missionaries in the British West Indies." *History of Education Quarterly* 21, no. 4 (1981): 429–47.

Ross, Andrew. *John Philip, Missions, Race, and Politics in South Africa*. Aberdeen, UK: 1986.

Ross, Robert. *Adam Kok's Griquas: A Study in the Development of Stratification in South Africa*. Cambridge: 1976.

———. "Congregations, Missionaries and the Grahamstown Schism of 1842–43." In de Gruchy, *London Missionary Society in Southern Africa*, 120–31.

———. *Status and Respectability in the Cape Colony, 1750–1870*. Cambridge: 1999.

Rupp, Gordon. *Religion in England, 1688–1791*. Oxford: 1986.

Said, Edward. *Culture and Imperialism*. New York: 1993.

———. *Orientalism*. New York: 1979.

Saunders, Christopher. "James Read: Towards a Reassessment." In *The Societies of Southern Africa in the 19th and 20th Centuries*. Vol. 7, Collected Seminar Papers, Institute of Commonwealth Studies. London: 1977.

Schoeman, Karel. "Bastian Tromp Writes 'The Very Truth': A letter to the London Missionary Society, 1812." *Quarterly Bulletin of the South African Library* 47, no. 2 (1992): 67–76.

Schwartz, Bill, ed. *The Expansion of England: Race, Ethnicity and Cultural History*. London: 1996.

Seed, John. "Theologies of Power: Unitarianism and the Social Relations of Religious Discourse, 1800–50." In Morris, *Class, Power and Social Structure in British Nineteenth-Century Towns*, 107–56.

Semmel, Bernard. *The Methodist Revolution*. New York: 1973.

Sen Gupta, K. P. *The Christian Missionaries in Bengal, 1793–1883*. Calcutta: 1971.

Sermons Preached at the Annual Meeting of the Missionary Society. London: 1795, 1807.

The Societies of Southern Africa in the 19th and 20th Centuries. Vol. 7, Collected Seminar Papers of the Societies of Southern Africa Seminar, Institute of Commonwealth Studies. London: 1992.

Solow, Barbara, and Stanley Engerman, eds. *British Capitalism and Caribbean Slavery: The Legacy of Eric Williams*. Cambridge: 1987.

Stanley, Brian. *The Bible and the Flag: Protestant Missions and British Imperialism in the Nineteenth and Twentieth Centuries*. Leicester: 1990.

———, ed. *Christian Missions and the Enlightenment*. Grand Rapids: 2001.

———. "Commerce and Christianity: Providence Theory, the Missionary Movement, and the Imperialism of Free Trade, 1842–1860." *Historical Journal* 26, no. 1 (1983): 71–94.

———. *The History of the Baptist Missionary Society, 1792–1992*. Edinburgh: 1992.

Statement of the Case of the Protestant Dissenters under the Corporation and Test Acts. London: 1827.

Stoler, Ann Laura, and Frederick Cooper. "Between Metropole and Colony: Rethinking a Research Agenda." In Cooper and Stoler, *Tensions of Empire*, 1–56.

Stuart, Doug. "Converts or Convicts? The Gospel of Liberation and Subordination in Early Nineteenth-Century South Africa." In Hansen and Twaddle, *Christian Missionaries and the State*, 66–75.

Stuart, Kenneth. *Restoring the Reformation: British Evangelism and the Francophone Reveil, 1816–1849*. Milton Keynes, UK: 2006.

Switzer, Les. "Christianity, Colonialism and the Postmodern Project in South Africa: The Comaroffs Revisited." *Canadian Journal of African Studies* 32, no. 1 (1998): 181–96.

Tawney, R. H. *Religion and the Rise of Capitalism*. New York: 1961.

Taylor, John. *The Apostles of Fylde Methodism*. London: 1885.

Temperley, Howard. *White Dreams, Black Africa: The Antislavery Expedition to the River Niger, 1841–1842*. New Haven: 1991.

Temu, Arnold, and Bonaventure Swai, eds. *Historians and Africanist History: A Critique—Post-Colonialist Historiography Examined*. London: 1981.

Thomas, Rev. Josiah. *Strictures on Subjects Chiefly Relating to the Established Religion and the Clergy*. London: 1807.

Thompson, David M. *Denominationalism and Dissent, 1795–1835: A Question of Identity.* London: 1985.

Thompson, E. P. *The Making of the English Working Class.* New York: 1963.

Thompson, F. M. L. *The Rise of Respectable Society: A Social History of Britain, 1830–1900.* Cambridge, Mass.: 1988.

Thompson, L. M. *The Unification of South Africa, 1902–1910.* Oxford: 1960.

Thorne, Susan. *Congregational Missions and the Making of an Imperial Culture in Nineteenth-Century England.* Stanford: 1999.

———. "Protestant Ethics and the Spirit of Imperialism: British Congregationalists and the London Missionary Society, 1797–1925." Ph.D. diss., University of Michigan, 1990.

Torr, A. Louise. "The Isaac Hughes Papers: An Examination of the Correspondence between the Rev. Isaac Hughes, Dr. John Philip and the London Missionary Society during the Period 1824–1867, with Particular Attention to Hughes' Work at Griquatown." *Africa Notes and News* 23, no. 4 (1978): 167–70.

Transactions of the Missionary Society. Vol. 2. 1803–1806.

Trapido, Stanley. "The Emergence of Liberalism and the Making of 'Hottentot Nationalism,' 1815–1834," in *The Societies of Southern Africa in the 19th and 20th Centuries*, 34–59.

Turley, David. *The Culture of Antislavery, 1780–1860.* London: 1991.

Turner, Mary. *Slaves and Missionaries: The Disintegration of Jamaican Slave Society, 1787–1834.* Urbana, Ill.: 1982.

Valenze, Deborah. *Prophetic Sons and Daughters: Female Preaching and Popular Religion in Industrial England.* Princeton: 1985.

Wallbridge, Edwin Angel. *The Demerara Martyr: Memoirs of the Rev. John Smith, Missionary to Demerara.* London: 1848.

Walls, Andrew. *The Missionary Movement in Christian History.* Edinburgh: 1996.

Walsh, John. "'Methodism' and the Origins of the English-Speaking Evangelicalism." In Noll, Bebbington, and Rawlyk, *Evangelicalism*, 19–37.

Walsh, John, Colin Haydon, and Stephen Taylor, eds. *The Church of England, c. 1689–c. 1833: From Toleration to Tractarianism.* Cambridge: 1993.

Walshe, Peter. *Black Nationalism in South Africa: A Short History.* Johannesburg: 1973.

Ward, W. R. *Faith and Faction.* London: 1993.

———. *The Protestant Evangelical Awakening.* Cambridge: 1992.

Watts, Michael. *The Dissenters*. Vols. 1 and 2. Oxford: 1978, 1995.

Wilberforce, William. *An Appeal to the Justice, and Humanity of the Inhabitants of the British Empire, on behalf of the Negro Slaves of the West Indies.* London: 1823.

Williams, C. P. "Not Quite Gentlemen: An Examination of Middling Class Protestant Missionaries from Britain, c. 1850–1900." *Journal of Ecclesiastical History* 31, no. 3 (1980): 301–15.

Williams, Donovan. "The Missionary Personality in Caffraria, 1799–1853: A Study in the Context of Biography." *Historia* 34, no. 1 (1985): 15–35.

———. "Social and Economic Aspects of Christian Mission Stations in Caffraria, 1816–1854." *Historia* 30, no. 2 (1985): 33–48.

Williams, Eric. *Capitalism and Slavery*. Chapel Hill, N.C.: 1944.

Williams, John. *A Memoir of Rev. Thomas Belsham*. London: 1833.

Wolffe, John. *God and Greater Britain, 1843–1945*. London: 1994.

Yeo, Stephen. *Religion and Voluntary Organizations in Crisis*. London: 1976.

Index

abolition, 53, 55–57, 65–66, 68–69, 70, 72–74, 86, 89, 91, 118, 122

Addington, Henry; *see* Sidmouth, Lord

antislavery; *see* abolition

Baptist Missionary Society, 11, 22, 57

Binney, Thomas, 99, 100

Bogue, David, 9, 11, 22, 25, 33

Bowker, John Mitford, 137–38

Bristol Remonstrance, 104

Brougham, Henry, 53, 54, 67, 74, 102, 104

Buxton, T. F., 64–65, 69, 86, 121–26, 137

Calderwood, Henry, 129, 131–36

Cape Constitution, 143

Carey, William, 11, 22, 26, 150, 152

Castlereagh, Lord, 43, 47, 51

Colonial Office, 62, 65, 76, 102, 105, 119, 121–22, 125, 127, 137, 142

Congregationalism, 3, 109–11; *see also* Independents

Congregational Union, 105, 110

Demerara, 10, 57, 60–67, 73, 106

Dutch East India Company, 76, 78

D'Urban, Sir Benjamin, 123, 125

Dissent, 4, 12, 17, 19; politicizing of, 48–51, 56, 58, 91, 96, 100, 106, 109; relationship to Evangelical Revival, 20–22, 29, 31–32, 34; response to Sidmouth's Bill, 38–43

Dissenting Deputies, 35, 37, 39, 41, 49, 68, 99

East India Company, 11, 24, 45, 76, 78

Emancipation Act, 60, 72, 101

Evangelical Revival, 7, 9, 12–13, 23, 29, 56

Eyre, Edward John, 143, 144

Fairbairn, John, 118

General Body of Dissenting Ministers, 72

Glenelg, Lord, 125–26, 128

Great Disruption, 108

Grey, Lord, 43–44, 101

Hankey, William Alers, 70
Harris, John, 98
Hawies, Rev. Thomas, 48
Holland, Lord, 39, 40, 42–45, 49
Home Missionary Society, 28
Hottentot Rebellion, 140–41

Independents, 9, 16, 20, 22 38,
    41–42, 53, 109, 111; *see also*
    Congregationalism

Jamaica, 57, 59, 60, 62, 66, 68–69,
    72–73
James, John Agnell, 103

Kat River Settlement, 7–8, 95–95,
    115–17, 122–24, 129, 132, 135,
    139, 140–41
Khoi, 76–79, campaign for rights,
    83–88, 90, 93–96, politics after
    Ordinance, 50, 115–25, 130, 132–
    34, 137–39, 140, 142, 145
Kitchingman, James, 75, 76, 84, 93

Liverpool, Lord, 40–42, 46, 62, 93
Locke, John, 132, 133, 134
London Missionary Society:
    Congregationalist identity, 110–13;
    early engagement in Cape politics,
    82–85, 95; early mission to the Cape
    Colony, 76–80; early mission to
    Demerara, 60–62; eastern Cape fron-
    tier, 123–26; founding, 9–10, 23–25;
    government grants controversy,
    101–8; Grahamstown controversy,
    131–35; Hankey controversy, 68–72,
    75; John Smith and Demerara rebel-
    lion, 62–67; Kat River, 116–17,
    119–21; legacy, 141–43; relationship
    to home missions, 26–29, 53

Mackay, William, 94
Methodism, 13, 16–17, 19, 32, 34, 42

Moffat, Robert, 129–33, 136
Murray, John, 61, 65–66, 67

Ordinance 50, 92–96, 117–20, 122–
    23, 139

Philip, Jane, 62
Philip, John, 75–76; background and
    arrival in Cape Colony, 80–82; con-
    flict with Robert Moffat, 129–31;
    early controversies with colonial gov-
    ernment, 83–85; first visit to Britain
    and publication of *Researches in South
    Africa*, 85–92; last years in South
    Africa, 135–40, 143; opposition to
    Vagrancy Law, 117–22; second visit
    to Britain, 115–17, 126–29; support
    for Ordinance, 50, 92–96; views on
    the Eastern Cape, 123–26
Pringle, Thomas, 82, 95
Protestant Society for the Protection of
    Religious Liberty, 38–39, 44–46, 50,
    97, 99–101

Queen Adelaide Province, 125–26, 137

Rattray, Charles, 106
Read, James, Jr., 7, 133–35
Read, James, Sr., 78–80, 83, 88, 93, 96,
    116–17, 120–22, 124, 126–27, 129,
    131–36, 138, 139–40, 144–45
Researches in South Africa, 85, 91, 93,
    97
Roby, William, 20, 22, 26

Schreiner, W. P., 145
Sidmouth, Lord, 31, 33–38, 40–42,
    48–51, 59–60, 62, 69, 73, 97, 104
Slave Trade, 24, 51, 54–55, 57, 73, 86
Smith, John, 62–67
Smith, William, 45, 53–54
Society for the Promotion of Christian
    Knowledge, 10, 14–15, 29, 90

Society for the Promotion for the Gospel, 10, 14–15, 29

South African Commercial Advertiser, 82

Stockenstram, Andries, 92–93, 95, 117, 123–24, 128–29, 142

Stoffels, Andries, 122

Test and Corporation Acts, 2, 33, 43, 48

Toleration Act, 31, 39, 59

Tshatshu, Jan, 115–16, 126–27, 129

United Committee, 91, 99–100

Vagrancy Act; Cape Colony, 117, 119–21, 122, 125

van der Kemp, Johannes, 10, 77–79, 80, 83, 88, 120, 124

Vorster, John, 143

Wesleyan Methodist Missionary Society, 10, 57, 102, 127

Whitbread, Samuel, 43–44, 49, 107

Whitefield, George, 13, 15–17, 19, 22, 29, 43

Wesley, John, 15–17, 20, 29

Wilberforce, William, 11, 24–25, 46, 55, 62, 64, 66–67, 73, 84, 86

Wilks, John, 38, 42, 44, 99

Wilks, Rev. Matthew, 9, 38

Wray, John, 60–64

Xhosa, 77, 80, 82, 95, 115–16, 122–25, 127–29, 131, 135, 139–40